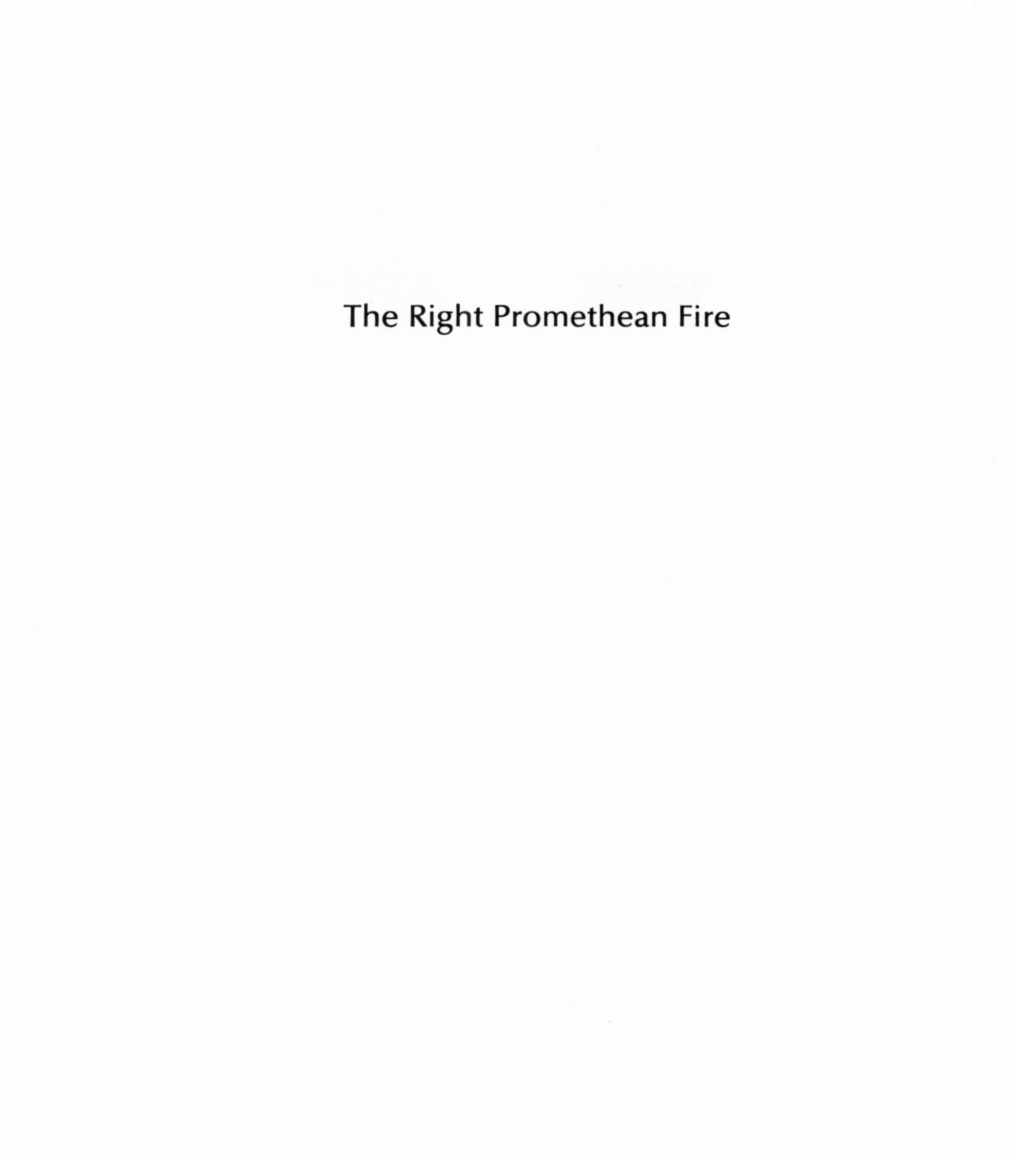

The Right Promethean Fire

The Right Promethean Fire

Imagination, Science, and Cultural Change

Ihab Hassan

University of Illinois Press
Urbana Chicago London

Manufactured in the United States of America

Library of Congress Cataloging in Publication Data

Hassan, Ihab Habib, 1925–
The right Promethean fire.

1. Civilization, Modern—1950- —Addresses essays, lectures. 2. Criticism—Addresses, essays lectures. 3. Science and civilization—Addresses, essays, lectures. I. Title.
CB430.H38 909.82 79-18844
ISBN 0-252-00753-0

CB
430
.H38

C1

From women's eyes this doctrine I derive:
They sparkle still the right Promethean fire;
They are the books, the arts, the academes,
That show, contain, and nourish all the world,
Else none at all in aught proves excellent.

Shakespeare, *Love's Labour's Lost*

*

Formation, transformation,
Eternal mind's eternal recreation.
Girt around by images of all things that be,
They [the Mothers] do not see you, forms alone they see.

Goethe, *Faust II*

*

Man, one harmonious soul of many a soul,
Whose nature is its own divine control,
Where all things flow to all, as rivers to the sea;
Familiar acts are beautiful through love;
Labor, and pain, and grief, in life's green grove
Sport like tame beasts, none knew how gentle they could be!

Shelley, *Prometheus Unbound*

*

What else am I who laughed or wept yesterday,
who slept last night like a corpse, and this
morning stood and ran? And what see I on any
side but the transmigrations of Proteus,

Emerson, "History"

*

Eve: To desire, to imagine, to will, to create. That is too long a story. Find me one word for it all: you who are so clever.

Serpent: In one word, to conceive. That is the word that means both the beginning in imagination and the end in creation.

Shaw, *Back to Methuselah*

For B. Hassan-Koten

CONTENTS

ACKNOWLEDGMENTS

My appreciation goes to the Vilas Trust Fund and the University of Wisconsin-Milwaukee, most particularly to Dean William Halloran; to the Camargo Foundation and the Rockefeller Foundation; and to the Council for International Exchange of Scholars (Senior Fulbright Lecturing Program)—who all helped to make this work possible.

Some sections in this volume, delivered first as addresses, have appeared in the following publications:

"The Critic as Innovator: A Paracritical Strip in X Frames," in the *Chicago Review,* 28, no. 3 (Winter, 1977).

"Culture, Indeterminacy, and Immanence: Margins of the (Postmodern) Age," in *Humanities in Society,* 1, no. 1 (Winter, 1978).

Two other sections, now greatly expanded and revised, also appeared earlier:

"The Re-Vision of Literature," in *New Literary History,* 8, no. 1 (Autumn, 1976).

"Prometheus as Performer: Toward a Posthumanist Culture?", in Michel Benamou and Charles Caramello, eds., *Performance in Postmodern Culture* (Madison, Wisc.: Coda Press, 1977); and *The Georgia Review,* 31, no. 4 (Winter, 1977).

Traces of ideas and of phrases in this book may also be found in "Toward a Transhumanized Earth: Imagination, Science and Future," *The Georgia Review,* 32, no. 4 (Winter, 1978).

At a time when many scholarly presses, feigning interest in "provocative" and "experimental" work, seek safety in academic consensus, the University of Illinois Press, under the editorship of Richard Wentworth, has proven an exception. I am happy that the publisher of my earlier work, *Paracriticisms,* is also publishing this new work; and I am grateful to Carole S. Appel for her punctiliousness and cooperation in editing this book.

The Center for Twentieth Century Studies at the University of Wisconsin-Milwaukee, directed by the late Michel Benamou (shaper, enabler, friend), was a place of intellectual gaiety where ideas, including some here, risked and found themselves. I owe it much, and celebrate his memory.

Finally, this book was coauthored by many authors, some living, others nominally dead. It was "written," too, in the complex ways of language and love, by my wife: Sally Hassan.

PERSONAL PREFACE

I

The subtitle of this speculative work indicates its three major concerns: imagination, science, and cultural change in our time, leaning into the future. Its informing sense is that imagination—empowered by science, extended by technology, enacted by us all—has shaped, and still continues to shape, a world which we awkwardly call postmodern, posthumanist. Thus we stand between history and hope.

As for the title, it evokes an ancient dream, an ineluctable perplexity. The dream has come of age, our age, come to crisis, our crisis. No doubt, every moment chooses its mythic hero, its double in desire and secret discomfitures, its doer. I thought Prometheus could serve that choice, flawed though he may be. Does not his flaw qualify him all the more to attest our condition, our feeling?

Five epigraphs help to put in play my meaning. Prometheus, imperfect redeemer, needs to be redeemed. This Shakespeare shows in the lines from which I take my title. Biron there is speaking; with sage dalliance, he recalls King and Courtiers to an erotic apprehension of experience; and so challenges all utopian schemes, all rigors and ascesis, that require an ablation of desire. The *right* Promethean fire sparkles in women's eyes because, mindful and loving still, they eschew the latent madness of Prometheus. What madness? Pride, will, rootless intelligence, what every Ahab or Faust, vulgarly speaking, refuses to acknowledge.

In Goethe's early dramatic fragment, Prometheus thinks he already possesses the earth, "the realm occupied by my action," with nothing above, nothing below it. Such is the *hybris* of heroes. Yet Prometheus also concealed a dark, moonlike side, some aspect of the feminine even gods and heroes can not ignore.

Goethe came to see this; his Faust, more lived and living than Prometheus, descends to the Mothers enthroned in boundlessness, there to seek awful knowledge of "Life's images, astir, yet lifeless forever," and surrender himself in "desire, love, adoration, madness." Poetically, the Mothers remain a high mystery—Goethe refused to explain them to Eckermann. Discursively, though, we may concur with Harold Jantz that they shadow forth "the matrices of all forms, at the timeless, placeless originating womb or hearth where chaos is transmuted into cosmos. . . ." They image, my second epigraph says, "formation, transformation," the power of the *ur*-imagination.

Yet greater even than the power of that imagination, or rather at the very center of it, is love. Earth sings in my third and pivotal epigraph a paean to it; and Demogorgon plangently calls on love to spring "from its awful throne of patient power / In the wise heart" to celebrate the deliverance of Prometheus, a redeemed universe. Skeptical though he may have been, Percy Bysshe Shelley renders here a true vision, one to which this work assents, and from which it must always recede. Assent is crucial: to the Satanic and solipsistic impulse in the Promethean myth there is no answer but love. Writing with *Frankenstein* in mind, Harold Bloom observes: "Though Mary Shelley may not have intended it, her novel's prime theme is a necessary counterpoise to Prometheanism, for Prometheanism exalts the increase of consciousness despite all cost." Here lies our peril, our self-amazement.

Shelley's Prometheus is like some luminous emanation: even as we behold it, we fall away into time. A more accessible figure of "eternal recreation" appears in my fourth epigraph: Proteus, whimsical master of metamorphoses. Emerson also believed him to be an embodiment of history. "The philosophical perception of identity through endless mutations of form makes him [man] know the Proteus. . . . I can symbolize my thought by using the name of any creature, of any fact, because every creature is man agent or patient." We, then, are "the Proteus" because language permeates existence, because mind is one and nature "its correlative."

This is also to say that time opens itself to the human imagination. So, at least, Shaw's Serpent advises his Eve in my last epigraph. Beginning in imagination, ending in creation—as Eve herself does and Lilith before her—we all move in time, which is the dimension of consciousness that creates reality by recreating it. The Serpent is merely lucid, Eve prophetic in the flesh. The story of earth's evolution may be in her keep.

That story continues, its vatic nature revealed in many myths. As Eve is mother to us all, so is Gaia or Themis mother (in one version) to Prometheus, the forward-seeing. C. Kerényi puts it thus: "Saved from destruction . . . the human race will also endure. But something different from this world *might* happen. Prometheus rises above this world, as it were, not from pride and defiance but on the strength of a vision derived from a profound maternal source. . . ."

May we not call such a figure a gnostic* Prometheus, which all five epigraphs assume, and assuming question still?

II

More symbol than concept, the figure of a gnostic Prometheus shifts and changes in these pages, remains to mock our hope. Yet a certain nexus of ideas relates it to our cultural exigencies, our proximate thoughts. Its fire is science and vision, technic and myth, language and dream, the whole ardor of life, pure spirit also, and many magical things. "Fire," Mircea Eliade notes, "turned out to be the means by which man could 'execute' faster, but it could also do something other than what already existed in Nature." But this fire is not blameless: stolen first, it perpetuates the pain of mind. The Renaissance Platonist, Marsilio Ficino, saw in its light an allegory of consciousness, "beset by the continuous gnawing of inquiry, the most ravenous of vultures." Still, it was fire that brought humankind through the Ice Ages and left its mark in all those depthless caves where men refused to stay "like phantoms huddled in dreams." No wonder that Aeschylus' Prometheus boasts: "Senseless as beasts I gave men sense, possessed them of mind. . . ." Pain of mind, torment of the vulture: what premonitions of a new order did Prometheus glimpse there, chained to his rock? His answers riddle time. Yet this much he may have come to realize: to the abstractions of air and fire he must wed the moist earth and generative mire. Perhaps the outcome will prove to be no rough beast but bright body, possessed of the full civility of articulate desire.

Prometheus shifts; he was ever a trickster. But he also en-

*In this work, gnostic, when not capitalized, refers to knowledge, wisdom, or spirit, rather than to ancient Christian cults. See p. 141 below for *O.E.D.* definitions.

gages our direct concerns: in criticism, in literature, in the arts, in the sciences, in the travails of a planetary society, as the five chapters or essays of this work try to show. The book begins with the critic's business, widens gradually into larger speculations, moving from rhetorical, through cultural, to visionary themes. Thus the first essay addresses the critic's freedom and responsibility within the changing frames of current theories; it means to affirm a larger role for the critical imagination than our professions permit. The second reviews the rhetoric of those theories, mostly French, that challenge our ideas of literature, and challenge our humanist measure of things; reviewing these, the essay also previews some concepts of imagination, and so may serve as a tentative invitation to vision. But our enterprise is not only visionary; it calls as well for cultural and epistemic redefinitions, which the third essay solicits; drawing on certain analogues from the physical and human sciences, this essay proposes indeterminacy and immanence, twin perspectives on postmodern society, inseparable. Science, the fourth essay maintains, molds more than society, molds cosmos to mind; beyond the "two cultures," in zones of conjunction still obscure, science and spirit reveal a universe that reveals them. This gnosis, the last essay supposes, constitutes the prophecy of Prometheus, a prophecy far more problematic in a posthumanist age than it ever was under the rule of Zeus.

Imagination, I confess, is my arch theme; teleological or not, it makes our future, *is* our fate, though we may come to it soon or late. Conjoined to that theme are other recurrent themes: desire, hope, change; ambitions and afflictions of the humanities; the immanence of languages, the indeterminacies of knowledge and action; a new play between wholes and parts, or the One and the Many as philosophers used to say; politics, history, the transhumanization of the earth; the role of mind—self-made and from itself concealed—in the universe; death, first literally, then as metaphor of change, finally as a language the cosmos speaks to us when we calm our fears. Are these fit topics or tropes for a gnostic Prometheus? I am certain only that they are part of the human project, our own gnosis.

III

Some singularities in the form of this work merit brief explanation.

Four interchapters occupy the space between five chapters, the former extracts from a journal I kept while writing this book. Do such journals intrude on a work of this sort? The question, ultimately, is for each reader to weigh; I can do no more here than rationalize a certain bias and procedure. Journals have served as a literary device for centuries; and since Gide's *The Counterfeiters,* they have brought an acute self-consciousness to the formal interrogation of forms. My journal also interrogates that genre we call academic criticism, strains at the model of linear discourse. Yet this nisus, which I began in *Paracriticisms,* invalidates neither; testing a limit, transgressing a line that history or habit has drawn, remains an act more often reflexive than revolutionary.

The journal discloses no intimate facts, events; still, it avows a degree of subjectivity, perhaps of intersubjectivity, which I hope can modify the incantatory abstractions of the Promethean theme. The journal suffers its own abstractions; indeed, it seems at times less journal than allegory—product, Allen Tate might say, of an "angelic" rather than "symbolic" imagination. Though less iconic in my tastes than Tate, I recognize this tendency in myself and try to texture it with travel notes, historical gossip, incongruous sources, sundry styles. The journal, after all, was not meant to muse eternity but to slip behind certain scenes of the writing self.

The self, advanced opinion now has it, is a "fiction." But so is everything else in so far as mind partakes of reality, and language itself is our supreme fiction. The self may be more fiction than we once allowed, and my journal tacitly admits this. Who, indeed, is the critic? How many in him speak? Yet "murmuring in various voices," as Japanese authors say, I can not pretend to have "dispersed" or "displaced" myself entirely: my sense of both self and self's other self, death, *finally* inhibits that game. Part diary and part allegory, a commonplace book and a little dictionary of quotations, the journal, in the end, neither answers nor confesses but patterns certain motifs, mild obsessions of a writing day.

If the journal expresses a subjective tendency or correlative, quotations express another antithetical to it. I do quote copiously throughout, and touch on the uses of citations in the first essay.

But the question is more complex than my (self)-mockery there admits. Roland Barthes believes that quotations seek to establish the paternity, authority, of a subject. But what if hundreds of "fathers" speak sychronously in many tongues? Susan Sontag understands: "The taste for quotations (and for the juxtaposition of incongruous quotations) is a Surrealist taste."

I should like to believe that quotations in this work act less as escutcheon than mosaic of a collective dream. Alternatively—since from time there is no escape—they may constitute a kind of music, gnostic yet full of noise, aspiring Babel and wise babble, the sound of our being here. Distinct from my language, in sound if not sense dissonant, these intertexts still offer a context for my text, can become themselves the text and my words quotations. Though the self may need sometimes to claim for itself uniqueness, isolateness, thought finds its identity not in quotes but in language, in mind, ubiquitously. This, too, is an aspect of the transhumanizaion of the earth.

Quotations offer one kind of break in what the eye can see, the ear can hear. But ruptures and diremptions can also be structural. There is calculated duplicity in calling the sections of this work "essays" and "chapters" interchangeably; for they stand neither in continuous nor discontinuous relation to one another. Written and many times rewritten, linked by various images, ideas, techniques, the work still wants to resist conventional unities, wants to preserve its internal lapses and its mixed modes, wants also to enliven inert uses of footnotes, margins, typography on the page. I am not certain that the interests of multivocation have been thus hugely enhanced. I know only that integrity or wholeness derives less from Unity than from interactions that contemporary science, art, philosophy, contemporary life itself, have all helped us to realize. In any case, a study of the postmodern imagination may be forgiven some defamiliarization, deformation, of traditional forms.

The deformations are mild; this will not make the work less moot. For critics who speak fluently of "deconstruction" or "decenterment" do little to apply either to their discourse; and reviewers who know all the right distinctions—Auerbach's between hypotaxis and parataxis, Jakobson's between metaphor and metonymy, Barthes's between writerly and readerly texts—will suffer experiments in every field but criticism. Such are the current aggravations of our humanities.

IV

My sense of the humanities may be a little alien to the acceptations of academe. Specialists, I suspect, will protest in the name of rigor my use of science in these pages. But specialists always protest whatever threatens specialization, not merely their specialties; and rigor remains the beginning, not end, of our critical enterprise. Nor was I free to limit my scope: cultural and epistemic mutations, the very subject of this book, compel us to unsettle boundaries, alter the fictions with which we work. Scientists themselves have taken to philosophic speculation; in doing so—science is not the monolith some humanists want it to be—they fiercely disagree. I trust that the more generous among them may find here no violation of their adventure in ideas.

It may also be that I impose too large, too exorbitant, a task on the humanities; Prometheus does prompt us to zealotry. Such promptings are patently ludicrous, if not thrasonical. Yet to bring the humanities into the Party of Hope (Emerson) as well as that of Memory is also to overcome the fear, crotchetiness, defeatism that pervade our profession. Who has not become weary of the old humanist vision, its intricacies of remorse, its pinched piety and riskless chatter? Bergson believed the universe a "machine for the making of gods." I take this as a summons, which imagination and science deliver to the humanities even as we are delivered to our future.

Perhaps it is time for us to recover the euchronic sense of existence. Oscar Wilde famously remarked: "A map of the world that does not include Utopia is not worth even glancing at, for it leaves out the one country at which Humanity is always landing." Precisely: utopia is both the dimension of the uncreated, which desire, imagination, and science create, and the country of the present, already here to be recreated. I do not plead for futurists, who can be thin of language and pale of vision. I plead for what needs no pleading: the reality of change, and the imperative of humanists to enter the regions of renewal. Kenneth Boulding proclaims: "The world of today is as different from the world I was born into as that world was from Julius Caesar's." This is easy, as easy to proclaim as to disclaim. The question remains: how can humanists, self-delighting in their complexity, now bring their resources of mind and feeling to incommensurate transformations?

This book provides no perfervid answers, though it poses

and transposes the question in various contexts. One of these I call the transhumanization of the earth. Nothing therein is mystical, though I dare say that Blake, Goethe, Emerson may serve us as well as our current masters of skepticism. No doubt, the process of transhumanization will prove more problematic than Teilhard envisioned; it may even prove cataclysmic. Still, as new gnostics realize, the powers of planetization are as much technological as spiritual. "To see technology in proper scale, we need cosmic consciousness, and that consciousness comes more often from meditation than from reading Marx or Freud," William Irwin Thompson says. The point is coenesthetic, not mystical.

And what precisely is "mystical," facile and dismissive epithet, favored by dogmatists intolerant of all but their narrow portion of reality? When William James concludes *The Varieties of Religious Experience* thus: "The whole drift of my education goes to persuade me that the world of our present consciousness is only one out of many worlds of consciousness that exist, and that those other worlds must contain experiences which have a meaning for our life also. . . ," is he mystical? Is Einstein or Heisenberg? Or is everyone who will not concede to meager paradigms and binding tempers the sovereignty of thought?

Though I have received no mystical illuminations, I would insist on the vast compass of human awareness, the energy of intuition, the turbulence and order of thought. I would insist as well that the frame of that thought may be greater than critics permit themselves to imagine; and that human history must account for biological evolution and the changing universe. Biology may or may not be destiny; imagination surely is; and history and cosmology converge even as myth and technology constantly meet. I would insist further that politics is what we have and must learn to do better than we do; but that in a complementary and coeval vision, politics is what we must work politically to make obsolete. I would insist finally that irony may be our present mode, expressing our fastidiousness, or perhaps simply our age in the universe; yet irony is also what we must, with due complexity, overcome. The "Nietzschean laugh" has begun to ring hollow; and heroism, which all the raillery of Nietzsche serves only to purify, abides as our "instinct for reality." "In heroism, we feel, life's supreme mystery is hidden. We tolerate no one who has no capacity whatever for it in any direction," notes Nietzsche's contemporary, William James.

V

But insistencies lack geniality, and this becomes tiresome; we have all had enough of terrorists. I hope the following texts will strike the reader as more probative and modest. I hope, too, that despite their singularities, they will prove more readable than recent criticism leads us to expect. Last, I hope these texts take certain risks.

Max Planck believed that no original scientist really convinces his colleagues; he simply outlives them. But in our era, we have all witnessed innovations, first furiously opposed, become common, invisible as the light of day. Thinking back on my works—without critical privilege—I think of three moments in which I have taken some risks: in *Radical Innocence* (1961), on the postwar American novel; in *The Literature of Silence* (1967), on the strategies of decreation in literature—these expanded in *The Dismemberment of Orpheus* (1971); and in *Paracriticisms* (1975), on the theory of postmodernism and paracritical discourse. The risks were partial, the success arguable—the success wider, I think, the lesser the risk. Now these subjects seem safe enough. What then was the fury all about? About our life in culture, about power over ideas and texts, about wagers on immortality, however exiguous the stakes?

Yet if this work has any intimation of something beyond itself, it is simply this: where Life truly matters, where it makes and remakes itself most fully, power and its human psychomachias dissolve. Where precisely is that blessed region? In the mind, of course, though where else I do not know. This book—fragment of an autobiography, meditation on science and imagination, small prayer for change—simply yields itself to that query.

Milwaukee, Wisconsin — February, 1979

THE CRITIC AS INNOVATOR

A Paracritical Strip in X Frames

—For S.

FRAME ONE

We have already begun. Invisible frames form our transactions as we read or think or dream in the verbal space of these pages. In *Frame Analysis,* Erving Goffman concerns himself with "realms of being," "codes of behavior," "constitutive rules," "worlds of make-belief"; he attends minutely to various "figures within frames" as these frames slip or shift or break:

> I start with the fact that from an individual's point of view, while one thing may momentarily appear to be what is going on, in fact what is actually happening is plainly a joke, or a dream, or an accident, or a mistake, or a misunderstanding, or a deception, or a theatrical performance, and so forth.

"What is really happening," then, is itself a function of frames, which are a kind of fiction. As Goffman concludes: "Life may not be an imitation of art, but ordinary conduct . . . is an imitation of the proprieties, a gesture at the exemplary forms, and the primal realization of these ideals belongs more to make-believe than to reality."

Our situation "in this time and place" thus is framed; the subject, criticism, is itself framed; and so is my own discourse, which will proceed in a series of frames broken by montages. These montages are superimpositions, or perhaps merely impositions, and they tend to be digressive, questioning, and rather ill-humored. But as my verbal strip moves, it slips, revealing inter-frames. I call these embarrassing flashes *slippage.*

Frame and Montage and Slippage: three modes of this strip, three tracks in a carping tape. It is all done in the hope of bringing inadmissible evidence into partial evidence.

Here comes the first Slippage.

SLIPPAGE

He recalls an exhibit of Renaissance picture frames at the Alte Pinakothek in Munich. The frames were empty, hung against white walls; elsewhere in the museum, the masterpieces of Altdorfer, Grünewald, and Dürer, of Breughel and Rembrandt, hung in their plenitude. He sensed that the museum had now become the frame of frames. And the frame of the museum? Finally, of course, the Universe.

But the Universe was an unspeakable fiction—a "thing" turned into fiction precisely in order to be spoken. Did framing and its opposite, deconstruction, then turn everything into fiction?

He refuses the thought. Desire and Death, he needs to assume, are "literal." Else the Universe is but a trope on the Void. This goes against something in him that hopes someday to be called his (Promethean) Hope.

FRAME TWO

In his celebrated work, *The Structure of Scientific Revolutions,* Thomas S. Kuhn argues that scientists tend to operate within a "consensus of research," which he calls a paradigm. Paradigms are not impervious to private or public influences: "An apparently arbitrary element, compounded of personal and historical accident, is always a formative ingredient of the beliefs espoused by a given scientific community at a given time," Kuhn admits. Nonetheless, scientific paradigms do take hold, organizing both theory and experiment, until an intolerable crisis in both compels scientists—or at least the most alert and inventive among them—to discard one paradigm for another. Paradigms are thus enabling structures. But these enabling structures also constrain; their enemies are anomalies, "*unexpected* novelty," genuine surprise.

Kuhn's argument is rather more complex; he was later to distinguish between *kinds* of paradigms and to call the most comprehensive a "disciplinary matrix." Still, even a naïve outline can underscore certain differences between the organization and development of knowledge in the sciences and in the humanities. For in the latter, the equivalent of a scientific paradigm seems to be a *school*. Now competing schools do sometimes exist in the sciences, but only in "pre-paradigmatic" periods, before a paradigm reigns. In the humanities, schools are less the exception than the rule. "If we doubt, as many do," Kuhn says, "that non-scientific fields make progress . . . it must be because there are always competing schools, *each of which constantly questions the very foundations of the others.* The man who argues that philosophy, for example, has made no progress emphasizes that there are still Aristotelians, not that Aristotelianism has failed to progress" (my italics). This is but another way of saying that scientists and humanists adopt very different views of their past. "Scientific education," Kuhn continues, "makes use of no equivalent for the art museum or library of classics, and the result is sometimes a drastic distortion in the scientist's perception of his discipline's past."

Applied to the humanities, Kuhn's ideas probably need a rest. But there are others, more sensitive to our enterprise, who also doubt the authority of paradigms in our indisciplines. Here is Victor Turner speaking very much to the point in *Dramas, Fields, and Metaphors:*

> The result of confrontation between monolithic, power-supported programs and their many subversive alternatives is a socio-cultural "field" in which many options are provided. . . . As my colleague Harold Rosenberg . . . has often argued, the culture of any society at any moment is more like the debris, or "fall-out," of past ideological systems, than it is itself a system, a coherent whole. Coherent wholes may exist . . . but human social groups tend to find their openness to the future in the variety of their metaphors for what may be the good life and in the contest of their paradigms.

To exchange "paradigms" for "schools" or "fields," then, is to exchange a *largely* epistemological view of a discipline for another that more freely admits history and desire. Indeed, the latter may have more to do with the principles and prejudices of Criticism than we ever confess.

Three points follow from this discourse so far:

a. Acceptability in criticism depends on our conscious or semi-conscious, hyperconscious or unconscious, loyalty to a critical school, including the Eclectic School. There are no dominant paradigms in the humanities; there are only some vague areas of "tacit knowledge" (Polanyi), which are becoming vaguer and fewer. Consequently, nothing I say here can possibly "invalidate" or render "obsolete" other critical persuasions. (Historical Scholars, Formalists, Marxists, Freudians, Jungians, Structuralists, Semioticians, Speech Actors—please relax.)

b. Fields, schools, and frames in the humanities lack military and, alas, economic power to back them, and so share a certain insecurity. Thus they pretend to ignore what disconfirms them. In truth, we work (read, write, teach) among breaking and intersecting frames. Thus we are all open to each other's discomforts—not to say animadversions.

c. More specifically, the absence of a sovereign paradigm in criticism makes innovation easier and more doubtful than in the sciences. For us, there are fewer constraints; there are also fewer enabling structures. We enjoy a certain "weightlessness"—and suffer from it. Such is the burden of our Freedom in this postmodern moment of unmakings.

MONTAGE

Some animadversions on the literary situation:

1. *American foundations have been generous to the Humanities. But what is their long-range impact on the American mind? Do they inhibit innovation or encourage it? Dedicated all to "excellence," do they not tend to define it in traditional terms, and so reward conventional work? These and more searching questions may be particularly pertinent to the National Endowment for the Humanities, which dispenses large governmental grants.*

2. *American universities often seem more open, their society more fluid, than their European counterparts. Why, then, do avant-garde trends in criticism originate in Europe rather than in America? And why do avant-garde critics meet with less suspicion there than in our universities?*

3. *Why does the reviewer of the year's work in literary criticism, writing in* The New Republic *of September 25, 1975, mention an article by a Yale colleague—it was an important article—yet overlook a major work by George Steiner,* After Babel, *which is of distinct relevance to the literary culture? Yet do plasma physicists, say, pretending to honor scientific paradigms, really behave differently?*

4. *Certain magazines are very much in the critical news today. For instance,* New Literary History, Critical Inquiry, Yale French Studies, Diacritics, Modern Language Notes, Salmagundi, The Georgia Review, Sub-Stance, *etc. They also happen to be quite fine. Yet do such congregations of talent contribute not only to the intensity but also to the constriction of critical discourse, and seduce critics into mannerisms of language and thought? For a small example: in certain quarters,* aufhebung *is now translated as "elation." For a larger instance: critical discourse now centers obsessively on a few names—Marx, French Nietzsche, French Freud, Heidegger, Derrida. Is there some benefit in decentering the circles of our intellectual reference? What about, say, Emerson or William James?*

FRAME THREE

The preponderance of schools in the humanities is an awkward condition of critical innovation. But there are others: for instance, the coincidence of critical and poetic talent in the same person. The classics of criticism, as the truism goes, were most often composed by poets: Sidney, Dryden, Pope, Wordsworth, Coleridge, Shelley, Poe, Eliot, to mention only those writing in English. Yet rarely have these authors illumined the relation between analysis and poesis in a manner that satisfies our modern sense of the creative process. Coleridge and Valéry, perhaps, remain among the exceptions to this cavil. Eliot in *The Sacred Wood,* however, only adds to our perplexity when he says about Swinburne, "This gives us an intimation why the artist is—each within his own limitations—oftenest to be depended upon as a critic; his criticism will be criticism, and not the satisfaction of a suppressed creative wish—which, in most persons, is apt to interfere fatally"—and then proceeds to demolish Swinburne, in his following essay, as too imperfect a critic.

I suspect that the issue of the poet as critic will remain problematic until we know more about the physiology of the human brain and the phenomenology of the creative process. The question, however, becomes more manageable if we formulate it thus: to what degree, and precisely in what epistemological sense, is all criticism a fiction? Far from shocking us, this formulation has a historic claim on our attention.

The claim was most cleverly advanced by Oscar Wilde at the turn of the century. Surprisingly, Wilde has been rehabilitated. Richard Ellmann has edited his essays, in *The Artist as Critic;* Lionel Trilling has referred to his ideas, in *Sincerity and Authenticity;* and current critics brightly associate him with an even more fashionable figure: Nietzsche, not the philosopher of Becoming but the darling and deconstructing dandy of poststructuralist thought. All this does not obscure Wilde's faults. His coyness distracts; his oxymorons can become tedious; his aphorisms sometimes pall. But the man had satiric genius, and perhaps even a darker, deeper genius within his gaiety.

Frame within Frame

With America's Bicentennial still in mind, I offer this Wilde passage:

> "The crude commercialism of America, its materialising spirit, its indifference to the poetical side of things, and its lack of imagination and of high unattainable ideals, are entirely due to that country having adopted for its national hero a man, who according to his own confession, was incapable of telling a lie, and it is not too much to say that the story of George Washington and the cherry-tree has done more harm, and in a shorter space of time, than any other moral tale in the whole of literature."

The passage is from "The Decay of Lying," first published in 1889. Wilde could not have known about Cambodia, Watergate, and the grisly antics of the CIA. Would the renascence of lying in America have cheered him? I think not. Wilde believed that true lying is imagination, a faculty wholly beyond the powers of politicians, who can only misrepresent. Yet more than most nations, America manufactures dreams, nightmares, *and* profound critiques of both.

For our purpose, Wilde's most pertinent essay is "The Critic as Artist." Matthew Arnold, we recall, enjoined critics (in 1864 in "The Function of Criticism at the Present Time") "to see the object as in itself it really is." This precept soon began to shift toward a more subjective focus in the criticism of Ruskin and Pater. But it remained for Wilde to stand Arnold on his head, and scandalously to suggest that the aim of the critic is to see the object as it really is not. There is method in Wilde's scandal, however, and we do well to allow him to speak for himself through the infamous Gilbert:

> The antithesis between them [the creative and the critical faculties] is entirely arbitrary. Without the critical faculty, there is no artistic creation at all.

*

> But, surely, Criticism is itself an art. . . . Why should it not be? It works with materials, and puts them into a form that is at once new and delightful. What more can one say of poetry? Indeed, I would call criticism a creation within a creation. For just as the great artists, from Homer and Aeschylus, down to Shakespeare and Keats, did not go directly to life for their subject-matter, but sought for it in myth, legend and ancient tale, so the critic deals with materials that others have, as it were, purified for him, and to which imaginative form and colour have been already added. Nay, more, I would say that the highest Criticism, being the purest form of personal impression, is in its way more creative than creation, as it has least reference to any standard external to itself, and is, in fact, its own reason for existing, and, as the Greeks would put it, in itself, and to itself, an end.

*

> The artistic critic, like the mystic, is an antinomian always.

Scandal, sacrilege, and high camp—all of us who have been trained in Positivist Scholarship or the New Criticism want to cry! (Indeed, I shudder to think of the ruin of Graduate English Departments, should everyone suddenly take after Wilde; fortunately, graduate students are much too sensible thus to jeopardize their future tenures by committing premature academic suicide.) Yet frivolous, perverse, or extreme as Wilde's statements may seem, his position in some sense anticipates that of many other critics, including W. K. Wimsatt on the "intentional fallacy," Harold Bloom on "poetic misprision," Wolfgang Iser on the "implied reader," and Roland Barthes on the illicit "pleasures of the text." For the basic impulse of Wilde—no matter how mauve or *fin de siècle* his manner may appear—is to deny the author a privileged view of his text, deny the text itself any ultimate concreteness or unity. The critic, Wilde insists, should not be fair, sincere, or rational. "There are two ways of disliking art. . . . One is to dislike it. The other is to like it rationally," he has Gilbert quip; and again: "What people call insincerity is simply a method by which we can multiply our personalities." Here Wilde approaches that notion of the "empty" or indefinite "subject" so crucial to later structuralists, who believe with Nietzsche that what we call a self is at best a rendezvous of several people.

For Wilde's "critic as artist," then, the act of reading is constitutive; it is an act of creation. The text (or object) is multiple and "shifting," a word dear to Wilde; so is the self (or subject). Indeed, subject and object sometimes shift or exchange their places. And transgression (stepping across), in life as in criticism or art, "is an essential element of progress." Here are all the elements of the critic's epistemological Freedom—and all the unresolved problems too.

MONTAGE

But why think of the critic only? Isn't his/her activity as constitutive awareness or creative agonism a political fact as well? Wilde brings to mind Karl Marx. Here is Marx, in his letter of July 22, 1861, to Ferdinand Lassalle, on political "misprision:"

> Otherwise it might be said that every achievement of an older period, which is adopted in later times, is part of the *old misunderstood*. . . . Thus, too, all modern constitutions rest in great part on the *misunderstood* English constitution. . . . The misunderstood form is precisely the general form, applicable for general use at a definite stage of social development.

History as "misunderstanding"? Criticism as the politics of literary misunderstanding?

And who, precisely, tends to become a critic, instead of a doctor, computer technician, or diplomat? Are there innumerable types, or are there certain identifiable, certain recurrent types? Should we pursue such dismaying queries? Or should we rather assume that Criticism is best defined abstractly, without reference to Person, defined in terms of such institutions as Literature or the University?

The questions are perhaps worth mooting: the politics of criticism (more of this later) is not altogether alien to the personae of critics.

SLIPPAGE

He thinks of Hegel's primal beast called Recognition.

Having waited decades to meet it, he chose then to seek it out in the world, its lair. Vain quest. Once, sitting in his study alone, he felt behind him some immense breath, raw, ontic, older than time. Turning slowly, he saw . . . nothing. A small heap of ashes on the carpet may have dropped from his cigar.

He continues to seek the Beast, as a formality, suspecting all the time that it is tracking him to his grave.

FRAME FOUR

Oscar Wilde was not the only writer to bruit the case for the critic as artist. His French contemporary, Rémy de Gourmont, did quite as much and possibly with greater consequence. Half a century later, a man who had little in common with either Wilde or Gourmont made an even stronger case for the liberty of the critic as everyman. I mean Jean-Paul Sartre. In *What Is Literature?*, Sartre scathingly portrays the traditional critic:

> The critic lives badly; his wife does not appreciate him as she ought to; his children are ungrateful; the first of the month is hard on him. But it is always possible for him to enter his library, take down a book from the shelf, and open it. It gives off a slight odor of the cellar, and a strange operation begins which he has decided to call reading.

It is this operation, this activity we call reading (which has become even more problematic in our day), that Sartre wants to redefine, to revitalize. Sartre's dialectical bias is already clear:

> But the operation of writing implies that of reading as its dialectical correlative and these two connected acts necessitate two distinct agents. It is the conjoint effort of author and reader which brings upon the scene that concrete and imaginary object which is the work of the mind. There is no art except for and by others.

This leads Sartre to conclude what now seems to us so obvious: that reading is a "synthesis of perception and creation." True, in this synthesis the great Existential Marxist does not give to language the primacy that both Structuralists and the New Critics were to accord it. Yet in his conception of the literary work, created by the reader's freedom, and of literature itself, as the subjectivity of a society in permanent revolution, he offers a moral and historical basis for the act of critical innovation. For its philosophical basis, Sartre demands that we surpass even Kant in declaring the work of art without finality or end, a work constituted by each glance of the beholder, responding to each appeal, "a pure exigence to exist."

Those other neo-Kantians, our own old New Critics, took an antithetical view of the matter. Yet even during their reign, there were some who kept the possibility of the critic as innovator alive. Thus, for instance, in the *Kenyon Review* Symposium of 1950–51, entitled "My Credo," Leslie Fieldler argues for an "amateur criticism," and Herbert

Read movingly speaks of the "critic as a man of feeling." Even that collage of New Critical ideas, R. W. Stallman's *The Critic's Notebook* (1950), has for an epigraph these lines from Martin Turnell: "The critic possesses a dual personality. He is at once an 'artist' and a 'thinker,' the 'man of feeling' and the 'intellectual'. . . . He is an artist, *but a special kind of artist*" (italics mine).

This formulation may strike us as philosophically naïve. Consider, however, a later writer: Paul de Man, surely one of the most subtle critics now writing in America, steeped in the European tradition, inward with current thought. De Man knows that the relation of "authentic criticism" to literary studies is at best problematic; he does not want to force criticism upon a propadeutic endeavor to which it might be alien. In *Blindness and Insight*, he candidly notes:

> Whether authentic criticism is a liability or an asset to literary studies as a whole remains an open quesion. One thing, however, is certain; namely, that literary studies cannot possibly refuse to take cognizance of its existence. It would be as if historians refused to acknowledge the existence of wars because they threaten to interfere with the serenity that is indispensable to an orderly pursuit of their discipline.

Furthermore, de Man realizes that "all true criticism occurs in the mode of crisis"; for him, a crisis in criticism is in some measure redundant since crisis makes for genuine insight, for critical authenticity. He also notes that genres are no longer as pure as we once liked to believe. "The gap between the manifestoes and the learned articles," he says, "has narrowed to the point where some manifestoes are quite learned and some articles—though by no means all—are quite provocative." Thus criticism, in becoming cousin to the manifesto, proclaims its right to newness.

More significantly, perhaps, de Man clearly perceives the implications of Heidegger's "hermeneutic circle" to the art of critical interpretation: the latter becomes endless. No totality of meaning or closure of form can suffice. "The hermeneutic understanding is always, by its very nature, lagging behind: to understand something is to realize that one had always known it, but, at the same time, to face the mystery of this hidden knowledge." And again, speaking now of Derrida, de Man observes: "not only does the critic say something that the work does not say, but he even says something that he himself does not mean to say. The semantics of interpretation have no epistemological consistency and can therefore not be scientific." Thus the "authentic" critic begins his job by accepting the inevitable discrepancy between the original text and his critical discourse. On this point, de Man is emphatic:

> The necessary immanence of the [critic's] reading in relation to the text is a burden from which there can be no escape. It is bound to stand out as the irreducible philosophical problem raised by all forms of literary criticism, however pragmatic they may seem or want to be. We encounter it here in the form of a constitutive discrepancy, in critical discourse, between the blindness of the statement and the insight of the meaning.

It is precisely this "constitutive discrepancy" in critical discourse, recognized intuitively by Wilde as by later critics, that makes for the initial condition of innovation in criticism—again, its Freedom. But is it also a *sufficient* condition? I think not.

FRAME FIVE

The critic's Freedom is anxious and fractious; it is initiative, responsive, and reflexive all at the same time. But it can provide only the ground for innovation. A critic needs more, needs an erotic sense of Style and an intuition of the New.

An original style neither seeks nor evades "difficulty," though a degree of "defamiliarization" (*ostranenie,* the Russian formalists called it) may be an aspect of it. True, critical languages, as we all know, now suffer with jargon, neologism, and abstraction; they have become technical and idiolectic at the same time. (God guard us against the transumptions, metalepses, paronomasias, catabases, and apotropies that afflict our eristic discourse.) Yet we also sense that the style of a Blackmur or a Barthes, uncouth as it may seem to limpid minds, expresses a curious energy—a kind of love?

Blackmur now is half forgotten. Yet in such essays as "A Critic's Job of Work," "A Burden for Critics," and "The Enabling Act of Criticism," Blackmur, despite his inclination to dense technical analysis, maintains the stance of an artist or lover, both disciplined and freed by what he loves. "Criticism, I take it, is the formal discourse of an amateur," he writes in *Language as Gesture*. "When there is enough love and enough knowledge represented in the discourse it is a self-sufficient but by no means an isolated art. It witnesses constantly in its own life its interdependence with the other arts." But it is Blackmur's style, more than anything else, that betrays the artist in him; dark, original, poetic, the style is forever at the point of re-creating everything that it touches. It is itself touched by that perversity of the critical genius, that quiddity of the artistic temperament, which evokes two other wholly different critics: Marxist Walter Benjamin and Structuralist/Poststructuralist Roland Barthes.

About Benjamin I will have nothing to say here except that he must be counted with Barthes among the rare critical geniuses of our century. As for the latter, protean structuralist, cunning semiotician, oblique amateur (lover) of language, he has from the start averred the privileges of the critic as a "special kind of artist." Thus in *Critique et vérité,* Barthes desires both "criticism and works always to say: *I am literature,*" since the critic can only "continue the metaphors of the work, never reduce them" to any intelligibility. In his later works, Barthes is even more explicit and paradoxical about the role of criticism. Here he is in *Critical Essays:*

> It is by acknowledging itself as no more than a language (or more precisely, a metalanguage) that criticism can be—paradoxically but authentically—both objective and subjective, historical and existential, totalitarian and liberal. . . . Thus begins, at the heart of the critical work, the dialogue of two histories and two subjectivities, the author's and the critic's. But this dialiogue is egoistically shifted toward the present: criticism is not an "homage" to the truth of the past or to the truth of "others"—it is a construction of the intelligibility of our time.

This paradoxical conception need not paralyze criticism, though it does betray the structuralist tendency to oscillate between the poles of logic and fantasy, science and solipsism. For Barthes, such oscillations are checked by a complex commitment to *pleasure.* "The pleasure of the text," as Barthes says in a recent book by that name, is perverse and polymorphous; it is erotic, constituted by the intermittences not only of the heart but more of the body. "The text is a fetishistic object and that fetish desires me," he confides. Criticism—or more precisely, critical style—becomes the fumbling response to that requited desire. Far from obeying the imperatives of logic as Barthes had earlier suggested, critical style embraces the text, only to discover its own muteness, discover, that is, its inability to say anything except: "this is it for me! This 'for me' is neither subjective, nor existential, but Nietzschean. . . ." But critical muteness now recovers speech under another imperative: neither the imperative of Logic nor simply of erotic Style but of *Novelty.* Here is the crucial passage in *The Pleasure of the Text,* which finally defines for Barthes the function of the critic as innovator:

> The New is not a fashion, it is a value, upon which is founded all criticism: our valuation of the world no longer depends, at least directly, as in Nietzsche, upon the opposition between the *noble* and the *base*, but rather upon the opposition between the Old and the New. . . . To escape from the alienation of present society, there is only one way: *escape forward:* all old languages are immediately compromised, and all languages become old as soon as they are respected.

Barthes's insight into the role of the critic as innovator is difficult—some would say crepuscular or impenetrable. It is an insight based, as Susan Sontag had hoped, upon an erotics rather than a hermeneutics of texts, an erotics *and* politics of the New. And the secret agent of that insight is for Barthes, as it was for Blackmur and Benjamin, critical Style!

Style may be the secret agent; but in structuralist circles, of which there are many, the public demand is to abolish familiar distinctions between "criticism" and "literature." Thus Eugenio Donato summarizes this assumption in *The Languages of Criticism and the Sciences of Man:*

> Derrida's enterprise also reveals within our modern context the impossibility of drawing an essential line between literature and criticism. Literature can only be a denunciation of literature and is not therefore different in essence from criticism. Criticism, in as much as it is a denunciation of literature, is, itself, nothing but literature.

The name of Derrida, magus of grammatology, has been uttered. Soon, I must speak of his and others' unmakings; for therein lies another aspect of critical innovation. But a montage once again clouds my frame.

MONTAGE

Do I quote from others too much? Very well, then, I quote too much, and I must need quote some more. But what does it mean "to quote"?

We rarely quote nowadays to appeal to authority—Leonardo: "Whoever refers to authorities in disputing ideas, works with his memory rather than his reason"—though we quote sometimes to display our sapience and erudition. Some authors we quote against. Some we quote not at all, offering them our scrupulous avoidance, and so make them part of our "white mythology." Other authors we constantly invoke, canting their names in cerebral rituals of propitiation or ancestor worship. Others still, we quote for the pleasure or prestige of their company. (It is a little like being seen in public with Raquel Welch or, in another time, with the Duke of Windsor.) And there are authors, finally, whom we quote in the spirit of true sodality.

Do will, vanity, and desire (Blackmur's Moha?*), then, always insinuate themselves in our quotation marks? I can not answer without quoting further. This exposes another problem.*

In a statement on "the critic as innovator," quotations seem a bizarre aporia or contradiction. Yet aporias may have uses that reason refuses. By playing texts against texts, voices against voices, do I permit language to open a new space, begin an intertextual discourse (Kristeva) that may "say" what I cannot say? And is this still another aspect of the critic's Freedom?

I leave the "dear reader" to decide. But as a pacifier to that reader's conscience and mine, I must recapitulate my argument. Here is a quick flash-back of my five frames:

1. *Frames or fields shape our actions and utterances, including critical discourse; frames are really a kind of fiction.*

2. *Schools (in America, this often means Graduate Schools) rather than paradigms prevail in criticism; schools render critical innovation both easier and more ambiguous within shifting frames. For they are open to history and desire.*

3. *Criticism is a constitutive discourse, like literature itself; thus the critic as a frame-worker, a "special kind of artist," enjoys some epistemological Freedom.*

4. *The critic as a "special kind of artist" reveals him/herself in Style, and in a complex, erotic attitude toward the New.*

5. *All this, as we shall see, leads into politics, the critic's multiple Concern, and into the bounds and circumference of imagination.*

FRAME SIX

All my comments so far evade the peculiar provocations of our postmodern thought. It is an antinomian moment that assumes a vast unmaking in the Western mind—what Michel Foucault might call a postmodern *épistémè*. I say "unmaking" though other terms are now *de rigeur:* from deconstruction to dispersal to a variety of virtual "deaths." Such terms express an ontological rejection of the traditional full subject, the *cogito* of Western philosophy. They express, too, an epistemological obsession with fragments or fractures, and a corresponding ideological commitment to minorities in politics, sex, and language. To think well, to feel well, to act well, to read well, according to this *épistémè* of unmaking, is to refuse the tyranny of wholes; totalization in any human endeavor is potentially totalitarian.

Two recent examples may impart some sense of this postmodern will to unmaking. They are, in their intellectual styles, strikingly divergent. Yet both clearly share certain assumptions about our moment.

In *La Révolution sans modèle*, three men—François Châtelet, Gilles Lapouge, and Olivier Revault d'Allonnes—discuss informally the possibilities of radical yet unmediated change. The paradox seems inescapable: all human effort is in time, and time decomposes as well as consolidates. Thus innovation becomes inheritance. Furthermore, all human effort is in language. (Indeed, the word revolution itself may signify an obsolete concept of change; that is why Jean-François Lyotard likes to speak of volution instead of revolution.) And language imposes all its patterns on our thoughts and actions. How then escape the structures of discourse? Model, anti-model, without-model?

The authors circle and circle around. Is a model-in-the-making still a model? Can a model convert, subvert, or pervert its own versions, and so keep itself incomplete? What if various models were set against one another, without dominance of a single model? How does an under-determined model (anarchic) suddenly become over-determined (totalitarian or utopian)? Or is every model of "perfection" really an image of the void?

They quote Julio Cortazar: "One cannot change man without changing his instruments of knowledge, language itself." They quote Roland Barthes: "Today, there is an area of language exterior to bourgeois ideology: our language comes from it, returns to it, remains locked within it. The only possible answer is neither confrontation nor destruction but only theft: to fragment the old texts of culture, of science, of literature, and to disseminate and disguise the fragments in the same way that we disguise stolen merchandise."

The authors finally wonder: is the concept of a revolution without a model not a model itself? Or is a revolution without a model a pleonasm, since all "true" revolutions are indeed without a model, the model coming afterwards? Or again, should the model of every revolution be designed only for one purpose, to engender a revolutionary *movement?* These and other queries suggest how the will to unmaking declares itself in an exoteric work, a work of intellectual journalism at its liveliest.

In contrast, *L'Anti-Oedipe* by Gilles Deleuze and Félix Guattari seems esoteric, formidably learned and speculative. Subtitled *"Capitalisme et schizophrénie,"* the book envisions history as the coding and uncoding of an erotic flux, the flux of a *"machine désirante,"* which controls all human effort. The desiring machine has defined three stages of history: *"Sauvages"* (primitive, tribal, prehistoric societies), *"Barbares"* (ancient, despotic states), and *"Civilisés"* (modern, immanent capitalism); these correspond to the "full body," "paranoia," and "schizophrenia." The authors describe themselves as "schizoanalysts," and relentlessly attack the Oedipus complex, which they perceive as a rank misunderstanding of the forms of desire in history.

But what, specifically, is their theory of unmaking? In a complex and technical argument, which considers the material as well as the epistemological basis of capitalism, Deleuze and Guattari conclude that the latter represents a new creativity of "schizoid time." "Civilization," they say, "defines itself by the uncoding and deterritorialization of [erotic] fluxes in capitalist productions." There is thus an "affinity" between capitalist and schizophrenic fluxes, but no exact identity. On the contrary, as schizophrenia represents the *limit* toward which capitalism tends, so does it also represent the destruction against which capitalism must struggle. (Capitalism attempts to save itself from ultimate schizophrenia by coding and "axiomatizing" with one hand what it constantly uncodes with the other.)

Schizophrenia, in short, heralds and hastens the end of capitalism. Thus Deleuze and Guattari designate schizophrenia, not schizophrenics, as the essential revolutionary condition, and paranoia as the essential despotic or fascist state. Schizophrenia fragments, unmakes; it refuses totalization, as in Antonin Artaud, William Burroughs, R. D. Laing, John Cage, as in nearly all postmodern arts. "We no longer believe," the authors say, "in an original totality nor in a totality of destination." For Deleuze and Guattari, then, schizophrenia has become the historical agent of the liberation of desire, which is the source of all production. Unmaking is the human project *par excellence.*

These two works, quixotic in their contrast, are part of a larger frame of deconstruction that must include the work of Derrida, Foucault, Barthes, Kristeva, and Sollers, among others. And that larger frame, is it not a historical development of that still vaster configuration we call modernism in the arts?

In the arts, we know, the will to unmaking began to manifest itself earlier, around the turn of the century. Yet from the ready-mades of Marcel Duchamp and the collages of Hans Arp to the autodestructive machines of Jean Tinguely and conceptual works of Bruce Nauman, a certain impulse has persisted, turning art against itself in order to remake itself. Sometimes, the artist has turned not only against his art but even against his flesh. Thus Vito Hannibal Acconci, a "body artist," bites himself in public; Chris Burden arranges a party to have himself shot in the arm; and the Viennese, Rudolph Schwarzkogler, slowly amputates his penis before a moving camera—and bleeds to death. The artist's body has become his medium, and the dismembered medium his message. In this, literary authors lag only a short distance behind.

But the main point is this: art, in process of "de-definition" as Harold Rosenberg says, is becoming, like the personality of the artist, an occurrence without clear boundaries: at worst a kind of social hallucination, at best an opening or inauguration. That is why Jean-François Lyotard enjoins readers "to abandon the safe harbour offered to the mind by the category of 'works of art' or of signs in general, and to recognize as truly artistic nothing but *initiatives* or events, in whatever domain they may occur."

Art as "initiative," as "event"; texts that are, in the words of Barthes, "*scriptible*" rather than "*lisible*"; a postmodern *épistémè* of unmaking. What imperatives of innovation do these impose upon the critic? What new rigors and exigencies? And what omissions or remissions?

MONTAGE

Working with Frames and Montages, how do I select or exclude? Tendentiously, of course, as any maker must. Tendentiously, yes—but also, like The Three Princes of Serendip, *with some happy accidents and fortunate pratfalls? It may be comforting to think so. Yet given the inter-debtedness of language and mind, each to itself and each to each, how can anything finally be excluded? Even a catch phrase, "the critic as innovator," creates the very contexts from which it is absent, clusters of thought to which it wants to return. How imply these contexts of absence? In a bibliography of silences?*

Here, for instance, are some omissions in my treatment of the critic as innovator:

1. *Criticism and language games. See Ludwig Wittgenstein,* Philosophical Investigations, The Blue and Brown Books, *and* Zettel.

2. *The problem of "subjective," "objective," and "transactive"*

paradigms in literary interpretation. See the essays by David Bleich and Norman N. Holland in New Literary History, *VII, no. 2 (1976).*

3. The role of literary tropes and fictions in historical narratives, including literary history. See Hayden White, Metahistory; *Louis Mink, "History and Fiction as Modes of Comprehension,"* New Literary History, *I, no. 3 (1970); and Paul Hernadi, "Clio's Cousins: Historiography as Translation, Fiction, and Criticism,"* New Literary History, *VII, no. 2 (1976). Some essays of "The Bellagio Symposium,"* New Literary History, *VII, no. 1 (1975), are also relevant, as is Ralph Cohen and Murray Krieger's* Literature and History.

4. The limits of "objectivity" in American criticism, endless debate. See essays by Murray Krieger, Northrop Frye, and E. D. Hirsch, in L. S. Dembo, ed., Criticisms; *as well as the essays by M. H. Abrams and E. D. Hirsch, in Morton W. Bloomfield, ed.,* In Search of Literary Theory.

·5. The phenomenology of the reading process, in its innumerable versions. See, for instance, Georges Poulet, "Phenomenology of Reading," New Literary History, *I, no. 1 (1969); Gaston Bachelard,* The Poetics of Reverie; *and Wolfgang Iser,* The Implied Reader.

6. The question of innovation or initiation in language generally. See Edward Said's Beginnings; *for instance, this passage: "Or, in radical criticism, it is the deep anterior claim of the writing, sometimes willfully forgotten, sometimes deliberately attenuated, but always haunting the critic whose reading abuts the mountains and the caverns of another's, an author's, mind at work: such critics write critical poems imitating the behavior of the mind."*

Yet why, in rectifying some of my "omissions," do I include in my "bibliography" articles from only a single journal? And how does such a bibliography, arbitrary still in its own *omissions, clarify the imperatives of innovation?*

FRAME SEVEN

Inevitably, the imperatives of innovation lead us, through politics, to the critic's Concern. The politics are triple: politics of the page, of academic criticism, and of language and society in general.

Consider the periodical *College English*. Revitalized in the last decade by left/liberal editorial policies, it has set out to change the profession from within. Yet its arguments appear invariably in serried, double columns of an unvarying typeface. They appear, more significantly, in a format that challenges none of the social or technical or sensuous conventions of its own medium: editorial policies, printing rules, subscription forms, advertising practices, etc. Thus, whatever reform *College English* attempts, it does so on the level of abstract rational discourse; that is, on only one level of human discourse in culture. Yet had it attempted more, would it not have lost its credibility for many of us? Our passion may sometimes be our task, but the slogan of our "critical inquiry" remains linear "reasoned discourse"—reasoned, alas, ironically or blandly, aggressively or fearfully, but seldom reasoned to express the full measure of human awareness.

This is not the place to develop a rationale for the Mallarméan project of breaking up the type, the line, the page, the language. Still, any cursory look at certain works by Michel Butor, Philippe Sollers, Maurice Roche, Ernst Jandl, Eugen Gömringer, Helmut Heissenbüttel, Christine Brooke-Rose, Raymond Federman, Ronald Sukenick, Donald Barthelme, Walter Abish, Dick Higgins, Eugene Wildman, Campbell Tatham, or John Cage, among many others, can convey, through expanding eyes, intimations of that project.

Who then will carry this project to criticism and how?

Frames within a Frame

Essaying collections recommended
by Richard Kostelanetz

Bann, Stephen, ed. *The Tradition of Constructivism.* New York: Viking, 1974.

Brockman, John. *Afterwords.* Garden City: Doubleday Anchor, 1973.

Burnham, Jack. *Great Western Salt Works.* New York: Braziller, 1974.

Cage, John. *M.* Middleton, Conn.: Wesleyan University Press, 1973.

Depew, Wally. *Nine Essays on Concrete Poems.* Alamo, Calif.: Holmganger Press, 1974.

Ferguson, Gerald. *The Standard Corpus of Present Day English Usage.* Halifax: Nova Scotia College of Art and Design, 1973.

Gillespie, Abraham Lincoln. *Collected Works.* Edited by Hugh Fox. Forthcoming.

Hassan, Ihab. *Paracriticisms.* Urbana: University of Illinois Press, 1975.

Kostelanetz, Richard. *Recyclings: A Literary Autobiography.* Volume One: 1959–67. New York: Assembling Press, 1974.

LeWitt, Sol. *Arcs, Circles & Grids.* New York: Paul Bianchini, 1972.

Lippard, Lucy R. *Six Years.* New York: Praeger, 1973.

Olson, Charles. *Additional Prose.* Bolinas, Calif.: Four Seasons, 1974.

Queeney, Shiva & Michael Goodenough. *The Be-Cause Look Book.* New York: Links, 1973.

Themerson, Stefan. *Logics Labels and Flesh.* London: Gabberbocchus, 1974.

To which we can add:

Barthes, Roland. *Roland Barthes par Roland Barthes.* Paris: Éditions du Seuil, 1975.

Calvino, Italo. *La cittá invisibile.* Milano: Giulio Einaudi, 1972.

Derrida, Jacques. *Glas.* Paris: Galilée, 1974.

Kostelanetz, Richard, ed. *Essaying Essays: Alternative Forms of Exposition.* New York: Out of London Press, 1976.

The politics of the page, no less than its erotics or stylistics, intrudes upon us precisely because, as Barthes said, "all old languages are immediately compromised, and all languages become old as soon as they are respected." And the languages of criticism?

SLIPPAGE

Be serious, he thinks; think of power, of politics.

He fancies that he has accepted his death, or at least lived with it on terms of intimate forgetfulness, ever since that morning in the Alps, an adolescent still, he saw a black hearse wind its way *upwards* through snow and blue ice. Or was it only an imaginary scene, painted by Caspar David Friedrich?

He fancies that he has accepted his death, and so become an amateur of change, mediating between Time and Value. Why, then, should he heed politics?

Politics: a repetition compulsion, oppression or revenge made licit, the actor always excluding much of him/herself from the act in order to act. But also politics: feeding the hungry mouth, stopping the torturer's red hand, giving human Hope its patient due.

He recalls a line from Mao to Chou En-lai: "Our mission, unfinished, may take a thousand years." Perhaps more. But the struggle, he thinks, must always be double: to struggle and *at the same time* struggle to empty all struggle.

FRAME EIGHT

The politics of the page may be part of the inhibiting politics of criticism as an academic institution. The critical article and the scholarly book now reign; they mediate our imagination and knowledge. But why not *also* the essay, the ideal essay rooted etymologically in risk, trial, examination, balance, rooted in *both* risk and balance? "The essay—" someone always asks, "but is it criticism?" Perhaps it is not. But perhaps also what criticism now requires is a text that puts itself in jeopardy with other texts.

Criticism, like Literature, is a historical institution; it is neither a Platonic triangle nor a stone pyramid enduring Time under a yellow sun. Our ideas both of Criticism and of Literature are changing, have changed. Even Northrop Frye, more given to heroic schemata than most of us, understood in his *Anatomy of Criticism* a point we tend to miss: "The total Logos of criticism by itself can never become an object of faith or an ontological personality"; and again: "The presence of incommunicable experience in the center of criticism will always keep criticism an art, as long as the critic recognizes that criticism comes out of it but cannot be built on it."

Yet for some critics—or let us simply say, for some writers of texts—the age demands less building than *bricolage* (Lévi-Strauss), than forage or rummage. This demand may wrench the writer out of the university's noetic frame, perhaps out of literature itself, out and back in again. Edmund Wilson, Edmund Wilson, Edmund Wilson: we intone his single name forever, as if to prove that the man of letters is but recently defunct in America. In France, however, the names of great and eccentric essayists roll easily off the tongue: Bachelard on fire, Caillois on the octopus, Leiris on tauromachy, Bataille on eroticism, Blanchot on absence, Butor on nearly everything—not to mention Sartre or Camus!

The temptation, of course, is to conclude that the natural enemy of the free essay is the university: that society of specialized knowledge and power which has become the main custodian of the critical mind since literature began to be studied in the vernacular (see Walter J. Ong's *The Barbarian Within*). Yet the university itself may be more symptom than cause of intellectual enervation in America. Behind the page, behind the essay, behind the humanities, vaster dispositions of culture loom into view. These are recognized by Serge Doubrovsky in *The New Criticism in France:*

> Criticism is an inoffensive and distant activity only on the surface. In reality, it is the machinery of censorship, the ultimate policing force that a society produces as a means of keeping strict watch on the expression of thought within it and ensuring the preservation of its values.

The emphasis here is perhaps too heavy. But it serves to elicit the ultimate implication of the topic: namely, that innovation in criticism finally aspires not only to epistemological, existential, or aesthetic freedom but also to basic political change. This statement, of course, cries anxiously for qualification. Yet it underscores the present need to move beyond the Arnoldian position, as restated by Northrop Frye in *The Well-Tempered Critic:*

> But it seems clear that Arnold was on solid ground when he made "culture," a total imaginative vision of life with literature at its center, the regulating and normalizing element in social life, the human source, at least, of spiritual authority. Culture in Arnold's sense is the exact opposite of an elite's game preserve; it is, in its totality, a vision or model of what humanity is capable of achieving, the matrix of all Utopias and social ideals.

Culture may be the "matrix" of all human possibilities; yet the societies in which we act still remain at a bitter distance from those "imaginative visions" that culture constantly generates. Can the critic as innovator help to close the Gap of Hope? Can we all begin to understand the disposition of power, avoiding both the etherealizations of the avant-garde ("the consciousness industry," Enzensberger called it) and the reifications of troglodytic Marxism? How would a genuine post-Marxist theory both articulate and change reality? And admit imagination?

MONTAGE

The Gap of Hope. It will certainly not be closed simply by typographic experiment or paracritical play. But neither will it be closed by a criticism that ignores its potential as performance, a performance affecting our societies, our institutions, our languages, and indeed our very senses. *A Promethean performance?*

Why is it, I wonder (ungraciously? unjustly?), that so many American critics, despite their intellectual brilliance, lack prescience about culture, lack also in the power of enabling moral ideas? (There are of course some exceptions—how many?) Is it because so few critics are willing to step out of their academic frame, out of the scholarly book or critical essay? Or is it because, as Frank Kermode pretends, critics are not expected to make sense of our lives as other writers are expected to do? (Has any truly great critic ever held that view?) And why not? Why must criticism invariably *be so discrete, so technical, so exclusive an activity of mind, denying mind so large a part of itself?*

I realize the dangers of making inordinate claims for criticism: bad religion, bad politics, bad prose. (I have sometimes come close to all three myself.) But no danger, I feel, should now inhibit our search for a new liveliness, a new capaciousness, a new potency in criticism. Can humanists otherwise hope to enter the future, release imagination, subvert power with a more equivocal (and so hopeful) power?

The Gap of Hope grows.

FRAME NINE

The question persists: what, beyond the critic's Freedom, Style, and intuition of the New, defines Concern, and so empowers the critic's language to enter history? In his *Theory of the Avant-Garde,* we recall, Renato Poggioli thought the judgments of great critics to be posthumous or prophetic: "Great criticism starts with the *Zeitgeist* but tends to anticipate posterity," he wrote. Through such anticipations of concern, the critic's Freedom returns as Responsibility, taking hold of history.

Concern, however, is often a shadowy and shifting thing. From Lukács to Eliot, critics have filled the ideological spectrum with doctrines and myths of concern. My own view of the matter is neither doctrinal nor mythic. The critic's concern is a double wager: one with history, the other with eternity. It determines both his/her politics and moral life. No critic, I suspect, can enlarge the possibilities of a sullen craft without exceptional force and generosity of concern, though no concern alone, however fierce, could make a critic artful. Most obviously, critical concern expresses itself in formative subjects, arch themes. The point is recognized by conservative no less than by radical critics.

In an obscure essay, titled "Experiment in Criticism" and published in *The Bookman* in 1929, T. S. Eliot affirmed: "The various attempts to find the fundamental axioms behind both good literature and good life are among the most interesting 'experiments' of criticism in our time"; such attempts, he thought, showed "that the modern literary critic must be an 'experimenter' outside of what you might at first consider his own province." Eliot had in mind the New Humanism of Babbit and More, and its French equivalent, the Christian Humanism of Ramon Fernandez. We, of course, now have very different matters in mind; indeed, some of us may feel that we may soon enter an altogether posthumanist phase. Yet the conjunctions Eliot made half a century ago between intellectual scope, moral significance, and critical experiment still hold; only their focus and our concerns have changed.

Our concerns: what formative subjects do they now provide criticism? Here I can only wager or guess in rubric form:

a. Theories of the Imagination: a general theory of fictions, including criticism, which can take into account current neurological, psychological, philosophic, and linguistic research.

b. The Politics of the Imagination: how imagination takes power and when it fails to do so, and the nature of the power that imagination *can* take.

c. The Future: prophetic or utopian fictions—models of desire, dream, and hope—that become agents of transformation, become concretions of the future.

d. Mythology and Technology, Mysticism and Science: convergences between their structures in the deeper structures of postmodern culture, and the implications thereof.

e. The One and the Many: the emergent role of mind, extended by technology, in mediating between unity and diversity, organization and chaos, the ecumenical will and the will to secession on earth—toward a new vision, not of sameness but of wholeness.

Stark and huge as some of these Promethean subjects seem, they are of profound practical and theoretical interest to our literary business. Yet in the end, I would not wish simply to identify innovative with self-conscious criticism. It is not merely that "the owl of Minerva takes its flight only when the shades of night are gathering" (Hegel); it is also that the best criticism, like the best art, finds its source in a region unavailable to either theory or action. This is a region that tempts us into both language and silence.

SLIPPAGE

Silence, he thinks, is itself the slippage. But what peeps through, as poor Pip saw, is not I but the Cosmos.

No life wholly fulfilled in literature can bring to it the highest vision. No life entirely satisfied in criticism can bring to literature the deepest insight. Slippage or silence: where biographies begin and very quickly end. Something else begins to happen. . . .

He wonders: "what language of childhood can I call my own?" Having reinvented himself in a "foreign" tongue, has he lost all sense of "foreignness"? Having escaped his "first" language, has he also escaped the primal censor or authority?

Thus, silence or slippage becomes the eternal text of Imagination.

FRAME TEN

It is time to clip this paracritical strip. The Imagination, elsewhere I have maintained, may be the teleological force in human evolution; language and metaphor create time continually, and may finally redeem it in a "silence" we can not yet imagine. To what does the road from Babel lead? We do not know. In *After Babel,* George Steiner offers these apposite meditations:

> We need a word which will designate the power, the compulsion of language to posit "otherness." That power, as Oscar Wilde was one of the few to recognize, is inherently in every act of form, in art, in music, in the contrarieties which our body sets against gravity and repose. But it is preeminent in language.

*

> The dialectic of "alternity," the genius of language for planned counter-factuality, are overwhelmingly positive and creative. . . . Language is centrally fictive because the enemy is "reality," because unlike the Houyhnhnm man is not prepared to abide with "the Thing which is."

Insofar as Criticism is made both of language and silence, strip and slippage, it participates in the "dialectic of alternity" in ways we have yet to discover. This gives it the ineluctable aspect of arbitrariness, to which history also contributes. Our concept of Literature—like our concept of the Child, the Madman, the Criminal, or the Professor—is no more than two centuries old. "The view that there is an art of literature," René Wellek says, "which includes both poetry and prose in so far as it is imaginative fiction, and excludes information or even rhetorical persuasion, didactic argumentation or historical narration, emerged only slowly in the 18th century." There is no reason to assume that this exclusion will remain permanent, or that it is central to our verbal projects now or in years to come. All change, if innovative, seems at first gratuitous.

The fear of arbitrariness in criticism qualifies our very hopes for it. For criticism may be the Unnecessary Angel who can still cry: "in my sight, you see the earth again."

Alas, the trouble with all angels is their transparence.

From
THE CAMARGO JOURNAL
I

. . . there is no theory that is not a fragment, carefully concealed, of some autobiography.

Paul Valéry

The Camargo Journal

From September, 1974, to June, 1975, I was a Senior Fellow at the Camargo Foundation in Cassis, a small fishing village some twenty kilometers east of Marseilles. The Foundation was endowed by Jerome Hill, scion of J. J. Hill, renowned railroad magnate.

The Camargo Foundation provided my wife and me with a simple apartment overlooking the Mediterranean; the brochure described the view as "incomparable," which it was. The Foundation also provided us with the most precious "commodity" in our world: time. Time to think, to read, to write—and of course to live. Travel was tolerated—up to a point.

At that time, I was more interested in the thinking, the reading, the traveling, than in the writing—possibly to the chagrin of the Foundation's director. For that time was something (as the French say, *n'exagérons rien*) of a turning point in my intellectual life: not only "between books" but also between "outlooks." Now, in retrospect, I am not sure that my outlook has greatly changed, though it certainly found leisure to vex itself.

After some months, I began to write a journal with a fountain pen, erasing nothing, crossing out little. My concerns were still inchoate, as the journal reflects; yet they included some central ideas of the present work, and included as well the lived context of these ideas. I knew, somehow, that I wanted to approach Prometheus, but it was Faust, all-too-humanly flawed, who kept coming to mind.

What follow are edited and revised exerpts of this journal. The sequence—roughly chronological though no dates are given—errs in Time; for Time like Imagination or Science was also something I meant to vex. What follow, above all, remain queries, musings of a reading man between idleness and work, not renditions such as poet or novelist might assay of things of this world. A variety of styles and voices, patterned disjunctively, put reflection in doubt even as they insinuate an obscure hope. Is not every question a solicitation of desire?

Some believe the end of a book is one's own end. Not I.

Six months now without a word on paper. What happiness!

"I no longer know how to speak" (Rimbaud). But the task is to place oneself beyond all such agonies. Let the hand pick up the pen again, the words start or cease like a familiar disease. No finger on pulse. Pulsars will throb, in any case, at the edge of mind.

■

In Cassis, during this autumn and winter, every night the stars. Whatever the mood of the day, these bodies shine. Sally and I walk, lifting our faces to the sky: striding Orion, Taurus's red eye, Aldebaran, jagged Cassiopeia, Perseus in tangles, the Pleiades faint and clustered, Deneb highest, Sirius brightest.

Is it only by night that we see beyond our sun? Light is the jealousy of the sun, shutting out brighter bodies and farther suns. But at night, there may be another light revealing worlds in darkness. Death, I know, is clairvoyant. So is Imagination, which inhabits inner and outer spaces.

Novalis thought all that inspires us "wears the colors of Night," mother of "Creative Love." I put it thus: Imagination (notwithstanding Nietzsche, crazed by the sun) is less solar, less lunar even, than sidereal, which is to say androgyne.

■

The "Panorama" of the Camargo Foundation, where we live, overlooks Cap Canaille. The fishing port curves to the left; the Mediterranean fills the horizon. Canaille itself glows ochre and yellow in the morning sun, humped like a majestic whale over the sea. We rise naked, surprised every morning by ourselves and this scene. And every morning, we continue to be surprised by our surprise.

I make coffee. We eat croissants, dunking them in a strong brew with cream. The light streams through the French windows. We sit a little heavy with our dreams, which I, unlike Sally, rarely recall.

Perhaps dreams and certain metaphors are the body's deepest speech. A philosopher, Merleau-Ponty, says: "It is through my body that I understand other people, just as it is through my body that I perceive 'things.'" And a poet, Stanley Burnshaw: "Poetry begins with the body and ends with the body. . . . Creature and world flow into each other on their own. . . . Much of the time, perhaps most, we are being lived."

A seamless web: metaphor and flesh, dream and beast, centaurs. But what Language does live us all?

■

We are back from a lecturing visit to Vienna: massive, imperial, gray in its waning season. I think of a Sunday morning at the Spanische Reitschule.

Capriole

Courbette

Levade

Piaffe

Here art and instinct, imagination and nature, will and matter, seem perfectly to meet. This requires rigor, patience, intuition, grace—supreme breeding of Lippizaner horses. But what does "breeding" mean? Intelligence invading evolution, human purpose moving in stud and mare? The grand hall of the horses, despite dark clouds framed in its windows, seems light. The light of centaurs? Let us say instead: in the wedding (or struggle) of man and beast each completes the other, a tacit exchange of energies. Perhaps we can go even farther to say: consciousness is never wholly absent from nature, from the foal cavorting in the craggy hills of Lippiza. The program book notes:

> The Lippizaner going a piaffe merely repeats what the wild and unbroken horse does when meeting an unsurmountable obstacle on its headlong rush across the pasture. . . . The whole is dominated by music, not the music produced by the band but that created by the vibrations of the thoroughbred horses.

That vibrant music of thorough breeding, at certain moments, comes like an intuition of intelligent Being. But the moment turns. As the courtly riders of the Reitschule move into their finale, the Great School Quadrille, the hall bursts into applause. Pomp and pride, the sound of circumstance—we slip into history again, without disdain. Those Sunday centaurs, after all, are richly politic. The "seamless web" is made of many threads and strains.

Faust contemplating suicide on an Easter Sunday:

> Wie alles sich zum Ganzen webt,
> eins in dem andern wirkt und lebt!

■

Our windows face south in Cassis. I also face my fiftieth year. My hair has begun to thin. Just now I think: "I have never felt better!" Then I recall

Faust again. (Back in September, we had seen a production at the Residenz Theater in Munich; Ulrich Haupt played a bumbling Faust, Hans Korte a consummate Mephisto.) The aging Doctor complains:

> Ich bin zu alt, um nur zu spielen,
> zu jung, um ohne Wunsch zu sein.
> Was kann die Welt mir wohl gewähren?
> "Entbehren sollst du! Sollst entbehren!"

Perhaps each of us is vouchsafed only one great decision: the decision to die. But "ripeness is all." Die not too soon or too late; for there is cowardice in both.

Jung believes that the integration of the Self takes place only in later life, on that gentle slope downward, toward the second childhood, toward penultimate innocence. Youth thrusts to forget the first childhood and so comes of age; age attempts to recover the first childhood in preparation for the second. The two childhoods are never the same.

Yet I feel no more need to recover my childhood than my dreams. The lines of Life and Heart in my left hand, someone once told me, do not meet—most rare. I am, it seems, a westering spirit, with back turned on orients and origins. Still, the earth is round: there is never escape in movement or metamorphosis.

■

Our windows face south: Morocco, Tunisia, Algeria, Libya, Egypt. When the mistral blows cold and hard from the Alps, carrying the fine grind of Provence, the chimney sings for nights on end, a film of dust covers everything; then the sky suddenly clears, scoured, an azure space. But when the sirocco blows from the south, it brings leaden clouds, the heavy breath of Africa. I feel no nostalgia, almost none.

I gaze across the Mediterranean, imagining Alexandria and Port Said where I once landed, Arion-like, on a dolphin.

(Sally wonders: why are these bright creatures so amicable? Is their helpfulness prescient? Or is it rather a kind of evolutionary pathos?)

I imagine Cairo. I can only imagine, not recall these cities. That childhood we all feel so huge, and that "mother's tongue"—whose invention are they? Arabic was the only subject I ever failed in school.

■

A rare event. I woke this morning remembering a dream: without fear or joy, simply as a decision in the night, I shot myself in the head with my father's old Webley—and never died.

(A few months after, my father died.)

■

I sit in the November sun, feet propped on the window sill, reading the Oxford Anthology of English Poetry. *The sea interminably sparkles. What kind of mood comes from this superfluity of warmth and light? Certainly not Shakespeare's:*

> Fear no more the heat o' the sun
> Nor the furious winter's rages;
> Thou thy worldly task hast done,
> Home art gone, and ta'en thy wages.

Nor yet Dunbar's:

> The state of man does change and vary,
> Now sound, now sick, now blyth, now sary,
> Now dansand mirry, now like to die:—
> *Timor mortis conturbat me.*

Nor even that anonymous poet's:

> Hey nonny no!
> Men are fools that wish to die!
> Is't not fine to dance and sing
> When the bells of death do ring?

Nor Shakespeare's again, close as it may come:

> Nothing of him that doth fade,
> But doth suffer a sea-change
> Into something rich and strange.

Poetry does not mediate all our moods. Yet struggle as we may, culture returns to possess the very movement that attempts to evade it. Octavio Paz somewhere says: "death condemns to culture. Without it there would be no arts or trades. . . ." Like, say, Cranach's "Fountain of Youth": the dream of renewal, or art itself as the form of eternal return.

I raise my eyes from the page to look upon rocks that Odysseus's foot might have trod.

■

I write too much of death, Sally says. Who can believe that I scarcely mind it? Yet the body, quick and fit, can be transparent as a huge eyeball, and so careless in death's sight.

■

Homer in the south, Shakespeare in the north, both long dead. Whatever it was they wrote, their lives have now become figurative. Keats in a famous letter of 1819 wrote: "A Man's life of any worth is a continual allegory—and very few eyes can see the Mystery of his life—a life like the scriptures, figurative. . . ." Perhaps we are lived as language is spoken or a text written. St. Paul: "Not me, but Christ in me." Our lives: Allegories of Reality?

But if a poet's life is figurative and his works are a comment upon it, then criticism is a comment upon a comment, and a journal, which comments both upon itself and criticism, is—what? An allegory so many times removed from the mystery? Allegory removes, displaces—and returns us finally to language, locus of all displacements. We are caught between reflection and reflexion. Yet we retain the urge to crack all mirrors.

■

The crack in the mirror may be Eros, cosmic desire. In L'Érotisme, *Georges Bataille quotes Rimbaud:*

> Elle est retrouvée.
> Quoi? L'éternité.
> C'est la mer allée
> Avec le soleil.

This we see every day in Cassis. But "this" is also poetry. Hence Bataille concludes:

> La poésie mène au même point que chaque forme de l'érotisme, à l'indistinction, à la confusion des objects distincts. Elle nous mène à l'éternité, elle nous mène à la mort, et par la mort, à la continuité: la poésie est *l'éternité.*

Desire, Death, Eternity are here (romantically) compact; we participate in them through Imagination.

The imagination of Bataille is one of transgression, "le frisson de dépassement"; *this he invests too much. To Sade he attributes a heroism of the imagination there where I perceive only a calculus of sex, a tumescence of number. Yet Bataille carries Freud's argument farther than the latter cared or dared to take it. Transgression defies the work imperative, defies society and every limiting form, seeking beyond eroticism itself eternal continuity, which only death, only the release from discrete and discontinuous being, can finally provide. Consciousness—Promethean, Faustian, even Adamic—is created by transgression, creating itself by crossing the very limits that it has created and must in crossing somehow maintain. In doing so—that is, in transgressing and restraining itself—consciousness aspires erotically to its opposite: the void, non-being. Hence also its aspiration to silence, the limit toward which language tends.*

"De l'érotisme," *Bataille says,* "il est possible de dire qu'il est l'approbation de la vie jusque dans la mort." *Always "dire," always this saying, which holds violence and violation in abeyance, preserves individual being. To speak, then, is not necessarily, as William Burroughs claims, to lie; it is rather to insist on self and other, on constraints that consciousness must unmake in order to make and remake itself. This places Wittgenstein in perspective:* "Wovon man nicht sprechen kann, darüber muss man schweigen." *The statement is more challenge than interdiction; we can never wholly answer it even as we continually try. Thus is poetry born.*

Imagination: a cat crossing thresholds silently.

■

Cassis is full of cats. They curl in the sun, lick their feet. At night, they hunch on garbage cans, pupils dilate. Through fishbones they know the sea. Their forms move sensually in the brain's alleyways. Yet they neither write nor speak.

Is human consciousness made of bad conscience? They used to say: ontogeny recapitulates phylogeny. Does the birth trauma of the individual then recapitulate that of the race from a simian womb? The acquisition of language is a paradoxical state: bad conscience toward all animals and a consciousness of superiority to them all.

I have never seen a cat mate.

■

French women: olive beauties, quick and crisp, perfectly made up, with their unsmiling presence of mind. (The smile in France is weakness unless legitimized by an exacting code.) High-pitched melodious voices, birdlike gestures. Why do they, unlike fairer women, seldom attract me? The romance of the archetypes, the geography of desire, south to north and east to west, reciprocally?

These musings lead nowhere; I read L'Anti-Oedipe *instead. For Gilles Deleuze and Félix Guattari,* "les machines désirantes" *energize all our actions. Desire requires no sublimation to become a social fact; it invests or disinvests directly the entire cultural field. The despot, of course, distrusts the fluidity of sex: "When I hear the word desire, I take out my revolver!" Still, it is Desire that conjoins Nature and History, making cruelty the primordial script.*

> . . . elle *[cruelty]* est le mouvement de la culture qui s'opère dans les corps, s'inscrit sur eux, les labourant. . . . Et si l'on veut appeler "écriture" cette inscription en pleine chaire, alors il faut dire . . . que c'est ce système cruel de signes inscrits que rend l'homme capable de langage, et lui donne une mémoire des paroles.

*Even the despot's desire creates out of sperm and excrement the hieroglyphs of time: the history of the "*flux graphique,*" the authors say, moves from the sperm at the tyrant's cradle* "jusqu'au flot de merde dans sa tombe-égout."

The way out: uncode all fluxes, push schizophrenia to the end. Paranoia is authoritarian, schizophrenia revolutionary, the Oedipus Complex the supreme fiction of totalization. What, then, is the Imagination of Schizophrenia, of uncoded languages, babbling voices, crumbling alphabets? The authors give this hint:

> C'est l'art, dès qu'il atteint à sa propre grandeur, à son propre génie, crée des chaînes de décodage et de déterritorialisation qui instaurent, qui font fonctionner des machines désirantes.

Like Marcel Duchamp, alias Rrose Sélavy?

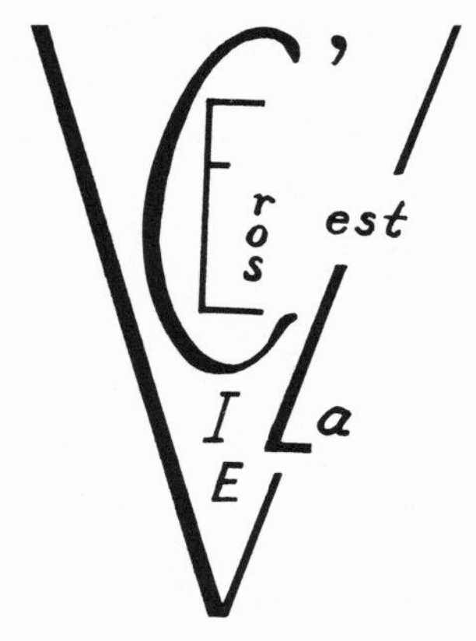

■

A yellow rose stands in a slender vase on the table. Sunlight. Yellow on yellow. Transparency.

I have taken up watercolors. I have no draftsmanship, no mimetic sense—I seem to speak all languages with a slight accent—only a curious sense of color and impetuous shape. I do bright landscapes, seascapes, really inscapes.

Though Mont Sainte-Victoire is not far away—we drive past it on the way to Aix or Avignon—I dare not even sketch it. Who can after Cézanne? All those paintings he made of it: enormous beyond their modest frames, they apprehend sensuously a strange presence. All those colors and all those shapes, summoning something that has neither color nor shape, what patience they still possess, as if matter could expiate itself infinitely into an essence.

Archly, Cézanne says: "The time will come when a single carrot will be pregnant with revolution." A revolution of forms beyond forms? As in a single yellow rose.

■

Matisse's (Dominican) Chapel in Vence.

We have visited the place many times, and visit it this year again. It is empty. Inside, the feeling of a mysterious power (as at Epidaurus), silent, joyous, healing.

The Virgin and Child on the white wall barely presage the Crucifixion; they speak rather a benediction, blessing the viewer, all. The Mother does not overwhelm the Child; He is already manifest, the Redeemer. Harmonious blend of Male and Female archetypes: the yellows of the Sun streaming through the stained glass windows lights up blues and greens of the Sea.

(Sally says we have two mothers, blue and green, Sea and Earth. The former is supportive, easy on life; the latter exigent. We move between them.)

In the white chapel, a figure stands out: the Monk in his cowl, St. Dominic. He is the Human, carrying a Book. Man, Woman, and Child are here, and the Book. And Nature also: light falls on an altar stone which looks like a great loaf of freshly baked country bread.

Sally, who believes in Happiness, reads this statement about Matisse: "Proud, civilized, and sensitive, he wanted his art to celebrate his faith that a profound life could be a happy life."

■

A profound life: what place does it hold for revolution?
A happy life: what place does it allow for desire?
Dante, Marx, Nietzsche, Freud.

■

"Le désir nommé Marx." *(Jean-François Lyotard leaves out Dante.) In* Économie libidinale, *Lyotard tries to articulate* "la grande pellicule éphémère," *a giant Moebius strip of desire, without exterior or interior, without "depth," ubiquitous. Blake and Brown also tried to speak that sacred strip. But Lyotard remains closer to Nietzsche, Sade, Klossowski:*

> Nous désirons l'athéisme de la bande libidinale. . . . Nous avons ainsi à sauter par dessus deux frontières, celle qui sépare la politique de l'a-politique, mais aussi celle qui sépare le religieux du laïc. . . .

The realization of desire demands permanent revolution. Yet even revolutions are figurative. Klossowski had postulated a "fantasme," *a fabrication of life's pulsional forces, deflected somehow from its "normal" expression. Lyotard accepts the postulate but refuses the deflection, which implies somehow "perversity." For him, the phantasm, ineluctable production of the libido, is affirmative; neither "real" nor "unreal," it invents itself "incandescently." No "truth" external to itself in this figuration, no signification as part of a universal Signifier. Pen in hand, I jot remarks in the margin and wonder.*

■

Shem the Penman, "sniffer of carrion." Including one's own?

On the Plage du Bestouan, *which our balcony overlooks, a ray has begun to rot. Why do I need to write another book? We had agreed to take a "year off"—travel, read, think—anything but this writing. Schopenhauer says:*

> The *pen* is to thought what the stick is to walking; but you walk most easily when you have no stick, and you think with the greatest perfection when you have no pen in your hand. It is only when a man begins to be old that he likes to use a stick and is glad to take up his pen.

Sally, Vermont in green spring, uses no stick. She also writes and writes. . . .

■

I watch La Vieille de Cassis trudge up the hill, wrapped in tattered black, with a stick more crooked than her back, and a frightened mongrel at her heels. Every day she shuffles past our window, bent more than half her height, her weather-worn legs finding their way to some unknown place, her mouth working at her dog in some toothless speech. Her other hand clutches always a fresh green sprig.

Cars speed by, grazing her elbow; they could swerve or lurch, leaving behind a heap of bones. What preserves this woman for her daily trudge?

We greet her sometimes on the street, see in her eyes a sudden ironic gleam. Otherwise, the eyes are vacant, watery, salt of the Meditteranean in their ancient stare.

She grips the green sprig tightly in her fist.

■

The sensuality of witches. The mind leaves the Mediterranean, traveling northward on a broomstick. To the Harzgebirg. Or to that city where, a friend once told me, there are houses specializing in hags. Walpurgisnacht: eroticism, transgression, uncouth fancies. But Mephisto does not really understand any of it; as usual, he takes the sliding view of things. Goethe knows better the "Faustian" sexuality of his countrymen.

(Where else is eroticism so will-full, imaginary, death-driven? The grotesque as aphrodisiac: in a fashionable shop window, a naked mannequin with flies on her white skin, a tin dagger through her tongue. SS uniforms, all black, little white skulls on the caps. Eros palaces and sex supermarkets. All this Genet knows and Pynchon—neither a German!)

And so Goethe tried to effect the spiritual marriage of Faust and Helena, North with South, Romanticism with Classicism, in his phantom Arcady:

Alles ist sodann gefunden:
ich bin dein, und du bist mein,
und so stehen wir verbunden;
dürft' es doch nicht anders sein!

Their issue is Euphorion, personification of Poesy, whom the Phorkas describes: "Nackt, ein Genius ohne Flügel, faunenartig ohne Tierheit."

But Helena dissolves into a cloud, Euphorion vanishes as an aureole, the Phorkas proves to be Mephisto masked. The scene ends with a wild hymn to Dionysos:

> Nichts geschont! Gespaltne Klauen treten alle Sitte nieder,
> alle Sinne wirbeln taumlig, grässlich ubertäubt das Ohr.

Still, in a transhumanized world, Germany may serve the cause of civilization more profoundly than any "civilized" country: Energy and Reason, Eroticism and Will, may be subject there to a richer transmutation than we suspect.

Faust failed though the Lord (or Mater Gloriosa) decreed otherwise. (In "dunklem Drang," *redeemed by a* "Liebe von oben.") *But the denouement may not be solely divine. Something in Goethe, something in Germany still, strives to reach beyond that failure. Is its name* "das Werdende"?

For the future, Faust will not suffice.

Dionysus, whom we must fear and honor, we may some day leave behind.

And Prometheus?

A little too abstract,

this business of

fire?

A little shrill?

THE RE-VISION OF LITERATURE: Rhetoric, Imagination, Vision

My "theme" is uncertain: perhaps it touches on something in literature that is best invoked by such words as Rhetoric, Imagination, Vision. The uncertainty is nearly excusable. A literary theory implies an ontology of literature, and an ontology is what we now call into doubt. The very concept "Literature," and not simply literary history, forces upon us radical queries. Hence my inordinate concern with the re-vision of literature. Yet the pun on revision has become rather stale and weary: we revise everything and rarely see anything anew. Can this failure be due to the frames of our vision?

This brings me to the "form" of this text: it is mildly paracritical. (There is no reason for alarm: I have no influence in the profession to corrupt the young.) Why paracritical? Consider for a moment this curious event we call "hearing a lecture," or "reading an article." Someone makes a claim on our attention, our time, our mortality—someone, including ourselves. The frame of this claim is often the same. Yet frames, we know, shape what we hear or see. Tilt the frame or crack it, and we perceive another thing; make it conscious of itself as frame and the perception is different again. I do no more here than alter a little the semantic typography of my text, and so call attention not only to the cultural problematic of frames but also to the current reflexive will of literature. Thus my discourse will follow a Text, interrupted by some Intertexts and Epitexts, moving back through a Retrotext, finally coming to its inconclusion.

And here ends my pretext.

EPITEXT I

We sit in Schloss Leopoldskron, in Salzburg; the rococo window opens on a large artificial pond. Suddenly there is a big plop, and rings begin to form on the green water: a fish. Sally, who is reading Emerson, quotes out loud: "The eye is the first circle; the horizon which it forms is the second; and throughout nature this primary figure is repeated without end. It is the highest emblem in the cipher of the world." Circles, frames, ciphers. I wonder where is that fat fish now, that was for an instant at the center of the circumference. The rings ripple out, empty, with gravity.

TEXT

I begin my proper text, knowing that anticipations of further disruption may hinder its reading. We need to re-cognize the primacy of vision in the arts. Even a sub-visionary critic, Hilton Kramer, exhorts us thus: "It is always a shock to be reminded that art is, after all, a spiritual enterprise. Our culture has developed in a way that makes it so much easier to think about art in terms of techniques or economics, as a game of personality cults and epochal 'breakthroughs,' that its spiritual attributes tend to be, if not wholly denied, then discreetly consigned to the ineffable. . . . we seem to lack even the rudiments of a persuasive vocabulary." Art, literature, as a spiritual force—that tattered Arnoldian doctrine is one we still esteem. Challenged many times, challenged by churchmen, moralists, aesthetes, and by critics as incongruous as T. S. Eliot and George Steiner, this prejudice of the spirit for art will not go away.

Steiner's challenge is the more recent and harsh. We have heard the grisly parable of the concentration camp *Kommandant* who loved to read Shakespeare, Goethe, and Rilke. But what do we mean by "read"? Steiner does not permit us to quibble or ask. "We do not know," he cries in *Language and Silence,* "whether the study of the humanities, of the noblest that has been said and thought, can do very much to humanize." Indeed, we do not; and our ignorance only proves that literature remains an aspect of our freedom. The great literary classics may or may not humanize; they certainly do not serve to condition or brainwash. Their "goodness" offers itself as a *choice.*

Steiner may be a moralist who expects too much (and why not?) from art; but there are skeptics and aesthetes who expect too little. They remind us that art provides no substitute for ethics or religion. It may provide no substitute, yet for many, the moral imagination has been kept vital in bad times by the perverse powers of art. Surely our own spontaneous response to Kent State, Watergate, or My Lai was itself thickly mediated by our experience *in* literature. Surely, such mediations quicken our values. Steven Marcus seems to think otherwise. In a piece entitled "The Demoralized Humanists," he writes:

"There is an undercurrent of expectation that the humanities are or should go into the business of creating values, new or old, for society." Professor Marcus prefers the task of "critical self-clarification." Yet "self-clarification" is no less a shibboleth—or an ideological stance. We choose one kind of clarity against another, and that assumes some value; moreover, we use clarification toward presumptive ends. If this does not make axiologists of us all, it may nonetheless expose the limits of our skeptical neutrality. The last is indeed cause for de-moralization.

In brief, to the shocking question that George Steiner asks we have no answer. But the answer to the *Kommandant* may be George Steiner himself: man, through language and silence, pitted continuously against the Inhuman. The morality of this confrontation is perdurable, and also too simple. Can morality help us to know vision? I much doubt it. Our path to the visionary question will be curious—and it may suddenly stop before the question starts.

INTERTEXT I

> Franz Kafka to Rudolf Steiner: "My happiness, my abilities and every possibility of being useful in any way have always been in the literary field. And here I have, to be sure, experienced states (not many) which in my opinion correspond very closely to the clairvoyant states described by you, Herr Doktor, in which I completely dwelt in every idea, but also filled every idea, and in which I not only felt myself at my boundary but at the boundary of the human in general."
>
> (Max Brod, ed., *The Diaries of Franz Kafka: 1910-1913.)*

If vision is not always discovered in a humanistic ethic, neither is it rediscovered in "literary content." Content is what lurks in Pandora's box itself. Open the box and out burst all those dreadful dualisms—literature as poesis &/or mimesis (*aletheia* came later), coherence &/or correspondence, pleasure &/or instruction, image &/or concept, mental event &/or physical object, presentational language &/or discursive statement, and finally as signifier &/or signified. I am not contemptuous of these dichotomies: they may be an aspect of the thinking mind, generated by the metalanguages of criticism rather than in the languages of literature itself. The dichotomies, so to speak, are the sound of only one hand clapping, while the other hand silently writes.

Far from being a formalist in criticism, I still find the question of content troublesome in three ways at least. First, it can lead and yield too quickly to ideology, a subject I am happier to engage in other terms. Next, it tends to confine the relation of literature and reality to older philosophical modes (Realist, Idealist, Nominalist) or else to restate its own question, as Käte Hamburger does in *The Structure of Literature* when she says: "literature is of a different nature from reality precisely because the latter is its material." Last, the evaluation of content implies a theory of interpretation, and the hermeneutic range extends from E. D. Hirsch to Wolfgang Iser to Roland Barthes, from validity in intentional interpretation to the phenomenology of an implied reader to the scandalous pleasure ("*atopiques*") and duplicities of the text.

Evaluating literary content may be troublesome; I would not call it trite. It may tempt us into ideology, ontology, or hermeneutics, and these are temptations we should not always resist. My own evasion on this occasion is simply a choice: I have construed the (para)critic's task as an invitation first to re-vision literature and then to prevision a new theory of the Imagination. For in the mansions of criticism, there are many divisions.

EPITEXT II

I sit in my study in Milwaukee; the walls are lined with books: The Unmediated Vision, The Visionary Company, The Tragic Vision, Beyond the Tragic Vision, The Classic Vision, The Vision Obscured, Vision and Response in Modern Fiction, Primal Vision, The Orphic Vision, Prelude to Vision, The Politics of Vision, The Armed Vision, Inventory *(Butor).*

I sit in my study; it is almost a perfect cube. Or is it really, with so many dimensions of vision in its walls, a hypercube? In the fourth, fifth, or n*th dimension, as in a hypercube, one may take away all the "contents" of a room, without disturbing anything. Are we ourselves memories of survivors in other rooms? (Doris Lessing).*

Obviously, the current revision of literature must proceed within the cultures of criticism itself. In America, it has been clear for some time that the exhaustion of the old New Criticism has left behind it a certain critical exhaustion. Quite possibly, the rise of popular culture as a matter of academic curiosity may provide a certain stimulus to criticism. But those critics seeking a new theoretical foundation for their discourse—where shall they look? Can they turn to England, as they did in the time of Hulme or of Leavis? Nothing in England now seems to compel theoretical attention. Some do turn to Germany, finding in Lukács and Adorno, in Bloch and Benjamin, a neo-Marxist source of literary ideas; or finding in Hans-Georg Gadamer and Hans Robert Jauss masters of the new hermeneutics; or finding in *Rezeptionsästhetik* a new field of interest.

But it is to France and again to France that American critics rush to learn about linguistics and semiotics, structuralism and post-structuralism—about the subtile New Rhetoric. Theirs is a dry but movable feast, the largest since Stein, Hemingway, & Co. descended upon Paris. One wonders if Edward Wasiolek can be right when he says: "We are a nation that is attached or condemned to scientism and the faith that the mind is an instrument for the analysis of given entities. Russian Formalism, if ever enough texts are adequately translated and if ever enough intelligent commentaries are produced, is likely to exercise a greater influence on American criticism than the French New Criticism." I suspect that if we do turn to Russian Formalism, it will be only after we have sacked Gaul.

The point is simple: nowhere is the revision of literature more advanced than in France. I say this with some qualms. For much as I admire French criticism, I want to put myself at a certain readable, a certain legible distance from its rhetoric and its lacks. The rhetoric has already turned into sesquipedalian cant; pick up any of our more ambitious quarterlies, and you will hear the poststructuralist chant. As for the lacks, they are those of signs dissolving perpetually into other signs, a metaphysics of absence, an ideology of fracture, a system wavering sometimes between science and solipsism—in short, a brilliant, rhetorical unmaking of the modern mind.

Let us attend for a while to some familiar voices of this unmaking, as they declare themselves in seven questioning (or questionable?) statements.

INTERTEXT II

A. The Unmaking of Man.
Claude Lévi-Strauss writes: "I believe the ultimate goal of the human science to be not to constitute, but to dissolve man. . . . I am not blind to the fact that the verb 'dissolve' does not in any way imply (but even excludes) the destruction of the constituents of the body subjected to another body."
(*The Savage Mind.*)

Michel Foucault writes: "One thing in any case is certain: man is neither the oldest nor the most constant problem that has been posed for human knowledge. . . . As the archaeology of our thought easily shows, man is an invention of recent date. And one perhaps nearing its end."
(*The Order of Things.*)

B. The Unmaking of Literature.
Roland Barthes writes: "All these endeavors may someday permit us to define our century . . . as the century of the question *What Is Literature?* (Sartre answered it from outside, which gives him an ambiguous literary position.) And precisely because this interrogation is conducted not from outside but within literature itself . . . it follows that our literature has been for a hundred years a dangerous game with its own death, in other words, a way of experiencing, of living that death. . . ."
("Literature and Metalanguage," *Critical Essays*.)

Tzvetan Todorov writes: "We must first cast a doubt upon the legitimacy of literature; neither the mere existence of the term, nor the fact that a whole university system is based upon it, can of itself justify its acceptance."
("The Notion of Literature," *New Literary History,* V, no. 1.)

C. The Unmaking of the Discrete Author, Reader and Text.
Roland Barthes writes: "In France, Mallarmé was doubtless the first to see and foresee in its full extent the necessity of substituting language itself for the man who hitherto was supposed to own it. . . . The absence of the Author . . . is not only a historical fact or an act of writing: it utterly transforms the modern text (. . . the text henceforth written and read so that in it, on every level, the Author absents himself)."
("The Death of the Author," in Sallie Sears and Georgiana W. Lord, eds., *The Discontinuous Universe.*)

Jacques Ehrmann: "The presence of a reader is no more explicit nor implied than is that of an author. This presence is just as indeterminate because these 'texts' are not addressed to any particular public. . . . Since the one who has assembled the 'texts' has a minimal control over how they are read, everything happens between the lines, in the whiteness that separates the 'texts' . . . in all that, unknowingly, has remained silent and that depends upon

the user. . . . In this manner the 'text' loses the sacred character which in our culture we have been pleased to confer upon it."
("The Death of Literature," *New Literary History,* III, no. 1.)

D. The Unmaking of the Book.
Roland Barthes: ". . . any upset an author imposes on the typographic norms of a work constitutes an essential disturbance: to deploy isolated words on a page, to mix italic, roman, and capital letters . . . to break the material thread of the sentence by disparate paragraphs, to make a word equal in importance to a sentence—all these liberties contribute in short to the very destruction of the Book. . . ."
("Literature and Discontinuity," *Critical Essays.*)

Philippe Sollers: "In our civilization the book was originally written language. Then it became printed writing. Perhaps it is in the process, and has been for a long time, of assuming a totally different significance which poses the real, misunderstood question of *writing,* of which the written volume would be only a limited particular case."
("The Novel and the Experience of Limits," in Raymond Federman, ed., *Surfiction.*)

E. The Unmaking of Genres (including Criticism).
Philippe Sollers: "On this level the distinctions between 'literary genres' destroy themselves. They are generally maintained only by a convention which permits falsified limits. . . . But we should not let our society dictate the definition of literary activity any more than our artificial roles as producers and consumers."
(*Surfiction.*)

Jacques Ehrmann: "In fact, if literary material rightfully extends to all linguistic signs, it is logical to think that every distinction between literary language, ordinary language, and critical language is also rightfully abolished because no inherent difference separates them essentially. The opposition between language and metalanguage would be obliterated thereby from the start. It would yield to a critical unfolding of signs stretching out infinitely and indefinitely, all in the same place, without any priority being attributed to a particular one. . . ."
("The Death of Literature".)

F. The Self-Unmaking of Semiotics.
Julia Kristeva writes: "Semiotics cannot develop except as a critique of semiotics. . . . Research in semiotics remains a process that discovers nothing at the end of its search but its own ideological moves, so as to recognize them, to deny them, to start again."
(*Semiotikè.)*

G. A Coda to Unmakings.
Jean-François Lyotard writes: "Oh, that exquisite polysemy, little tear of safe thinkers *[bien pensants]*, small carping disorder, sugared deconstruction. Do not hope to gather the libidinal in those nets.

"A final point, understood a thousand times: semiology is nihilism."
(*Économie libidinale.*)

And from an entirely different perspective, Werner Heisenberg: "It may also be the case today [1969] that the tendency to *unshaping* [my italics] springs from a sense of life that not only seems to perceive the unreliability of all past forms but also decries behind the forms connections that later, perhaps, may again be able to support life. This may possibly be the most important content of modern art."
(*Across the Frontiers.)*

Yet Heisenberg, unlike the New Rhetoricians, also knows: "But in the final analysis, the central order, or the 'one' as it used to be called and with which we commune in the language of religion, must win out."
(*Physics and Beyond.*)

Terrorism, travesty, or trivia?

These enunciations and denunciations do not represent a coherent movement or system. They are sometimes contradictory and often provisional; and indeed, later representatives of *Tel Quel* can be as critical of earlier structuralist theories as they are of traditional literary ideologies. As Barthes himself says, "Structuralist Man" is not the last word of time; a new language will arise (has arisen?) that will speak him in turn. Yet we cannot dismiss him without at least some struggle; he must be qualified in our consciousness before his is "overcome." His ambition, while it lasted, was after all a noble one: "*Homo significans*," his structures were simulacra of "intellect added to object."

The poststructuralist activity, however, may itself be part of a larger trend of our time. In searching for an epitome of that trend, I have used the simple Anglo-Saxon word, "unmaking" (*anglo-saxon,* by the way, as the French insist on calling Beowulf and Muhammad Ali, the Godfather and me). Yet I could have used trendier terms: for instance, deconstruction, decentering, dissemination, dispersal, difference, *différance,* discontinuity, demystification, decreation, disapperance, etc. All of these terms of unmaking share something with the concept of silence, variously articulated by George Steiner, Susan Sontag, myself; and they also evoke Harold Rosenberg's "de-definition" of art. But they go farther, suggesting a radical reorganization in our modes of knowledge, in the discourse by which we apprehend our very being—suggesting what Michel Foucault would call a postmodern *épistémè.*

Foucault, as we know, distinguishes between three *épistémès* or sovereign codes which organize culture and consciousness in the preclassical, classical (roughly the seventeenth and eighteenth centuries), and modern periods. In the latter, the failure of the heroic Mallarméan task of transforming all language into the ultimate Word confirmed "the disappearance of Discourse." But if language now returns in some postmodern era, with the shudder of new gods, if it returns, Foucault asks in *The Order of Things,* "with greater and greater insistence in a unity that we ought to think but cannot as yet do so, is this not the sign that the whole of this (modern) configuration is now about to topple, and that man is in the process of perishing as the being of language continues to shine ever brighter upon our horizon? Since man was constituted at a time when language was doomed to dispersion, will he not be dispersed when language regains its unity?" Foucault, of course, means the "dispersion" of man as a particular concept, as a constellation of images within a particular *épistémè;* but that is no minor matter. The "dispersion" of man into a universal language (like Teilhard de Chardin's "noösphere"?) or a universal desire would leave none of our categories, least of all "literary vision," intact.

I say desire because, as we have seen, that is also the term used by Gilles Deleuze and Félix Guattari in their flamboyant revision of psychoanalysis. Yet Foucault and Deleuze are not alone; Jacques Derrida seems most at ease with "deconstructed" realities. As a philosopher, he does not flinch from saying, "I am trying, precisely, to put myself at a point so that I do not know any longer where I am going." Following through with the "decentering" of thought begun by Nietzsche's critique of metaphysics, Derrida refuses "totalization," refuses transcendental meaning within any given system, affirming instead the joyous play of a world without "truth," without "origin," a world offered continually to our interpretations and our deconstructions, our absences. In his philosophical *epos* on writing, *Of Grammatology,* Derrida even hints that a future "meta-rationality" and "meta-scientificity" may surpass "in the same and single gesture, *man, science,* and the *line* (of the book)."

A radical reorganization in our modes of knowledge, in the discourse by which we apprehend our being, is indeed what French criticism insinuates into our midst—a re-vision of the Human even more than of Literature. The reaction of American critics to the situation is often uncertain, and sometimes queasy. Our tradition, after all, is pragmatic, and we are skeptical of the eccentricities and ethnocentricities of French intellectual life. Still, we yearn more than ever for vindication of the humanities in an age of technology, yearn especially for a bright new theory of literature. French theories, however, raise more questions about our business than they are willing to answer. Some critics attempt to neutralize or domesticate these questions, and so are able to pursue their business quite as usual. (Some, more *au courant,* "redouble" their "utterances" to "constitute" their "enunciations" by "liberating the signifiers"—which act, of course, both "diachronically" and "synchronically"—then proceed to "decenter" a "text" here, "deconstruct" an "*épistémè*" there, "demystify" an ideology elsewhere, while "adequating" the "textuality" of the whole through scrupulous observation of both its "paradigmatic" and "syntagmatic" "codes"—in short, they "disseminate" the impression of noisy "absence," perhaps as I myself have just done.) Others attempt to provide a searching, rigorous, and sympathetic critique of structuralism; already, we have the works of Richard Macksey, Eugenio Donato, Paul de Man, Geoffrey Hartman, Leo Bersani, Fredric Jameson, Edward Said, Robert Scholes, and Jonathan Culler, among others, and the list is quickly growing. As for myself, I want to explore a different way.

EPITEXT III

This text was originally an address, and in it I included here two blank pages, with a note reading: ' "Improvise orally on the aporias of this critical moment. Do so in two blank pages, i.e., *four voice minutes." ' But for readers rather than listeners, the improvisations cannot be simply my own. Still, if I were to impersonate a reader, rather than the writer I am impersonating, these would be among the topics I would choose for random queries:*

— *The erotics of critical dedications. Some critics dedicate their works to real or symbolic Parents (the past), some to Children (the future), others to Siblings (the present). Some dedicate to Male figures and others to Female. There are critics, for instance, who tend to dedicate to Fathers and Brothers, others to Mothers, others still to Wives—very rarely to Mothers and Wives. Then there are those who dedicate to a whole Family. A few critics dedicate to No One and fewer still to Every One. On the whole, dedications to the* Anima *seem under-represented in the world of criticism, as are dedications to Artists. Is there an erotics of critical dedications? Why not? How can the emblem of a critic's love be irrelevant to his work?*

— *Media and the illusion of a paradigm. Lacking the "paradigms" of science, the humanities tend to create "schools" of thought, which are then promptly assumed to be paradigms of knowledge. In Paris, New Haven, or Baltimore, critics and philosophers converge, giving intellectual density to their enterprise. Friendships and rivalries weave themselves into the epistemological fabric of discourse. This has always been so. But schools nowadays, whether of art or of criticism, become "media" before they harden into ideology. What is the role of such media, both public and covert, in the current formation of criticism? Do authors, critics, and readers respond to* images *they have of one another rather than to texts? Are such images, like all clichés, too packed with personal needs, and so finally inexpressive?*

— *Academic depression and critical spirit. The topic is sordid; everyone knows our tribulations. Ebbing funds, falling enrollments, shrinking jobs, wobbling tenures. The humanities, in general, dispirited. In these circumstances, how much error and/or terror of innovation can our disciplines permit? True, in a moment of exigency, we can will to renew—better still, to re-invent—"excellence"; and we can learn to dispense with "frills." But among the youngest professors, how many will accept intellectual risk? More interesting: is there a critical theory that satisfies the needs of an ungenerous moment better than another? Or is all literary theory profoundly anti-heroic?*

But enough of these crotchety queries. Myself, I hope to explore another way. I am not certain yet where it may lead. It may lead toward Imagination, and perhaps by an incommodious "vicus of recirculation" bring us face to face with Vision once again. Meanwhile, the (post)structuralist "adventure" beckons us. Certainly, it has accomplished a major revision in our literary thought. It may have also tempted us into sterile sophistries and subtle deprivations. For instance, speaking now in the first person:

a. The (post)structuralist metaphysic of absence and its ideology of fracture refuse holism almost fanatically. But I want to recover my metaphoric sense of wholes. The difference between Norman O. Brown and Gilles Deleuze (who fails to acknowledge Brown) is precisely this: Brown knows that open is broken and fractured is free, but knows also that reality is one (*Love's Body*). Subtle rhetoricians, materialists, the French only disconnect. Opposed to ontological bad faith, they cultivate an ontological brittleness. For them, the Platonic apple must remain both erotically and epistemologically split.

b. The (post)structuralist concept of literature is, as Richard Schechner has noted, entirely implosive. Everything collapses inward on language itself, on structures within/without structures. But I long for a concept of literature that is also explosive: outward into gesture and performance, outward into action, responsive to change. By textualizing existence, the new rhetoricians can safely become Heroes of Reality. But is rhetoric really the foundation of all contemporary praxis and thought? (See Fredric Jameson's *The Prison House of Language*.)

c. The structuralist idea of structure may be finally inadequate to both human history and cosmic evolution, to the reality of *process*. Physicists, biologists, information theorists now prefer to speak of systems rather than structures, "self-transcendent systems" that ensure both continuity and change (Erich Jantsch and C. H. Waddington, eds., *Evolution and Consciousness*). And some geneticists want to supplant the concept of "code" with the more dynamic concept of "instruction." No life-denying formalism here.

d. The (post)structuralist temper requires too great a depersonalization of the writing/speaking subject. Writing becomes plagiarism; speaking becomes quoting. Meanwhile, we do write, we do speak. I realize that the problematic of the "subject" is exceedingly complex (from Sartre's *Critique de la raison dialectique*, 1960, and Lévi-Strauss's *La Pensée Sauvage*, 1962, the controversy continues through to Kristeva's *La Révolution du langage poétique*, 1974). Yet I know that I myself must articulate my historical voice as well as silence it, lose my life and find it. I can not stand forever *beside* myself, nor reflexively *between* my selves.

e. The style of many (post)structuralists fascinates at first, and then—begins to repel? Consider the oblique and difficult styles of Lévi-Strauss, Barthes, Derrida, Foucault, Kristeva, Deleuze, Serres. But what does "difficult" mean here? Hegel, Heidegger, and Husserl are often more difficult to read. Is it because the (post)structuralists rightly transgress disciplines—they are not *only* philosophers *or* anthropologists *or* critics—and so must transgress certain received categories of "clarity"? Is it because of their deep sympathy for what the bourgeoisie calls "perversity"? Or is it because, having banished the "subject" from their epistemology, the subject returns perversely to assert its presence in idiosyncratic styles, in complex verbal ceremonies that pretend to shun the vulgarities of the signified?

f. The (post)structuralist activity, when all is said and done, does not sufficiently enhance the meaning, experience, force, value, pleasure of particular literary texts, enhance what draws *me* to literature or quickens *me* to it. For Barthes, pleasure is crucial, though it implies a process of coding and uncoding, making and unmaking, recuperation and loss—finally of "fading"—a process that is not central to my own temper (*Le Plaisir du Texte*). This touches on elusive questions: boredom, ennui.

INTERTEXT III

Jonathan Culler remarks: "A semiological criticism should succeed in reducing the possibilities of boredom by teaching one to find challenges and peculiarities in works which the perspective of pleasure alone would make boring." (*Structuralist Poetics.*)

This is astute; yet a problem remains. The question of "boredom" is perhaps more general: the compositions of John Cage, the films of Andy Warhol or Michael Snow, the books of Philippe Sollers, the plays of Robert Wilson, so much else in contemporary art, are all involved in it. After hearing Jean-François Lyotard speak brilliantly on the subject, and on the deeper question of ennui with regard to "*le corps inhumain,*" I wrote him a brief note: "I suspect we need a theory of ennui. How are we to distinguish in the postmodern arts between "boredom" and a deeper "ennui"; and in the case of the latter, how between one sense of alienation (Marx) and another sense (Baudelaire) conducive to a new type of consciousness, making traditional patterns of expectations obsolete? There is also Om, Om, Om—a holy repetition!"

Since then, I have come across Reinhard Kuhn's fine study of ennui, *The Demon at Noontide.* Less a theory than a phenomenology of a psycho-literary condition, the book concludes: As a negative force, ennui, if it does not engulf its victims, can and often does induce efforts to fill the void that it hollows out. It is the state that, if it does not render sterile, precedes and makes possible creation in the realm of the practical, the spiritual, and the aesthetic. . . . It is . . . against the power of nothingness that man defines himself and asserts his humanity."

Can we then surmise that there is an ennui (not just boredom) to which much current criticism is a response, a cultural condition more complex than our own boredom with much current criticism?

The foregoing strictures—in which, I fear, I have lumped too many authors together, using the epithet "poststructuralist" evasively—may finally appear too personal to sustain a genuine critique; yet they mark for me a virtual arc, passing through French criticism, leading out. The shift in taste, in need, from a literature of commitment (Sartre/Camus) to a literature of abstraction (Robbe-Grillet/Sollers) must itself shift again. As Barthes in his *Critical Essays* says of such shifts: "I am tempted to see in their alternation that entirely formal phenomenon, the rotation of possibilities, which precisely defines Fashion: an exhaustion of a language and a shift to the antinomic language. . . ." But "antinomic" does not always define new "possibilities." A shift to what?

Rhetoricians and prophets can neither tell nor always foretell; no prophet or rhetorician, I may still throw myself into the question pell-mell, expressing a critical desire more than a historical will. The shift, I repeat, may be to a renewed concern with Imagination. Is Imagination the teleological force in human evolution, predicting, guiding, fulfilling change? Can it take regenerative power in society? How may we re-vision its role under every aspect of the cultural lexicon, in all its imaginative duplicity and multiplicity, and not simply under the aegis of a single method or semiotic theory? Bizarre as it may now seem, the famed quarrel between André Breton and Roger Caillois over Mexican jumping beans addressed the question of Imagination seriously, more seriously than rhetoricians would nowadays permit.

EPITEXT IV

I sit in Cassis, reading Caillois's La Pieuvre. *In a certain slant of sun, the Mediterranean is a hard, blue mirror, giving nothing of itself. I wonder how light flows through the octopus's outrageous eye.*

Imagination and observation, fancy and fact, mingle in our vision of certain creatures, Caillois says: the narwhal, for instance, the praying mantis, the spider, the lion, the bat, the peacock, the serpent, the horse—and the octopus. Throughout history, the octopus has acquired within the imbrications of our fantasy certain qualities: it was considered thieving, adaptable, shy, self-devouring, clownish, hoarding, and very often lascivious. But not until the Romantic age—with Michelet, Lautréamont, Jules Verne, and especially Victor Hugo—did the octopus become malignant and horrific. It became, in Romantic myth, a figure of the Void. With countless tentacles and suckers, the octopus absorbed the human Self into its viscous maw, fixing the entire process with huge, silken eye.

*The conclusion of Caillois is nearly as startling. We deceive ourselves, he argues, in thinking that the Imagination obeys only its own needs, evolves only according to its unique structures. True as this may be on a certain level, on another level, the Imagination is "contiguous" with Nature, an extension thereof. "Substances and dreams," Caillois writes, "follow distant but analogous itineraries. . . . I hazard to say that the same 'innervation' traverses their unitary field. . . ." Yet in this unitary field of existence, figments of the Imagination compete, as do organisms and even species. Only those figments that "justify" themselves (Caillois speaks of "*une imagination juste*"), justify themselves in an evolving universe, take hold—precisely because "complex and disconcerting correspondences" seem to make that universe just.*

Sitting in Cassis, reading Caillois, I suddenly smell garlic and saffron in the air. Is Sally preparing a bouillabaise? *If so, some small octopus and I may soon meet. Another "correspondence"? Or is correspondence simply a metaphor? Simply? And of what? Of itself?*

INTERTEXT IV

The poet, Elizabeth Sewell, says:
"Human thought is not merely metaphoric in operation. Itself

> forms one term of a metaphor. The other term may consist of the cosmic universe. . . ."
> (*The Human Metaphor.*)

> The scientist, Jean Piaget, says it in a different way:
> "Languages are not in the habit of forecasting the events they describe; rather, it is a correspondence . . . a harmony, then, between . . . the human being as body and mind—and the innumerable operators in nature—physical objects at their several levels. Here we have remarkable proof of that pre-established harmony among windowless monads of which Leibniz dreamt. . . ."
> (*Structuralism.*)

Once more, I return to my text, trying to comprehend Sewell and Piaget. Do both secretly invoke a venerable doctrine of correspondence between mind and matter? (Emerson, we recall, remarked: "The whole of nature is a metaphor of the human mind.") Piaget, of course, is mainly concerned with the languages of science; he is easier to understand. After all, science must assume, as Max Planck put it in his *Scientific Autobiography,* "that the laws of human reasoning coincide with the laws governing the sequences of the impressions we receive from the world about us. . . ." After all, Albert Einstein, sitting alone in a room, wrote $E = mc^2$; and decades later, with the assistance of Hahn, Fermi, Szilard, Oppenheimer, an explosion annihilated Hiroshima. After all, Paul Dirac predicted the existence of the positron years before it was confirmed in cosmic ray experiments and calculated the exact weight of the monopole four decades before it was "captured" (perhaps) over Sioux City, Iowa.

But how are we to understand the mystic metaphor of Elizabeth Sewell? Should we refer it to that tradition of language and gnosis about which George Steiner has ably written in *After Babel*—a tradition of the *Logos* or *Lingua Mundi* or *Ur-Sprache* or Word of God, which variously includes Pythagoreans, Kabalists, and Pietists, includes Meister Eckhart, Paracelsus, Kepler, Jakob Böhme, and Angelus Silesius, includes, even, with complex qualifications, Leibniz, Hamann, Vico, Goethe, the Romantics, and on to Kafka and Borges? Or should we rather try to understand Sewell's "human metaphor" in the postmodern context? Imagination and Science, Myth and Technology, Earth and Sky, the Many and the One, begin to converge in a "new gnosticism"—by which I mean that tendency of mind to dematerialize reality, to gather more and more mind in itself, to turn nature into culture, culture into language, language into immediate consciousness. Can this tendency lead us finally to an enlarged conception of Imagination? Or was this conception "always already" (Derrida) latent in those mute reveries before ancestral fires, flickering with still inchoate desires, in caves that once housed primordial dreams?

RETROTEXT

Fire, metaphor, desire.

"According to the myths of certain primitive peoples," Mircea Eliade writes in *The Forge and the Crucible,* "the aged women of the tribe 'naturally' possessed fire in their genital organs and made use of it to do their cooking but kept it hidden from men, who were able to get possession of it only by trickery." In some ancient matriarchies, then, women were sexually related to fire. Then "trickery" intervened; as in the case of Prometheus, who stole fire and hid it in a fennel stalk. Patriarchy on the way? More to the point, the cluster of references begins to expand: fire and desire, light and language, metaphor and mind, archetypes of a gnostic Prometheus, "master of fire" before other smiths and shamans.

Consider: Hesiod tells how Desire first impregnated the Void; the Old Testament begins Creation with Light; the New Testament initiates it with the Word; and true Gnostics identify Solar Seed with the Spermatic Word. Giambattista Vico elaborated still more these archetypes: the gods spoke to mute, primeval giants of the earth in thunder (and lightning?). "But at the first clap of thunder," he says in *The New Science,* ". . . as they felt the aspect of the heavens to be terrible to them and hence to inhibit their use of venery they must have learned to hold in check the bodily motion of lust." The same symbols are evoked more spiritually by Blake:

> Reader! lover of books! lover of heaven,
> And of that God from whom all things are given,
> Who in mysterious Sinai's awful cave
> To Man the wondrous art of writing gave:
> Again he speaks in thunder and fire!
> Thunder of Thought, and flames of fierce desire.
> (*Jerusalem.*)

Writing, thunder, thought, fire, desire. No wonder that Norman O. Brown quotes the foregoing lines in his *Closing Time,* which is a discourse or intercourse between Brown, Vico, and Joyce—the Joyce of *Finnegans Wake,* with its "vicous circles" and "broken heaventalk"—a discourse on Imagination, Language, and Reality.

I return to the point: fire and desire, light and letter, metaphor and mind—"the signature of all things"—came first and together, or "always already." On this, visionaries (Vico, Blake, Brown) and poststructuralists (Derrida, Foucault, Barthes) may agree. There are clear Orphic resonances in this linguistic gnosis, but also some Promethean overtones. Of the latter, Steiner says: "The symbolic affinities between words and fire, between the live twist of flame and the darting tongue, are immemorialy archaic and firmly entrenched in the [sexual?] subconscious. Thus it may be that there is a language-factor in the Prometheus myth. . . ." Indeed, in one version of that myth, Prometheus gives men the alphabet as well as fire and all the sciences and arts.

There may be a simpler name for all these (fiery, erotic, gnostic) gifts: Symbolism. "For all mental processes fail to grasp reality itself, and in order to represent it, to hold it at all, they are driven to the use of symbols," Ernst Cassirer observes in *Language and Myth.* Linguistic symbols are cognate to the symbols of myth, which also "posit" their meanings out of "the undifferentiated whole." Once "given," do such symbols become the stuff of reveries? "Psychically, we are created by our reverie—created and limited by our reverie. . . ," Gaston Bachelard writes in *The Psychoanalysis of Fire.* "Imagination works at the summit of the mind like *a flame,* and it is to the region of *the metaphor of metaphor* . . . that we must look for the secret of the mutant forces" (italics mine).

Imagination is the living flame, metaphor of metaphor, a power dynamic, mutant, and transformative. A power, I repeat, sexual as well, deriving its metamorphic force from great Eros, as writers since Hesiod and Ovid—including Freud, of course—have variously perceived. Thus, for instance, Bachelard notes: "*Sexualized fire* is preeminently the connecting link for all symbols"; and even: "Prometheus is a vigorous lover rather than an intelligent philosopher, and the vengeance of the gods is the vengeance of a jealous husband." But the sexual power of fire, which the myth of Prometheus tends to displace or repress, also works through science, back to its primitive forms. Eliade discovers in the earliest images and rituals of metallurgy a cosmogonic apprehension of reality, at once sacred and erotic, wedding the human body to the universe: "when we come to consider mining and metallurgy, we find ourselves confronted with specific concepts relating to the earth as mother, to the sexualization of the mineral world and its tools, and to the inter-relationship of metallurgy, gynaecology, and obstetrics." Later, alchemy accepts this order of existence but tries to "hurry" Nature with reverence in its attempts to transmute lead or mercury into eternal gold. Alchemy thus appears as a paradigm of human desire acting through metaphors of fire to realize change:

> The furnace supersedes the telluric matrix; it is there that the embryo-ores complete their growth. The *vas mirabile* of the alchemist, his furnaces, his retorts, play an even more ambitious role. These pieces of apparatus are at the very center of a return to primordial chaos, of a rehearsal of the cosmogony. Substances die in them and are revived, to be finally transmuted to gold.
> (*The Forge and the Crucible.*)

Metaphor, fire, desire: these work in prototypal *homo faber* to create the human world and receive the divine. They act also to purify the former even as they sacralize "the Work of Time." Thus Prometheus—*when* his erotic nature awakens—may prophetically affirm the gnostic unity of mind, beyond Myth and Technology, beyond Science and Imagination. Is that unity contained "in language" still? Paul Ricoeur believes it can not be otherwise:

> . . . it is in language that the cosmos, desire, and the imaginary achieve speech. . . . Thus it is the poet who shows us the birth of the word, in its hidden form in the enigmas of the cosmos and of the psyche. The power of the poet is to show forth symbols at the moment when "poetry places language in a state of emergence," to quote Bachelard again, whereas ritual and myth fix symbols in their hieractic stability, and dreams close them in upon the labyrinth of desires where the dreamer loses the thread of his forbidden and mutilated discourse.
> (*Freud*.)

I myself wonder.

TEXT

Yet this Retrotext may reveal only rumors of retrospection. The fact remains that since Kant, Fichte, and Schelling, since Blake, Wordsworth, and Coleridge, we have lacked an adequate theory of Imagination. Blake, we know, accorded to the Imagination a divine and prophetic role. "Everything which exists today was imagined long ago." Wordsworth held the Imagination to be part love and part intellect: "absolute strength / And clearest insight, amplitude of mind, / And reason in her most exalted mood." As for Coleridge, we know how long, brilliantly, and obscurely he digressed in his *Biographia Literaria* on the "esemplastic imagination"—or *"Einbildungskraft,"* as his sources called it, which unites the Many and the One—distinguishing between Primary and Secondary Imagination, and between both and Fancy. "The primary Imagination I hold to be the Living Power and prime Agent of all human Perception, and as a repetition in the finite mind of the eternal act of creation in the infinite I AM," he famously wrote. The tradition of these Romantic English poets extends into the modern epoch, culminating perhaps in Wallace Stevens, who wrote: "God and the imagination are one"—but bringing us back full circle to Blake, who also remarked in his Marginalia to Reynolds: "The eternal body of man is the Imagination, that is, God himself. . . ."

I would not want to exclude from our concerns with Imagination certain Romantic evocations of Divinity, or Joy, or Genius, or Prophecy, or Spiritual Love. Yet the Romantic tendency to equate Imagination with the sum of human faculties can provide, at best, only the radical element in an epistemology. That element, we have seen, is mythic and gnostic: metaphor is (immanent?) mind. That same element may also be modern: all thought is fiction (Nietzsche). So is all language fiction; counter-factual, it reveals, Steiner says, "the absolutely central power of the human word to go beyond and against 'that which is the case.' " Still, in this (postmodern) moment, we have come to know something about brain structures, electro-chemical impulses, dream functions, linguistic systems, mechanisms of perception and cognition, biofeedback. Is it unreasonable, then, to expect that physiology, neurology, philosophy, psychology, and linguistics should collaborate to render a fuller account of Imagination?

Literary critics, when they concern themselves themselves with Imagination at all, tend to turn to certain modern thinkers. These offer powerful, if partial, insights into that capable and most equivocal faculty. I cite four different examples here, in barest outline.

A. *Sigmund Freud*

Eros and Ananke determine the human tragedy. Dream, fantasy, delusion are actors or mediators in the play. So is Imagination, which Freud by his own admission did not quite comprehend—except perhaps as an aspect of sublimation, rooted in primal scenes and archaic desires, fed on playful fantasies. *Geschichtlich* we imagine, turned childishly toward our origins, remembering, repressing, repeating. But in the subconscious itself, all our imaginings, or at least fantasies, remain indistinguishable from facts. All art thus carries a double burden, concealing and revealing inadmissible wishes.

Freud's great work, *The Interpretation of Dreams,* theorizes about various techniques (condensation, displacement, association, substitution, transvaluation, transposition of expressive modes, in short, all the cunning means of symbolism) which, though they may touch on the imaginative process, finally pertain to another (oneiric) realm of meaning. In later essays, however, Freud attempts to engage the Imagination more directly:

> Our procedure consists in the conscious observation of abnormal psychic processes in others, in order to be able to discover and express their laws. Our author [Wilhelm Jensen, author of *Gradiva*] proceeds in another way; he directs his attention to the unconscious in his own psyche, is alive to its

> possibilities of development and grants them artistic expression, instead of suppressing them with conscious criticism.
> ("Delusion and Dream.")

*

> Now the writer does the same as the child at play; he creates a world of fantasy which he takes very seriously; that is, he invests it with a great deal of affect, while separating it sharply from reality. Language has preserved this relationship between children's play and poetic creation.
>
> . . . the essential *ars poetica* lies in the technique by which our feeling of repulsion is overcome, and this has certainly to do with those barriers erected between every individual being and all others. The writer softens the egotistical character of the daydream by changes and disguises, and he bribes us by the offer of a purely formal—that is, aesthetic—pleasure in the presentation of his fantasies.
> ("The Relation of the Poet to Daydreaming.")

*

> The uncanny as it is depicted in *literature* . . . merits in truth a separate discussion. To begin with, it is a much more fertile province than the uncanny in real life . . . ; for the realm of phantasy depends for its very existence on the fact that its content is not submitted to the reality-testing faculty.
> ("The Uncanny.")

Freud implicated the Imagination in the fundamental drives of human existence, in sex and egoism, and later in the death instinct. Yet his understanding of it remains shadowy, skeptical: "The 'creative' imagination is incapable of *inventing* anything; it can only combine components that are strangers to one another," he remarks in his *Introductory Lectures on Psychoanalysis*. This may be close to the truth; it can not be the essential part of it.

B. *Henri Bergson*

Evolution is ceaseless creation; so is consciousness, which appears "as the creative principle of evolution," Henri Bergson asserts in *Creative Evolution*. Time itself is "invention or it is nothing at all." But the freedom of creation, indeed of the Creator, is not absolute; it must confront necessity, seize matter, "the movement that is the inverse of its own," and so strive "to introduce into it the largest possible amount of indetermination and liberty." All this the intellect cannot wholly grasp; nor can instinct—only the intuition succeeds in grasping true creation in its "upspringing," its "indivisibility," and its "fervor."

There is nothing about a specifically human Imagination in this cosmic process. But in a later work, Bergson postulates a "myth-making function," which he also calls "virtual instinct," intended to protect life from the encroachments of an aggressive intelligence. Thus he writes:

> If intelligence now threatens to break up social cohesion at certain points . . . there must be a counterpoint, at these points, to intelligence. If this counterpoise cannot be instinct itself, for the very reason that its place has been taken by intelligence, the same effect must be produced by a virtuality of instinct . . . : it cannot exercise direct action, but, since the intelligence works on representation, it will call up "imaginary" ones, which will hold their own against the representation of reality and will succeed, through the agency of intelligence itself, in counteracting the work of intelligence.
> (*The Two Sources of Morality and Religion.*)

Oddly enough, there is a certain similarity between this view and Freud's. Bergson, however, goes farther in his speculations about this phantasmagoric tendency of mind: "Who knows indeed if the errors into which this tendency led are not the distortions, at the time beneficial to the species, of a truth destined to be later revealed to certain individuals?"

For Bergson, then, Imagination is an element of the creativity of the universe, an element meant to enhance the possibilities of human life and possibly to prefigure its evolution.

C. *Martin Heidegger*

The key word for Heidegger is not Imagination but Poetry. It is central in that cluster of Heideggerian symbols: Joy, Proximity, Home, Earth, Source, and Being. For instance:

> The vocation of the poet is homecoming, by which the homeland is first made ready as the land of proximity to the source. To guard the mystery of the reserving proximity to the Most Joyous, and in the process of guarding it to unfold it—that is the care of homecoming.
>
> *
>
> Poetry is the foundation which supports history, and therefore

> it is not a mere appearance of culture, and absolutely not the mere "expression" of a "culture-soul."
>
> *
>
> The poet stands between the former—the gods, and the latter—the people. He is one who has been cast out—out into that Between, between gods and men. But only and for the first time in this Between is it decided, who man is and where he is settling his existence.
> "Poetically, dwells man on this earth."
> (*Existence and Being.*)

That is, Poetry is a fundamental feature of ontology. Heidegger elaborates this proposition with reference to Language ("the house of Being") and Saying, in *On the Way to Language;* and with reference to Art, Truth, and Origin, in *Poetry, Language, and Thought:*

> Truth, as the clearing and concealing of what is, happens in being composed, as a poet composes a poem. *All art,* as the letting happen of the advent of the truth of what is, is, as such, essentially poetry.
>
> *
>
> The origin of the work of art—that is, the origin of both the creators and the preservers, which is to say of a people's historical existence, is art. This is so because art is by nature an origin: a distinctive way in which truth comes into being, that is, becomes historical.

But Poetry is not only Origin; it is also Openness. Therein lies its imaginative capacity, Heidegger avers, taking his cue from Rilke; hence its Unshieldedness, its "conversion":

> The conversion points to the innermost region of the interior. The conversion of consciousness, therefore, is an inner recalling of the immanence of the objects of representation into presence within the heart's space.
> (*Poetry, Language, and Thought.*)

This "conversion of consciousness" may be as close as Heidegger comes to speaking mundanely of an imaginative faculty; for his ontological apprehension of Poetry is, no less than Bergson's, sweepingly metaphysical.

D. *Jean-Paul Sartre:*

Sartre's two early explorations of the imaginary owe more to Husserl than to Heidegger. In the first of these, *Imagination: A Psychological Critique,* Sartre offers less a theory than a history of philosophical errors, and so concludes about his predecessors:

> They failed to realize that an atomistic conception of images was already contained in the very manner of formulating the problem. There is no avoiding the straightforward answer that so long as images are inert psychic contents, there is no conceivable way to reconcile them with the requirements of a synthesis. An image can only enter into consciousness if it is itself a synthesis, not an element. There are not, and never could be, images *in* consciousness. Rather, an image is *a certain type of consciousness.* An image is an act, not some thing. An image is a consciousness *of* some thing.

The last statement, of course, assumes the phenomenological definition of consciousness, and brings Sartre to the theory he attempts to develop in his second work, *The Psychology of Imagination.* Husserl had maintained, in his *Ideas,* "that 'fiction' is the vital element of phenomenology as of all eidetic science, the source from which knowledge of 'eternal truths' draws its nourishment." Sartre, however, ends by according to Imagination a more ambiguous function. Acknowledging its spontaneity and freedom, he also accepts the "essential poverty" of the image; for once formed, the latter remains hard, isolate, refusing experience. The difficulty stems in part from the implicit confusion of Imagination with image. It stems also from the fusion of the image itself with a kind of "negative" perception, which Sartre cannot prevent much as he wants to establish the Imagination as an "essential structure of consciousness." Here he speaks for himself:

> . . . nothing can be learned from an image that is not already known.
>
> ⋆
>
> The characteristic of the intentional object of the imaginative consciousness is that the object is not present and is posited as such, or that it is not posited at all.
>
> ⋆
>
> Thus the imaginative act is at once *constituting, isolating* and *annihilating.*
>
> ⋆

> We may therefore conclude that imagination is not an empirical and superadded power of consciousness; it is the whole of consciousness as it realizes its freedom. . . .
> (*The Psychology of Imagination.*)

With the last statement, Sartre appears to rejoin Blake and Stevens, which must strike us as incongruous.

The four examples exhaust neither the possibilities nor the perplexities of the subject. We conceive the Imagination in as many ways as we find to use or misuse the word; we further abuse such conceptions with conflicting metaphysical claims. Hence all those aporias and hence those endless perspectives:

(single entry): Antonin Artaud, *The Theatre and Its Double*
(multiple entry): Gaston Bachelard, *The Poetics of Space*
Owen Barfield, *The Rediscovery of Meaning*
Frank Barron, *Creativity and Personal Freedom*
Roland Barthes, *Mythologies*
Georges Bataille, *La Littérature et le mal*
Albert Béguin, *L'Âme romantique et le rêve*
Alfred Biese, *Die Philosophie des Metaphorischen*
Max Black, *Models and Metaphors*
Maurice Blanchot, *Lautréamont et Sade*
Ernst Bloch, *Das Prinzip-Hoffnung*
Harold Bloom, *The Anxiety of Influence*
Maud Bodkin, *Archetypal Patterns in Poetry*
Jorge Luis Borges, *Other Inquisitions*
André Breton, *Manifestoes of Surrealism*
Christine Brooke-Rose, *A Grammar of Metaphor*
Norman O. Brown, *Love's Body*
Scott Buchanan, *Poetry and Mathematics*
Kenneth Burke, *A Grammar of Motives,*
& *A Rhetoric of Motives*
Stanley Burnshaw, *The Seamless Web*
(triple entry): Roger Caillois, *Approches de l'imaginaire*
Ernst Cassirer, *The Philosophy of Symbolic Forms*
Jean Chateau, *Les Sources de l'imaginaire*
(double entries): Jacques Derrida, *Of Grammatology &*
"White Mythology"
Gilbert Durand, *Les Structures anthropologiques de l'imaginaire*
Anton Ehrenzweig, *The Hidden Order of Art*
William Empson, *The Structure of Complex Words*
Ernest Fenellosa, *On the Chinese Written Character*
Northrop Frye, *Fearful Symmetry*
E. H. Gombrich, *Illusion and Reality*
Nelson Goodman, *Fact, Fiction, and Forecast*
Jacques Hadamard, *The Psychology of Invention in the Mathematical Field*

Ray L. Hart, *Unfinished Man and Imagination*
Roman Ingarden, *The Literary Work of Art*
Wolfgang Iser, *The Implied Reader*
Fredric Jameson, *Marxism and Form*
C. G. Jung, *The Archetypes and the Collective Unconscious*
L. C. Knights, ed., *Metaphor and Symbol*
Arthur Koestler, *The Act of Creation*
Jacques Lacan, *Écrits*
Susanne Langer, *Feeling and Form*
Jacques Maritain, *Creative Intuition in Art and Poetry*
Hugo Meier, *Die Metaphor*
J. Needham, *Science and Civilization in China*
Friedrich Nietzsche, "On Truth and Lying in an Extra-Moral Sense" & *The Birth of Tragedy* & *The Will to Power*
Charles K. Ogden & I. A. Richards, *The Meaning of Meaning*
Ortega y Gasset, "La metáfora" & "El 'Tabu' y la metáfora"
Morse Peckham, *Man's Rage for Chaos*
Jean Piaget, *Play, Dreams, and Imitation in Children*
P. Quercy, *Les Hallucinations*
Quintillian, *Institutio Oratorio*
Paul Ricoeur, *The Rule of Metaphor*
I. A. Richards, *Coleridge on Imagination*
Ferdinand de Saussure, *Course in General Linquistics*
Wallace Stevens, *The Necessary Angel*
Tzvetan Todorov, *Introduction à la littérature fantastique*
Colin Turbayne, *The Myth of Metaphor*
(incomplete entry): Wilbur M. Urban, *Language and Reality*
?
Hans Vaihinger, *The Philosophy of As If*
Paul Valéry, *Leonardo, Poe, Mallarmé*
Heinz Werner, *Die Ursprünge der Metapher*
Philip Wheelwright, *The Burning Fountain* & *Metaphor and Reality*
(no entry): ?
?
Kenneth Yasuda, *The Japanese Haiku*
William Butler Yeats, *A Vision*
Heinrich Zimmer, *Philosophies of India*
Theodore Ziolkowski, *Fictional Transfigurations of Jesus*

Profusion, diffusion, confusion? "It is as if the very availability and self-ensured success of imaginative experience hindered rather than helped its comprehension in theoretical claims," writes Edward S. Casey. Yet Casey also writes to maintain that "the imagination is an autonomous mental act: independent in status and free in its action." Such equivocations may account for all those perspectives that Imagination seems to generate. But the same "equivocations" may also reveal something intrinsic to Imagination itself:

In imagining, the mind moves in many ways. Imagination multiplies mentation and is its freest form of movement. It is mind in its polymorphic profusion. It is also mind in the process of self-completion, and as such includes an element of self-enchantment.
(Edward S. Casey, *Imagining: A Phenomenological Study*)

*

Nor this alone
appeased his yearning; in the after day
Of boyhood, many an hour in caves forlorn
And in the hollow depths of naked crags
He sat, and even in their fixed lineaments,
Or from the power of a peculiar eye,
Or by creative feelings overborne,
Or by predominance of thought oppressed,
Even in their fixed and steady lineaments
He traced an ebbing and a flowing mind
Expression ever varying.
(William Wordsworth, "The Peddlar," 1798.)

*

We have come then by a long and circuitous route to the place where Wordsworth led us. Imagination is our means of interpreting the world, and it is also our means of forming images in the mind. . . . The two abilities are joined in our ability to understand that the forms have a certain meaning, that they are always significant of other things beyond themselves.
(Mary Warnock, *Imagination.*)

*

The imagination is the rebel of those subjects on which a detached analytic eye throws its light . . . imagination is integrated intelligence, intellect attached to rather than detached from the totality of human life. Reason *alone* is helpless to bring the rebellious imagination to light precisely because it forgets that it is itself only a part, that the part cannot comprehend the whole. . . .
(Eleanor Wilner, *Gathering the Wind: Visionary Imagination and Radical Transformation of Self and Society.*)

Here, in Eleanor Wilner's inspired work, is another clue to the failures of theories about the Imagination. Their arguments, reflexive and unverifiable, often end nearly where they began. Should we then abandon such vain efforts to construct a "Theory of Imagination," the phantasm of a chimera?

I think that may depend on what we mean by "theory." In a sense, *all* Art already constitutes such a theory, and this may include certain forms of imaginative criticism. In another sense, all actions which innovate in History are already part of that theory. As Wilner recognizes, Blake and Marx here agree; the Imagination proposes what History disposes, and the latter returns to propose to the first again; thus radical changes in self and circumstances meet. In his *A Philosophy of the Future,* Ernst Bloch goes even farther: "the external self-encounter" of "the humanum" suggests that "dreaming ahead" may image "that which lay ahead." Perhaps that is also what Marcuse senses when, in *An Essay on Liberation,* he anticipates a moment in which "society's capacity to produce may be akin to the creative capacity of art, and the construction of the world of art akin to the reconstruction of the real world—union of liberating art and liberating technology." A theory of Imagination, then, is nothing if not both scientific and poetic, at once an invitation to knowledge and to praxis. This, alas, we do not yet, do not quite, have.

But would such a master construct not prove to be more myth or ideology than theory? And does not even vision sometimes freeze in the eye? Against the perils of ideology we can finally admit only our death and error, which may guard us against that greater Death which is congealed Error; for light always breaks there where death is rehearsed.

EPITEXT V

I sit in the dead of a Milwaukee winter before our fireplace. A fire burns there, the logs arranged as I had learned from Bachelard, glowing side to glowing side, so that flames may spring from each to each in a "calorific series" of effluent and radiant heat. Yellow and blue, orange and black, a quick crimson as the wood cracks and some secret substance or sudden draft alters the chemistry of that insubstantial show. I hardly think; yet in retrospect I somehow recall that what I thought, were I thinking at all, concerned death more than knowledge or desire. This death, if death it be, has no end we can call end; and so we mumble of eternity. What every Empedocles knows? Says Bachelard: "Death in the flame is the least lonely of deaths. It is truly a cosmic death in which a whole universe is reduced to nothingness along with the thinker."

I sit in Milwaukee before a fire, in the dead of winter, with the clear certainty that spring must come around, and with it a clearer certainty still that yet another spring must bloom in which I have no share in the greenness nor any part in the thaw. Can this knowledge be but another name for

Imagination, threshold of the infinite? "Through its sacrifice in the heart of flames, the mayfly gives us a lesson in eternity," says Bachelard once again. The "lesson," I note, is given to us, *not to the mayfly.*

I move to some end:
like Death or Eternity,
yet for reasons wholly other,
the Imagination is what we cannot "deconstruct."
For it remakes itself even as we unmake all it can make, its "poetics continually (self) reconstructed" (Murray Krieger).

I move to the end: I hope that when a new theory of Imagination comes forth to take hold of our intellectual energies, it will not be so remote as to ignore our familiar actions, in classroom or office, kitchen or factory. In-forming our languages and noetic passions, it may thus re-form our day. But whatever the Imagination may prove to be, it comes from afar in our biological history, which is that of the earth and all the stars. Neither Imagination nor Literature can be finally revisioned without apprehension of the cosmic fact.

This much we know: the Imagination connects (and disconnects) us to this fact, to our wall-less home in reality. It permits Absence, respects Fractures—and always seems to pass through new Thresholds. In Blake, say *The Book of Los,* such thresholds allow us to move between all the stages of life, natural or artistic, private or communal, till Los, or Imagination, "glorious / An immense Orb of fire he fram'd." Owen Barfield also speaks of thresholds in *The Rediscovery of Meaning,* multiple thresholds which separate Self and Not-Self (*The Bhagavat-Gita*), Mind and Matter (Descartes), the Knowable and the Unknowable (Kant), the Conscious and the Unconscious (Freud).

But the Imagination passes through these
and all others,
abolishing none,
and so constitutes human
existence,
perhaps all of it.
"Then it is," Barfield writes, "that the threshold becomes like Aladdin's ring, yielding new meanings for old and giving birth to a future that has originated in present creativity instead of being a helpless copy of the outwardly observed forms of the past."

Only Aladdin's ring? I suspect that Barfield knew more than he was prepared to write: the threshold opens on a visionary realm. It is there that Imagination and Spirit meet. Emanuel Swedenborg spoke of the spiritual thus: "although it is in man, man is nevertheless able by means of it *to be present as it were elsewhere, in any place however remote. . . . The Human is the inmost in every created thing*" (my italics). "The Human is the inmost in every created thing." Is this the tedious anthropomorphism, anthropocentrism of our race speaking out once again? Or is the Human some aboriginal principle, toward which all theories of Imagination, Creation, must finally tend? It behooves humanists to wonder, and posthumanists too. A re-vision of literature may give this wonderment an intellectual shape, and yet preserve the wonder. Beyond the rhetoric of fracture—what other thresholds?

From
THE CAMARGO JOURNAL
II

The great point to which the technician of the Spirit should direct his attention in dealing with human beings is to leave them the possibility of discovering themselves, in the transformation which he is seeking to bring about in them, and the freedom to differentiate themselves ever more and more.

Pierre Teilhard de Chardin

Six months now in Cassis: the faint, persistent scratch of anti-Americanism. My own ambivalence toward France: it provided a language of my childhood and now grates on my adopted land.

Irritation feeds on contrasts. We are just back from a trip to Switzerland and Germany: the French ethos strikes us as a little dry, pinched. Mesure *leads to parsimony, lucidity to brittleness. The distance between wit and malice contracts. Dogmatism often conceals incompetence; Cartesianism ignores its quirks. Independence can mean egoism, my freedom instead of yours. Unhelpfulness, the penchant for the negative. Racism, Algerians at the post office* tutoyed *casually. Logophilia, the perpetual scrimmage of words. Driving itself as an impatient debate on wheels, shattered glass at intersections. Skepticism even of the light: yellow* phares, *tinted eyeglasses shutters closed. Austerity and suspicion of comfort: straight-back chairs, bleak museums,* caillous *instead of grass in squares, the spine-chilling main streets of provincial towns. Vanity and pretension, the latter so often justified. Sally reads me this passage from Dumas's* Dictionary of Cuisine:

> In passing, I have this piece of advice to anyone who plans to tour Spain: let him tour Italy first. Italy is an excellent conditioner between France and Spain.
> In Italy, where one eats badly, the best hotels will tell you: "We have a French cook."
> In Spain, where one eats abominably, the great hotels will boast: "We have an Italian cook."

"By the way," Sally adds, "have you noticed how the French dance? Abstractly, as if they would rather sit down and talk. But a culture is its contradictions: women scowl on the street to avoid male attention yet bare themselves almost completely on public beaches. Once they hid their eyes with veils, now it's fashionable shades."

We suddenly pause. Whence all these spiteful clichés? A moment of ill-humor? A surly exchange with some saleswoman at the Librairie du Port? Jobert quipping about America to the French press? Clichés arouse, clichés appease, but their partial insights organize reality always for the comfort of their users. Interestingly, they never quite describe one's own friends.

Clichés are also self-confuting. La Belle France "pinched"? From Brittany to Provence, from Savoy to the Pyrenées, where else in Europe can one find so much abundance? "Measure" and "parsimony": the land of Rabelais, Villon, Stendhal, Balzac, Hugo? "Cartesianism": in Pascal, Nerval, Lautréamont, Rimbaud, Jarry, Breton, Artaud? "Negative": perhaps, but also tough-minded. And isn't negation, as Sartre has taught us, the very principle of consciousness? "Unhelpfulness": seldom in the provinces, decreasing in Paris. As for "egoism": is it not a kind of self-possession or compactness, ease within one's own culture and skin? (By contrast, we

Americans seem so vague and vulnerable, and violent withal; either under- or over-filling our personal space, soft-shelled.) And that notorious "impatience" of the French: does it not keep one alert, spirit on the stretch? Though it may not rival our "willingness of the heart," it is a readiness of intelligence. "Bleak museums" I said: like the Beaubourg, the Orangerie, the Marmottan in Paris? Like the Léger Museum in Biot or the Fondation Maeght in St. Paul de Vence? And concerning that "logophilia": at least it avoids all those phatic noises, those sorrys and thank yous, that fill Anglo-American speech. Who but a French gas station attendant would describe the oil level in my car as "impeccable"? *Who but a Frenchwoman would correct the unidiomatic sign in the Munich Airport Ladies Room (Sally tells me) from* "L'Utilisation de ces Toilettes est sans Charge" *to* "L'Utilisation des toilettes est gratuite."!

Yet clichés of cultural praise may be finally as insidious as those of national derogation. We think of them as a form of wit. But they are closer to instinct, the "instinct of obligation" of the anthill, Henri Bergson would say, which constitutes a "morality of pressure" rather than one of "aspiration." These two are related:

> That which is aspiration tends to materialize by assuming the form of strict obligation. That which is strict obligation tends to expand and to broaden out by absorbing aspiration. Pressure and aspiration agree to meet for this purpose in that region of the mind where concepts are formed.
> *(The Two Sources of Morality and Religion.)*

■

Reading Le Monde*—global title, fractious outlook, conceptual writing—I wonder about the prospects of a United States of Europe. The idea seems no closer to realization today than in the time of Napoleon or Charlemagne. How then will the "planetization of mankind" (Teilhard) take place?*

Heroes, Lincolns or De Gaulles, embody both obligation and aspiration, the instinct of cohesion and the intelligence of the universe. Bergson, a Jew, speaks of heroism in terms that Teilhard, a Jesuit, might well understand:

> The truth is that heroism may be the only way to love. Now, heroism cannot be preached, it has only to show itelf, and its mere presence may stir others to action. For heroism itself is a return to movement, and emanates from an emotion—infectious like all emotions—akin to the creative act.

Heroism, love, the creative act: coincidence with the generative effort of life. Is this how the planetization of the earth will proceed? I fear that it will not prove so simple. Still, heroism is the ability to reconceive reality, transform the past. For this, acting on an ancient instinct, we exact from heroes a price: immolation first, veneration last.

Perhaps heroism must now become gnostic, at once mythic and technological, Promethean with love, before it can heal the world. Heroism: the Concrete Universal?

Le Monde, *fractious, would have none of these "utopian" thoughts.*

■

Grey doves fly low over the sea. Their nests, I know, are in crags of the calanques, *in lemon groves, umbrella pines, and cypress trees. Grey doves over a choppy sea. I can barely imagine them with an olive branch in their beaks. Even less with tongues aflame.*

D. H. Lawrence has this to say:

> The Father had his day, and fell.
> The Son has had his day, and fell
> It is the day of the Holy Ghost.

So I jot some queries for a gnostic view of history: no fathers and sons, no generations, everything there and at once revealed? The Many and the One reconciled? Self-identity without discord, wholeness in diversity, neither "schizophrenia" nor "paranoia" (Deleuze)? But can this still be history as we know it? "History as her is harped"? Eugen Rosenstock-Huessy thinks that "the community of One Time and One History" may now be possible, dependent upon human speech: "All speech rides the future of a new heaven and a new earth. All speech draws out the speaker from behind his isolation . . ." (Rosenstock-Huessy). It may depend particularly on poetry or primal speech: "Man makes himself by making his own gods, and this is poetry" (Norman O. Brown).

Conclusion? Man making the gods, man unmade by his gods, no more man or gods: just that holy ghost we call imagination or immanent speech?

■

*Back from a * * * lunch at "La Baumanière" in Les Baux (not as fine as "L'Oasis" in La Napoule), taking the backroads, the countryside like a piece torn from the moon. Yet even the sandstone of Provence whispers history.*

Les Baux: sculpted first by some primeval sea, sculpted after by the winds, now sculpted by human hands. In La Vallée des Enfers, fantastic shapes wherein nature, myth, and history compete. Across the powder-blue sky, a military jet streaks, drawing a thin silver arc over this contorted scene.

Cannonballs preceded the jets here. An impregnable fortress once stood high on the hill. The feudal Seigneurs of Les Baux—"Race d'aiglon, jamais vassale," *Mistral invoked them—defied all comers; and one, Raymond de Turenne, amused himself by hurling his enemies down the horrendous cliff. Till the cannon made the fortress obsolete.*

The cannonball—like catapult, arrow, and spear before—helped to dematerialize history. Now jet and missile, and everything electric, permit that dematerialization more. Here is familiar McLuhan:

> The computer . . . promises by technology a Pentecostal condition of universal understanding and unity. The next logical step would seem to be, not to translate, but to by-pass language in favor of a general cosmic consciousness. . . .

Motion yields to language, ground of our immanence. What kind of language? Arnold Toynbee speculates about im-mediate communication sans *technology:*

> Mankind's earliest means of communication was probably extrasensory perception—a faculty that was, and still is, shared by man with many other species.

Languages, already immaterial, continually dematerialize, etherealize, and ultimately realize, existence. Perhaps ultimately. Meanwhile, I think at Les Baux of that figure sculpted in a rock wall by some artist: a drooping Christ, his passion powerless to rise, falls back upon the earth in chthonic prayer.

■

Russell Young guides us on a magical trip through the Vaucluse: Cassis, Marseilles, Cavaillon (melons), L'Isle-sur-la-Sorgue (Provençal library), Fontaine-de-Vaucluse (Petrarch), Gordes (Vasarely museum), Sénanque (Cistercian Abbey), Venasque (ancient baptistry), St. Didier, Carpentras, Vaison-La-Romaine (forum, baths), Aurel, Sault, Apt (ochre and lavender), Pont Julien (pure Roman arch), Lacoste (Sade's estate), Bonnieux, Lourmarin, Silvacane (Cistercian abbey), Aix-en-Provence, Cassis.

February and the season sere, small stunted oaks with few auburn leaves, prickly shrubs, scattered rosemary, thyme, myrtle giving their aroma to the sun, everything else russet or vermilion, except where a stream—the Durance, the Coulon, the Ouvèze—suddenly turns a valley into greenish hues, and vines, olives, or almond trees pattern the hills. The Lubéron and Mont Ventoux, flecked with snow, dominate the province, a landscape untamed, unsettled, farouche. *Yet here civilization was shaped and reshaped. Neolithic tribes, Celtic Ligurians, Roman legions, Ostrogoth and Visigoth hordes, Arab armies all swept the countryside. Here the Courts of Love flourished; the Antipopes resided in Avignon; the Counts of Provence and Bishops of Venasque reigned.*

But the picturesque villages perchés *of the region tell another (more essential?) story. Cramped, secluded, perched eerily on every peak, these declare their suspicion of the world, incarnating in their stones ancient fears. Their walls seem jagged extensions of the very rocks on which they rest. (Do lives of these villagers extend the virtues of stone as well?) Since the prehistoric* bories *that first served them as homes, more typical than the cypressed* mas *of latter day, these peasants have dwelt* in *the earth (see Giono's* Regain*) and drunk occasionally the light. Did they, I wonder, ever experience history? Or like the immemorial fellah, only suffer time?*

A pause at Camus' grave in Lourmarin: a rough rock inscribed only with his name, dates, on a hillock of rosemary and lavender, a fragrant, undulating cloud, Sally says, like a woman hovering over his grave. Which woman? His mistress still alive in town, or some other emanation, all flowers and air? He loved women, justice, and the light. We drive off, stopping briefly at half-ruined Silvacane: silence, a moment for the spirit's rest among the rude elements of Provence.

The elements: here they call the mistral master, but I feel only the presence of earth and sun. Back in Cassis, I inhale the sea. Empedocles was right: the spirit needs four elements, bound by Love.

■

I will report a twofold truth. Now grows
The One from Many into being, now
Even from the One disparting come the Many,—
Fire, Water, Earth and awful heights of Air;
And shut from them apart, the deadly Strife
In equipoise, and Love within their midst
In all her being in length and breadth the same.
Behold her now with mind, and sit not there
With eyes astonished, for 'tis she inborn
Abides established in the limbs of men.
(*The Fragments of Empedocles,* tr. by William E. Leonard.)

Some two millenia later, the Sirens in Faust II *sing a paean to the universe:* "So herrsche denn Eros, der alles begonnen!" *and* "Heil dem seltnen Abenteur!", *to which the response of all benign spirits is:*

> Hochgefeiert seid allhier,
> Element', ihr alle vier!

So ends the Klassische Walpurgisnacht, as ethereal Homunculus, recapitulating the primal cycles of his life, seeks his body in the presence of Galatea's beauty.

■

I am reading the "other Balzac"—alchemical, visionary, elusive.

For instance: La Recherche de l'absolu. *Art, Science, and Spirit in Alchemy meet. Balthazar van Claës, aristocrat, seeks to discover the stuff from which matter is made. The search literally consumes his health, his hearth, his wealth. This Flemish Faust turns his back first on his perfect wife then on all life. Thus mind in search of the absolute returns to meet itself, exhausted in paradox:*

> Quoique plongés dans les abîmes de la pensée, et incessament occupés à observer le monde moral, les hommes de science aperçoivent néanmoins les plus petits détails dans la sphère oû il vivent. Plus intempestifs que distraits, ils ne sont jamais en harmonie avec ce qui les entoure, ils savent et oublient tout; ils préjugent l'avenir, prophétisent pour eux seuls, sont au fait d'un événement avant qu'il n'éclate, mais ils n'en ont rien dit.

Eros denied, spirit at the limit of both wisdom and folly. Stoned by urchins in the town square, this wasted visionary retreats to die. His last word is, of course, "EUREKA," which often spells "DELUSION." Often—but not oftener than that!

Eros denied: Gold, the Absolute, unconditioned Spirit. But Eros rarefied, deflected, may lead to Spirit too, as in Seraphita *and* Louis Lambert, *may lead to the true limits of the Human, which we call Love.*

Can Love, then, be somehow Abstract?

■

Balzac's unerring fictional sense of money. Gold in the mattresses of

France. De Gaulle's passion for the gold standard. The Freudian equation between excrement and gold, anality and money. The alchemical search for immutability. I turn instead to the transcendental equation of Buckminster Fuller:

$$Wealth = Knowledge \times Energy$$

This confirms Balzac: money is energy. But Fuller makes explicit (too simply?) what Balzac leaves implicit: money is mind, a gnostic energy greater than gold.

America broke the atom; this was done with gold, energy, and knowledge. And atomic fission (van Claës's dream?) may some day lead to the "absolute" (a unified field theory of cosmic forces?). But Sally in the meantime asks: why is fission always easier than fusion?

Fusion: fiery love potion of the stars.

■

The search for the absolute in art: Balzac's Le Chef-d'oeuvre inconnu. *(When Cézanne read it, he cried.) The aspirant is young Nicolas Poussin, introduced by the painterly Porbus to a true master, Frenhofer, who has the gift of bringing a canvas into blazing life. For ten years now, Frenhofer had labored in secret to realize his picture of womanhood, "La Belle-Noiseuse," which awaits only the advent of some matchless beauty to confirm the artist's final insight. She appears in Gillette, Poussin's radiant mistress, pandered by himself. The portrait is at last unveiled to the four: an unspeakable botch of paint,* "une multitude de lignes bizarres qui forment une muraille de peinture." *Still, there in the corner, the perfect tip of a female foot is visible to all, only the tip. Old Frenhofer cannot believe that his friends see nothing. They must be envious, the whole world is envious; he burns his "masterpiece" and dies.*

Aspiration, genius, love, jealousy sacrifice the self-obsession of all great art, death. A tumult of forces, a whirl of contradictions, and at the center—yes, there is one!—Gillette, who absorbs them all, and "inartistic" though she may be, recreates from all these passions the condition of life. Her true horror: not that she may be "used," not even that her lover may love her less than he loves his art, but simply that she may herself lose the capacity to love. No "passive" woman this, to Poussin she cries: "Je serai une infâme de t'aimer encore, car je te méprise. Je t'admire, et tu me fais horreur. Je t'aime et je crois que je te hais déjà."

Art, like Science, always tested at its limit by Love?

■

"Time is passing"; the Camargo Foundation "gave us time"; and as everyone in America knows, "time is money." In this case, a dead man's money, untaxed.

The man, Jerome Hill, was exceptional: "l'homme le plus évolué que j'ai connu," *Madame Beuchat, herself the exceptional librarian of the Camargo, once told us. His grandfather was J. J. Hill, sometimes called "the pirate of St. Paul." Call the grandfather what you will, his ruthless energy and mind found their way into the dream life of Jerome Hill.*

I am curious about this stranger, fellow American whom I never saw, who gives me leisure and memory, who left his native land as I left mine in order to "meet" here in Cassis. (Born in St. Paul in 1905, attended Yale, settled in Cassis in 1932, died in 1970.) I am intrigued by his versatile imagination: Jerome Hill painted, composed music, wrote poetry, made films (one, on Albert Schweitzer, won an Oscar) never married, spoke flawless French. An accomplished man, some say; a dilettante, *say others; but Schopenhauer remarks: "the* dilettante *treats his subject as an end, whereas the professional, pure and simple, treats it merely as a means." I am curious and intrigued, above all, by the motion of genes and dreams which yields a Jerome from a J. J.*

Jerome Hill seems to have been quizically aware of this enigma, which informs his autobiographical film. Its great Proustian theme is art and time. Images—wry, poignant, complex—images of what is, was, might have been, still could be—images of absolute childhood and the gratuitousness of existence—coalesce suddenly on the screen. For instance: a snow fight with his brother, an enforced afternoon nap in his mother's boudoir, the discovery of perspective through a hole in the window shade. The hole opens on childhood and on the magic box of the world, memory and reverie. It is also the hole through which we watch the film in a darkened room of "Pierrefroide" in 1975. (How many times has Russell Young, Hill's friend, seen this film, and what does he now think, sitting there behind the fussy machine?)

The moment, as they say, is frozen, though the film whirs from reel to reel. Motion of genes and dreams. Not far from here, at La Ciotat, the brothers Lumière invented "motion pictures," time running through a primitive machine.

■

The Camargo Foundation: a cluster of stone buildings standing at the edge of the sea. La Batterie served as a fort, and once housed Lieutenant Bonaparte; Pierrefroide was a studio in which Churchill painted; and in La Lèque, Brigitte Bardot and Grandma Moses found a weekend's rest. Today, we have a different kind of guest: Mr. and Mrs. Clark of St. Paul, Trustees of the Foundation. Courteous, shrewd, fair, they exemplify all the virtues of "good Americans," and suggest others which the stereotype sometimes conceals. For instance: a quality of genuine introspection, hedged in self-consciousness. Is the latter the "sacred disease" of Americans?

I am reading The Ambassadors *with my* aggrégation *students at the University of Nice. James knew, of course, the "complex fate" of Americans: brief history, immense space, unappeased yearning for the uncircumstanced. He knew also that self-consciousness comes from being "thrown forward" upon a "life-long trick of intense reflection." The insight applies to Strether, apostate of Puritanism. Though Puritanism has now receded, the insight may still apply to Americans. A Black writer, Ralph Ellison, maintains: "it is our good-and-bad fortune that we Americans exist at our best only when we are conscious of who we are and where we are going."*

But who is this "we"? James, born in New York City, lived in London; Ellison, born in Oklahoma City, lives in New York City; Hill, born in St. Paul, lived in Cassis; I, born in Cairo, live in Milwaukee. Americans all. Yet everyone persists to ask: "where are you from?*" The fiction of decisive origins, which instinct creates and culture re-creates—and mind transcends.*

The self-consciousness of Americans, Sally says (her father born in England), is perhaps a consciousness of displaced origins, but perhaps also a premonition of universal consciousness. Is Lewis Lambert Strether from Woollett or from some meridian of mind to which Balzac's Louis Lambert also belongs?

■

On a still day in Cassis, smoke ascends from a mas *in a spiral. La Couronne de Charlemagne—less like a crown than a giant collapsed sandstone soufflé—sits askew on the horizon. Below our balcony, the sea eddies lazily as waves splash and recede and gulls circle in the air. I try to watch all these gentle motions; time passes; the earth spins, turns about the sun.*

Curls and coils, whirls and whorls, rotations and revolutions. The wheels of myth; the reincarnations of Hinduism; the spirals of Faust's life; the cycles of Spengler and Toynbee; the gyres of Yeats; the cosmic involutions of Teilhard de Chardin. Never really a perfect circle, and only the circle knows its true "origin."

And now this about human gnosis: Kurt Gödel's mathematical proof, according to Piaget, leads us to envisage knowledge not as a "pyramid or building of some sort," but "as a spiral the radius of whose turns increases as the spiral rises."

Like smoke on a still day in Cassis—or Van Gogh's cypresses seen upside down.

Upside down: after health, sudden sickness. My dentist has given me an antibiotic to which I prove savagely allergic. All the symptoms of high fever, insurrection of blood and lymph. Hurriedly, a doctor flushes out my system; I am wasted; after two weeks of exhaustion, I recover. Something in my body loathes this matter foreign to it.

Self and Other: concepts of immunology and psychoanalysis, disease as language.

Georg Groddeck claims that diseases are our most secret and subtle discourse with the universe. More than a discourse—collusion, really, between the I and It—diseases serve as guerrilla forces, freedom fighters, against the tyrants of organic repression. But "freedom" is just another slogan; the It will have nothing less than Childhood, or the Loving Mother who lives in us all, Paradise.

Paradise: therapeutic concept and "creative space" of all ages. In Groddeck et le royaume millénaire de Jérôme Bosch, *Roger Lewinter writes:*

> Le corps, après la naissance, est ainsi le lieu de tout dehors, où l'être se représente la relation paradisiaque initialement vécue dans la matrice. . . . Dans le "Jardin des délices" [of Bosch], l'être humain défait sa chute en Enfer . . . par réaction en l'innocence originelle d'Adam. . . . Le paradis, comme l'indique l'intelligence psychosomatique de la maladie, est "perversion polymorphe": mise en jeu de toutes les modalités de vie du corps, en sorte que sa puissance existentielle soit épuisée, et que la mort intervienne non plus avant terme. . . .

Groddeck and Bosch: Disease and Art conjoined in a paradisiac vision of satisfied Desire. Paradise: not Void or Nirvana, but the Plenum of a consciousness we can imagine though not possess.

*Paradise regained: Utopia. Bosch points to Bloch for whom Dream, not Disease, is the basis of "anticipatory consciousness," a consciousness enhanced, imperiled, by anxiety about Death (*Todesangst*) as by anxiety of the Not-yet Known (*Noch-nicht bewusst*). Dream deconstructs reality and realizes Desire; so does Art, especially the most "utopian," Music. But for Ernst Bloch, the utopian project demands a permanent alliance between Art and Science, Imagination and Reality, Hope and Technic. This is the dream of Prometheus.*

I lie in a white bed, depleted by my "disease," sunk in a vague reverie, anticipating health. Is this, even this, inspired by the Principle of Hope?

■

Imagine, Sally once said, we all have a white garden within, a place where we meet the universe. I nod though I have also read of Melville's pallid and leprous universe.

3

CULTURE, INDETERMINACY, AND IMMANENCE
Margins of the (Postmodern) Age

The Argument:

The play of indeterminacy and immanence is crucial to the episteme of postmodernism, a term that may have now outlived its awkward use. Between shifting margins and maieutic fragments, the argument concerning this age of "indetermanence" proceeds in seven orderly parts:

I. Anarchy or Indeterminacy?
II. The Question of Epistemes
III. The New Science
IV. Of Herrings: Red, Silver, and Purple
V. The Cultural Evidence of Our Time
VI. In the Arts
VII. Human and Inconclusive

The Counter-argument:

This text is itself an inconclusive fiction of our time. The present remains always concealed from us, and true prophecy requires madness, unseemly on this occasion. Indeterminacy and immanence are as ageless as language; "indetermanence" is a barbarism; and epistemes are diversions from the imperative of our world, just praxis. Less maieutic than mystical or sophistical, the argument is itself marginal.

I. ANARCHY OR INDETERMINACY

We are enjoined to reflect upon the order and disorder of knowledge in our time. But I also wonder about our time, the margin of our mortality, and how we shall name ourselves as we die to meet posterity half way. Uncouthly, do we say:

The order of knowledge is founded on exclusions, Michel Foucault asserts. The task is to expose (include?) these exclusions. *L'Ordre du discours* (Paris, 1971).

we are children of the Postmodern Age? Yet why ponder the question? What, after all, is in a name? Partly our presence, our hope in part. Call it parturition and play. We always raise our voices to invoke ancestors whom we then proceed to remake.

Think of "Lucy," three and a half feet tall, not *Homo sapiens* but *Homo erectus* nonetheless, lying more than three million years on the Afar plain. Gracile hominid, was she mother of us all? They say not. She looked curiously at our "true ancestors" as they began to walk the earth. Thus, with every turn of the page, our "ancestors" recede; and the fiction of origins meets the fiction of differences. From paleontology to grammatology.

I call upon Matthew Arnold and Friedrich Nietzsche, who have been summoned so often they no longer come bearing the odor of clay.

Arnold has nearly preempted the concept of culture among academic Anglophiles of our day. His work, *Culture and Anarchy,* certainly casts a shadow on my subject, which I may seek to dispel in vain. Culture for Arnold—we know this all too well—was an "inward operation," a fruitful and passionate "curiosity," a "general intelligence" in "pursuit of our total perfection by means of getting to know . . . the best which has been thought and said in the world." It demanded civility of the "best self," harmony "in developing all sides of our humanity," and in "developing all parts of society" as well. In these dicta, "harmony," "totality," and "perfection" are key. Their absence leaves us open to anarchy or, worse still, harsh morality; at both, Arnold thought, Americans tended to excel.

Culture and Anarchy, ed. Ian Gregor (Indianapolis and New York, 1971), pp. 5-8.

"From Maine to Florida, and back again, all America Hebraises," Arnold complains (p. 15). This was in 1869. What might he think of Southern California today?

I have American culture particularly in mind. Is it given more than ever to either transcendent Hebraism or plain anarchy? Or is it transmuting itself into something Arnold would scarcely recognize, something indeterminate, immanent, rich and strange? For indeterminacy surely need not deny an ideal of harmonious perfection; nor is strangeness sometimes but the action of an immanent future in our lives. Arnold wrote: "So that, for the sake of the present, but far more for the sake of the future, the lovers of culture are unswervingly and with a good conscience the opposers of anarchy." The difficulty has become this: how to recognize "anarchy," which like "nihilism" can simply serve as objurgation of the New.

(p. 17)

How much of our intellectual rhetoric is mainly magical or apotropic?

Yet there is another case, and it is flamboyantly made by Nietzsche. No sweetness and

The Will to Power, ed. Walter Kaufmann (New York, 19€7), pp. 13, 39,

light here; instead, the hammer and dying sparks off the anvil. I quote at some length:

149, 163, 181, 199, 267, 283, 291, 309, 380, 418, 548.

What we find here is still the *hyperbolic naïveté* of man: positing himself as the meaning and measure of the value of things.

*

The period of clarity: one understands that the old and the new are basically opposite . . . that all the old ideals are hostile to life (born of decadence and agents of decadence, even if in the magnificent Sunday clothes of morality).

*

My chief proposition: there are no moral phenomena, there is only a moral interpretation of these phenomena. This interpretation itself is of extra-moral origin.

*

Play-acting as a consequence of the morality of "free will". . . . Personal perfection as conditioned by will, as consciousness, as reasoning with dialects, is a caricature, a kind of self-contradiction—A degree of consciousness makes perfection impossible—Form of *play-acting*.

*

It seems to me [why this sudden access of modesty?] important that one should get rid of the all, the unity, some force, something unconditioned; otherwise one will never cease regarding it as the highest court of appeal and baptizing it "God."

*

The "subject" is only a fiction: the ego of which one speaks when one censures egoism does not exist at all.

*

"There are only *facts*"—I would say: No, facts are precisely what there is not, only interpretations. . . . Insofar as the word "knowledge" has any meaning, the world is knowable; but it is *interpretable* otherwise, it has no meaning behind it, but countless meanings.—"Perspectivism."

*

So many features of postmodernism are implicit in these chips and shavings of 1883-88. For instance:

a. the decenterment of man

b. the vitality of the new

c. hermeneutics

d. the demystification of reason

e. the refusal of unity

f. the empty subject

g. fact-fiction, perspectivism

h. the liminality of language

i. thinking in fictions

j. the denial of origins

k. the energetics of value

l. ludic arts, the metaphysics of play

Language depends on the most naïve prejudices.

Now we read disharmonies and problems into things because we think *only* in the form of language—and thus believe in the "eternal truth" of "reason". . . .

We cease to think when we refuse to do so under the constraint of language ["the prison house of language" in other translations]; we barely reach the doubt that sees this limitation as a limitation.

m. the collapse of being and becoming, a new ontology

*

Parmenides said, "one cannot think of what is not";—we are at the other extreme, and say, "what can be thought of must certainly be a fiction."

*

Knowledge is referring back: in its essence a *regressus in infinitum*. That which comes to a standstill (at a supposed *causa prima,* at something unconditioned, etc.) is laziness, weariness. . . .

We tend to forget that Nietzsche's contemporary, William James, may also prove a source of postmodern tendencies. For instance: "The mind is at every stage a theatre of simultaneous possibilities." Or even Ralph Waldo Emerson: "But man thyself, and all things unfix, dispart, and flee."

*

Value is the highest quantum of power that a man is able to incorporate—a man: not mankind! . . . mankind is merely the experimental material, the tremendous surplus of failures: a field of ruins.

*

The world as a work of art that gives birth to itself. . . . "Play," the useless—as the ideal of him who is overfull of strength, as "childlike."

*

The new world-conception.—The world exists; it is not something that becomes, not something that passes away . . .—it maintains itself in both. It lives on itself: its excrements are its food.

No doubt, some will judge this catena of musings half demented and in any case rebarbative, though I admit to a certain pleasure that two great Europeans, near contemporaries—Nietzsche went mad within a year of Arnold's death—should perceive the human condition so differently. Against Arnold's hope for a universal culture, and for a criticism founded upon "a

Walter Kaufmann: "The publication of *The Will to Power* as Nietzsche's final and systematic work blurred the distinction between his works and his notes and created the false impression that the aphorisms in his books are of a kind with these disjointed jottings" (p. xix).

centre of taste and authority," Nietzsche speaks with irony, poetry, and truculence to exalt a perspectivism so radical as to appear to beggar nihilism itself.

There are, of course, many Nietzsches. One is the German Nietzsche, slayer of God, herald of the Overman, Dionysian psychologist, prophet of the transvaluation of all values, of whom Freud, Spengler, Heidegger, Jaspers, and Wittgenstein were acutely aware, as were Rilke, George, Kafka, Mann, Musil, Benn, and Ernst Jünger. But there is now another Nietzsche, French Nietzsche, perhaps less modern than postmodern, magus of deconstruction, geometer of decenterment, philosopher of language. Georges Bataille and Pierre Klossowski have written about him, and more recently, Jacques Derrida, Gilles Deleuze, Jean-François Lyotard, Henri Lefebvre, and Michel Foucault, among many others.

"Among all the thinkers of the nineteenth century he [Nietzsche] is, with the possible exceptions of Dostoyevsky and Kierkegaard, the only one who would not be too amazed by the amazing scene upon which we now move. . . . Much, too much, would strike him as *déjà vu:* yes, he had foreseen it; and he would understand. . . ." Erich Heller, *The Artist's Journey into the Interior* (New York, 1968), p. 173. Nietzsche himself cried: "Oh grant madness, you heavenly powers! Madness that at last I may believe in myself . . . ," *Ibid,* p. 197.

Whatever avatar of Nietzsche we choose to invoke, we must now acknowledge a radical counter-tradition that redefines for us both culture and anarchy, one that Arnoldians can only find dismaying. Yet the task, of course, is to avoid the tendency of one tradition to lapse into nihilistic chic and the other into pious beneficence—to avoid, that is, the strut and shuffle of our intellectual performances.

Contrast Norman O. Brown's "Apocalypse: The Place of Mystery in the Life of the Mind," *Harper's*, May 1961, with Lionel Trilling's *Mind in the Modern World* (New York, 1972).

MAIEUTIC

How is belief suspended, desire delayed, affect shunted or contained? Perhaps through Imagination, through all its evasions and tropes. Yet Nietzsche claims: "It is our needs that interpret the world; our drives and their For and Against. Every drive is a kind of lust to rule . . ." (p. 267). Lust to rule: what then is an academic conference? A colosseum of ideas or gladiatorial show, with Andabates, Retiariuses, Mirmillons, Samnites, and Thracians, vying for victory, or if they fall, hoping for a swarm of thumbs pointing heavenward? And the outcome of all this: what can it be? "Clarification," as we all half hope and half of that half half believe? Or is there an ontology of conferences, more precisely an onto-erotics and onto-politics, a presence anyway that shapes and gently mocks all our epistemes?

II. THE QUESTION OF EPISTEMES

Nietzsche's radical perspectivism, not merely his skepticism, challenged the grounds on which philosophy, from Plato to Hegel, had sought to build. Nature, language, and mind, no longer congruent, defied the articulations of a sovereign code. This view has now become banal. Yet the question remains: is such indeterminacy itself part of a new episteme?

Les Mots et les choses (Paris, 1966), pp. 219-21, 313.

In *The Order of Things*, Michel Foucault identifies three major *"epistémès"* of Western history; the last, beginning early in the nineteenth century, is the "modern." Two modern forms of reflection arise: science, which explores the relation of logic to ontology, and history, which explores that of signification to time. But the decisive trait is this: putting in doubt the reciprocities of being and meaning, modernism finally generates a self-reflexive discourse, a radically intransitive language, which can only affirm its own "precipitous existence," its ludic "dispersal." We call that language modern literature.

In our quotidian and comfortable humanism, "ought we not to remember that we are bound to the back of a tiger?" Foucault asks (p. 333). The tiger of an emergent posthumanism?

The dispersal of language—shall we say its near immanence?—marks for Foucault the "disappearance" of man, not literally, to be sure, but as a particular idea, a concrete figuration of history. This "disappearance" turns out to be yet another Nietzschean prophecy, its realization coming nearer every day. The prophecy fulfills itself in a field of lexical play; for as Foucault says:

(pp. 394 ff.)

> In the interior of language experienced and traversed as language, in the play of its possibilities stretched to their extreme point, what announces itself is that man has "come to an end," and that in reaching the summit of all possible speech, he arrives not at the very heart of himself, but at the edge of what limits him: in that region where death prowls, where thought is extinguished, where the promise of the origin indefinitely recedes.

Referring to Artaud, to Roussel, to Bataille, Blanchot, and Kafka, Foucault hints at yet another summit, at a luminous transformation still to come. There where the episteme of modernism begins to dissolve and the human face explodes beneath its masks in laughter, Foucault envisions the return of some unspeakable unity in language and wonders: "Is this not the sign that the whole of this configuration is now about to topple, and that man is in the process of perishing as the being of language continues to shine ever brighter upon our horizon?" Thus the being of all our languages seems to summon the future immanence of mind.

Foucault is a materialist, yet his vision here seems concordant with Teillhard de Chardin's. Foucault, however, senses that behind the apparent logophilia of every culture hides a profound logophobia, an obscure fear of "the great buzz, chaotic and continuous, of discourse." *L'Ordre du discours*, p. 53.

But we need to pause: where does Foucault's argument precisely rest? I put it for him baldly: the modern episteme, starting early in the nineteenth century, has nearly run out its course; during its movement, the dispersal of discourse, the indeterminacy of knowledge, the disappearance of man occur gradually; we may be approaching now a new logos, a new immanence of language. For Foucault, then, the moment of dispersal has been two centuries in the making; and what literary historians call Romanticism, Victorianism, Modernism, and Postmodernism are all subsumed by it. But this is macrohistory, and metahistory as well. For Michel Foucault could have scarcely performed his dazzling archaeology of knowledge were he not writing with a hindsight that, say, Gibbon, Michelet, Henry Adams, or Spengler could not possess. Where Arnold saw anarchy, Foucault sees indeterminacies betokening another order of discourse. Thus his concept of dispersal is itself part of the postmodern ethos. Whether a valid episteme of postmodernism, a new organizing principle of culture and mind, can be enunciated at this time is still moot.

Again, Nietzsche may be here an exception. Yet modernity itself is always complex. As Paul de Man says: "Modernity invests its trust in the power of the present moment as an origin, but discovers that, in severing itself from the past, it has at the same time severed itself from the present. Nietzsche's text [*The Use and Abuse of History*] leads him irrevocably to this discovery. . . ." *Blindness and Insight* (New York, 1971), p. 149.

But the time has surely come to probe the term indeterminacy itself, which so far has remained indeterminate, before it congeals into yet another critical slogan.

MAIEUTIC

All thought hardens; abstract thought hardens absolutely. Even metaphor becomes archetype, neotype, stereotype; and "deconstruction" may soon provide a base more solid than the one on which the tomb of Lenin rests. Is there a permanent revolution in language? We call it poetry. But what is the place and play of poesis in criticism? And what if the poetry should prove too thin even for critical discourse? Must we thus choose between critical ideology and critical doggerel? Perhaps we require a form for the critic's SUFFERING: *for there is fluency in pain when its sources are in gravity and grace. Yet this may seem too fierce an exigency to put in the way of criticism. Might we not also ask? what are the* PLEASURES *of the critical text? Poesis, suffering, pleasure: how do we acknowledge their presence in the shapes of our critical discourse?*

III. THE NEW SCIENCE

I wish to acknowledge here an excellent paper: Teresa Ebert's "The Tolerance of Ambiguity."

Science, according to Foucault, is one of the two modes of "reflection"—the other being history—that marks the emergence of the modern episteme in the nineteenth century. But the science of our century is sufficiently distinctive to warrant epistemological demarcations of its own, which Husserl somewhat adversely began in *The Crisis of European Sciences and Transcendental Phenomenology* late in the thirties.

We may consider 1905 as a turning point. In that year,

Albert Einstein published his paper on the Special Theory of Relativity. Events are always perceived with reference to a particular frame; in another system of coordinates, the "same" events are not the same. As Einstein succinctly put it: "There is no absolute motion." Nor is there absolute time or space. A moving clock ticks slower, a moving rod measures shorter, as their speeds approach the constant speed of light *in vacuo* (c). But the theory, which assumes the transformations of Maxwell and Lorentz, is no mere legerdemain. It has led to a new understanding of space, time, and motion; obviated the concept of absolute simultaneity; clarified the equations of electro-magnetism; unified the laws of conservation of momentum and of energy; and, as we all devastatingly know, proven the equivalence of mass and energy.

Out of My Later Years (New York, 1950), p. 41.

$\ell = \sqrt{1 - \frac{v^2}{c^2}}$

$t = \frac{1}{\sqrt{1 - \frac{v^2}{c^2}}}$

In 1915, Einstein formulated the General Theory of Relativity, which reckoned with gravity and inertial systems as elements of a unified field: "according to that theory, the physical properties of space are affected by ponderable matter." The theory also dispensed with Euclidean geometry, adopting instead "curved" or Riemannian space. "The fundamental concepts

$E = mc^2$

Essays in Science (New York, 1934), p. 52, 58.

Einstein also wrote: "There is no place in this new kind of physics both for the field and matter, for the field is the only reality." Quoted by Fritjof Capra, *The Tao of*

Physics (Boulder, Colorado, 1975), p. 211.

of the 'straight line,' the 'plane,' etc., thereby lose their precise significance in physics," Einstein notes. Much, much more was, of course, at stake, including the "singularities" of black holes in space. Suffice it now to say that with both theories Einstein forced the universe of Galileo and Newton to reveal an entirely different face.

To which Niels Bohr responded: "Nor is it our business to prescribe to God how he should run the world." Werner Heisenberg, *Physics and Beyond* (New York, 1971), p. 81.

Still, as Einstein thought, God does not "play dice with the universe." The witticism was a serious reproach to the new theoreticians of quantum physics, most particularly to Niels Bohr and Werner Heisenberg, authors of the "Copenhagen interpretation." For Heisenberg had published in 1927 his famous paper on the Uncertainty Principle: either the momentum of a particle or its position could be precisely determined, not both, thus betraying the ineluctable complicity of observer and observed, measuring system and field of measurement. That same year Bohr formulated his Principle of Complementarity: since light seemed to behave both as waves and as quanta of particles, logical contradictions in certain phenomena could be heuristically viewed under the aspect of complementarity. The mathematical formalism of these principles, which I have rendered in a few ill-

Werner Heisenberg: "What we observe is not nature in itself but nature exposed to our method of questioning. . . . In this way quantum theory reminds us, as Bohr has put it, of the old wisdom that . . . in the drama of existence we are ourselves both players and spectators." *Physics and Philosophy* (New York, 1962), p. 58. W. B. Yeats: "How can we know the dancer from the dance?" "Among School Children."

N.B. When Bohr was knighted, he chose as his *motto: contraria sunt complementa.* He had also visited China in 1937, and been struck by *t'ai chi.*

chosen words, has an awesome elegance, though their philosophical implications are to this day in passionate debate.

Einstein to Jacques Hademard: "The words of the language, as they are written or spoken, do not seem to play any role in my mechanism of thought." And Mozart in a letter of doubtful authenticity: "Nor do I hear in my imagination the parts *successively*, but I hear them, as it were all at once (*gleich alles zusammen*)." Quoted in Brewster Ghiselin, ed., *The Creative Process* (New York, 1952), p. 43.

Certain features of the new physics, however, seem provisionally clear. As a non-iconic science, physics now dispenses with geometric models to describe subatomic events. As a largely non-verbal discipline, it avoids both the ambiguities and conceptual constraints of natural languages. Instead of discrete objects, the new science also speaks of probabilities, tendencies to exist, thus blurring the ontological lines of being. As Heisenberg put it:

Across the Frontiers (New York, 1974), p. 115.

> . . . the new experiments have taught us that we can combine the two seemingly conflicting statements: "Matter is infinitely divisible" and "There are smallest units of matter," without running into logical difficulties.

Causality proves to be a concept of dubious use, and continuity in "matter waves"appears merely nominal. Thus electrons may "jump" from one "orbit" to another without traveling through intervening spaces. As for objectivity, that too seems a fiction transposed from classical concepts, useful only if the object is distinguished not from a

Zeno's paradox? No, simply the probability function Ψ explains the quirk. There are also quarks, neutrinos, and other ghosts of matter with "charm," "resonance," or "strangeness," that populate our cloud chambers.

subject but from the rest of the universe. Mechanism, determinism, materialism recede before the flux of consciousness, a kind of noetic Heraclitean fire. There is fright as well as elation in this recognition, to which Heisenberg attests:

Physics and Beyond, p. 61.

> At first, I was deeply alarmed. I had the feeling that, through the surface of atomic phenomena, I was looking at a strangely beautiful interior, and felt almost giddy at the thought that I now had to probe this wealth of mathematical structures nature had so generously spread out before me.

EXCURSUS ON GÖDEL'S PROOF

EVEN THE "WEALTH OF MATHEMATICAL STRUCTURES" HAVE THEIR LIMITS. THREE YEARS AFTER HEISENBERG'S PAPER ON UNCERTAINTY, KURT GÖDEL DEMONSTRATED THAT EVERY LOGICAL STRUCTURE MUST BE PART OF A LARGER AND "STRONGER" STRUCTURE; NONE CAN BE COMPLETE. AS STROTHER B. PURDY PUTS IT: "WITH THE LIMITATIVE THEOREMS OF KURT GÖDEL (1930) AND ALONZO CHURCH (1936) IT BECAME CLEAR THAT THE UNSOLVABILITY OF CERTAIN PROBLEMS, THE UNANSWERABILITY OF CERTAIN QUESTIONS, BASIC TO THE NATURE OF MATHEMATICS, HAD TO BE FORMALLY RECOGNIZED. IN THESE AREAS, MATHEMATICS SEEMS NOW MORE LIKE A GAME OF HUMAN INVENTION THAN AN UNCOVERING OF REALITY" [*THE HOLE IN THE FABRIC* (PITTSBURGH, 1977), P. 5]. THUS THE INCOMMENSURABILITY OF MIND AND THE WHOLE OF REALITY IS SUGGESTED. RECOGNIZING THE THEOLOGICAL AURA OF THE ARGUMENT, JEAN PIAGET WHIMSICALLY NOTES: "BUT GOD HIMSELF HAS, SINCE GÖDEL'S THEOREM, CEASED TO BE MOTIONLESS. HE IS THE LIVING GOD, MORE SO THAN HERETOFORE, BECAUSE HE IS UNCEASINGLY CONSTRUCTING EVER 'STRONGER' SYSTEMS [*STRUCTURALISM* (LONDON, 1968), P. 141].

ALL THIS, I SUSPECT, HARDLY ACCORDS WITH ARNOLD'S SENSE OF DIVINITY. MORE TO OUR POINT: SINCE THE IDEAL OF A STRUCTURE OF ALL POSSIBLE STRUCTURES SEEMS UNREALIZABLE, KNOWLEDGE MUST REMAIN *FINALLY INDETERMINATE.*

In such rarefied realms of reason, a humanist, modern *or* postmodern, gasps for breath. We need to return to our primary concern: contemporary culture and its singular indeterminacies. Granting that we inhabit neither a Newtonian nor a Laplacian universe, how then can the new sciences contribute to a definition of postmodernism?

The question must be answered by admitting first its obduracies. Scientific concepts, we are cautioned, should not be confused with cultural metaphors and literary tropes. Nor is there unanimity among scientists themselves concerning the implications of their discoveries. Against the instrumentation of Bohr, Einstein to the end clung to his realism, while Schrödinger stood uneasily in between. We encounter another difficulty when we coerce mathematical forms to yield philosophical statements about the nature of reality; the former tend to vanish, leaving behind only an abstract grin. (In this regard, the ingenious efforts of Carl Friedrich von Weizsäcker to modify classical logic and so correlate verbal and mathematical patterns proved inconclusive.) Finally, we need to recall that science, however tolerant of ambiguity, can not easily renounce the

Schrödinger's Cat Paradox:

"Imagine a cat confined in a chamber containing the following 'torture device' which cannot be operated by the cat itself. A Geiger counter with a very tiny amount of radioactive substance is placed in the chamber, so that in an hour *perhaps* one of the atoms decays. . . . If an atom decays, then the counter reacts and, by a relay mechanism, triggers a hammer which releases a pellet of cyanide. On leaving the system alone for an hour one would say that the cat is alive *if* no atom has decayed in the meanwhile, while the

Capra, *The Tao of Physics*, p. 138.

premise of immanence on which it rests. "Quantum theory forces us to see the universe not as a collection of physical objects, but rather as a complicated web of relations between the various parts of a unified whole," writes a contemporary physicist, thus echoing the organicism of Whitehead, so masterfully expressed in *Science and the Modern World* half a century before.

first atomic decay would have poisoned it. The function of the whole system would express this situation by containing in itself the fact of the living and the dead cat mixed or smeared out in equal parts. . . . the indeterminacy which is originally restricted to the atomic realm becomes a macroscopic sentient indeterminacy which can only be decided by direct observation." Erwin Schrödinger, quoted in Jagdish Mehra, *The Quantum Principle* (Dodrecht, Holland and Boston, 1974), pp. 72 ff. But should it be a black, ginger, or Siamese cat?

Yet in these same perplexities may lie some answer to our initial query: how can the paradoxes of physics contribute to an understanding of contemporary culture? For however alien quasars or quarks may seem to humanists—and I find them no more so than certain social structures we inhabit—it is now clear that science, through its technological extensions, has become an inalienable part of our lives. More, the new Prometheus, quite as in the adamantine days of Zeus, assays nothing less than the unification of mind. The project is not altogether mythical; its evidence is equivocally in our midst. Of this we can be more certain: the epistemological concerns of science must concern us all the more in that scientists themselves, defying difficulties I have noted, insist on philosophizing, speaking not in mathematics but in natural languages. Even Heisenberg admits:

See the next two chapters: "The Gnosis of Science" and "Prometheus as Performer."

Physics and Philosophy, pp. 201 ff.

> We know that any understanding must be based finally upon the natural language because it is only there that we can be certain to touch reality, and hence we must be skeptical about any skepticism with regard to this natural language and its essential concepts. . . . In this way modern physics has perhaps opened the door to a wider outlook on the relation between the human mind and reality.

In brief, relativity, uncertainty, complementarity, and incompleteness are not simply mathematical idealizations; they are concepts that begin to constitute our cultural languages; they are part of a new order of knowledge founded on both indeterminacy and immanence. In them, we witness signal examples of the "dispersal of discourse." In them and in other *Gedankenexperimente*—concept science seems to have preceded concept art—we may also discover models for our own historical moment. Admittedly, current analogies between science, culture, and sundry artistic and spiritual phenomena can prove too facile. Yet it is possible to be at once too rigorous and too timorous in exploring the cognitive possibilities of homologies. The semiotician Umberto Eco has put it thus:

"In the order of mental things, there seem to be certain very mysterious relations between *the desire and the event*. . . . That is because the mind when reduced to its own sole substance does not have the power to *finish*, and absolutely cannot bind itself by itself." Paul Valéry, in Ghiselin, ed., *The Creative Process,* p. 101.
Also:
"a literary object never reaches the end of its many-faceted determinacy." And: "Thus it is perhaps one of the chief values of literature that by its very indeterminacy it is able to transcend the restrictions of time and written word and to give to people of all ages and backgrounds the chance to enter other worlds and so enrich their own lives." Wolfgang Iser, "Indeterminacy and the Reader's Response in Prose Fiction," in J. Hillis Miller, ed., *Aspects of Narrative* (New York, 1971), pp. 10, 45.

Quoted and translated from *Opera aperta* by Teresa de Lauretis, "Semiosis Unlimited," *Journal for Descriptive Poetics and Theory of Literature* 2 (1977), pp. 367 ff.

An analogy ceases to be undue when it is posited as a starting point for further verification: the problem now consists in reducing the various phenomena (esthetic and otherwise) to more rigorous *structural models* and to identify in them not analogies, but rather similarities of structure, structural *homologies*.

Such homologies may help us better to define not only a cultural episteme but also the inadequacies of other models, including those of science itself, which is now as fully charged with promise as with menace.

MAIEUTIC

This solemn excursion into science, where precisely does it lead us? Toward an acceptance of immanence and *indeterminacy, holism* and *idiomorphism, integration* and *chance, totality* and *freedom? Physicists and biologists find such terms compatible; and so should humanists who live with the enabling contradictions of Imagination.*

Why then must critics choose between naïve scholarship and obsessive deconstruction, presence and play, "cognitive belief" and "cognitive atheism" (E. D. Hirsch)? Either humanism, with all its weary assumptions, or else dreary language games? Humanism speaks of "man," "values," "excellence," and the "critical intelligence" quite as if these could be legislated by the National Endowment for the Humanities. Deconstruction, calling happily upon the Sophists, ends by "troping" every "trope" and "demystifying" all "texts" in an ironic regress ad nauseam. *On the one hand, mental sloth, sometimes even "bad faith" (Jean-Paul Sartre); on the other, sterility, a "science" without true "gaiety" (Friedrich Nietzsche). What is finally missing in both?* Poesis, *intuition, some sense of the numinous?*

Consider Nietzsche again, our genius of this time-place: was he not both *overcomer and ironist, an "artistic Socrates" (Walter Kaufmann)? And how is culture itself founded? In his proleptic essay, "Truth and Falsity in an Ultramoral Sense," Nietzsche says:*

There are ages when the rational and the intuitive man stand side by side, the one full of fear of the intuition, the other full of scorn for the abstraction; the latter just as irrational as the former is inartistic. Both desire to rule over life. . . . Whenever intuitive man, as for instance in the earlier history of Greece, brandishes his weapons more powerfully and victoriously than his opponent, there under favorable conditions, a culture can develop and art can establish her rule over life.
(The Philosophy of Nietzsche, *ed. Geoffrey Clive [New York, 1965], pp. 514 ff.)*

A "culture can develop." Has the time come to defy our own "belatedness" (Harold Bloom) and to remake ourselves by that power which made our science and our poetry in the first and still present place?

IV. OF HERRINGS: RED, SILVER, AND PURPLE

We are approaching determinedly the problematic of postmodernism. There are certain problems, however, which I should like to clarify at the outset, and others that I intend to bracket or ignore in this context.

1. The sense of supervention (*post*modernism) is itself part of a larger phenomenon that I can not pause to explore. Lionel Trilling has entitled one of his best works *Beyond Culture;* Kenneth Boulding has argued that postcivilization is an essential part of *The Meaning of the Twentieth Century;* and George Steiner may have well subtitled his essay, *In Bluebeard's Castle,* "Notes Toward the Definition of Postculture." Before them, Roderick Seidenberg published his *Post-Historic Man* exactly in mid-century; and most recently, I have speculated about an emergent Posthumanism ("Prometheus as Performer"). Perhaps Daniel Bell is right: "It used to be that the great literary modifier was the word *beyond*. . . . But we seem to have exhausted the beyond, and today the sociological modifier is *post*. . . ."

The Coming of Post-Industrial Society (New York, 1973), p. 53.

2. Postmodernism and postmodernity are not necessarily identical; the latter is a more inclusive historical term, implying the end of a cycle that began with the European Renaissance. As Rich-

Richard E. Palmer, "Postmodernity and Hermeneutics," *Boundary 2*, v. 5, no. 2 (Winter, 1977), p. 236.

ard E. Palmer notes, postmodernism suggests a contemporary artistic movement, postmodernity points to a coming era of time. In the present essay, I acknowledge a certain aporia in these terms: that is, postmodernism as a current movement may also prefigure certain elements of postmodernity, including posthumanism and postculture.

"Joyce, Beckett, and the Postmodern Imagination," *TriQuarterly* 34 (Fall, 1975); *Paracriticisms*, Ch. 2.

3. Nor do I mean, in the present essay, to distinguish trenchantly between modernism and postmodernism. I have elsewhere risked this task, which must wait for its completion upon fuller retrospection; that is, upon our ability to write a more abstract, a more selective, historical narrative. On a certain level of abstraction, modernism itself may be assimilated to romanticism and its varied aftermaths. This view has been cogently argued by some critics, in accordance with their scholarly interests and their premodern temper.

For Paul de Man, modernism is the living or innovative element in literatures of all periods, the perpetual moment of crisis. *Blindness and Insight*, Ch. 8.

4. What we call a "literary period" is often not a period at all: its definition is not simply chronological but also typological. Thus we may find "antecedents" to postmodernism in Sterne, Sade, Blake, Lautréamont, Rimbaud, Jarry, Hofmannsthal, Stein, Joyce, Pound, Duchamp, Artaud, Roussel, Bataille, Queneau, or Kafka. This means that we have created in our mind a model of postmodernism, a particular typology of imagination, and have proceeded to "rediscover" the affinities of various authors and different moments with that model.

See Elinor Wylie's "The Eagle and the Mole." Must we either "stare in the sun" or "live among disembodied bones"?

5. Between successive periods, indeed throughout history, *both* continuity and discontinuity may be discovered. The Apollonian view, rangy and abstract, perceives only continuities; the Dionysian, discontinuous, clings to the immediate present. Yet we cannot finally choose one perspective against the other, though in viewing the recent past a certain degree of polarization seems inevitable.

Hence the needless opposition between "spatial" and "temporal" char-

6. Thus it seems we require a fourfold vision of complementarities, embracing continuity and dis-

acter of postmodernism: see Jürgen Peper, "Postmodernismus: *Unitary Sensibility*," *Amerikastudien*, v. 22, no. 1 (1977); and William V. Spanos, "The Detective at the Boundary," in Spanos, ed., *Existentialism 2* (New York, 1976).

For a brief history of the term, see Michael Köhler, "Postmodernismus: Ein begriffgeschichtlicher Überblick," *Amerikastudien* v. 22, no. 1 (1977)

continuity, diachrony and synchrony. But we require no less a dialectical vision; for defining traits are often antithetical, and to ignore this tendency of historical reality is to lapse into Newton's dreamless sleep. Defining traits must also be plural; to elect a single absolute trait is to exercise oneself in historical tautology.

7. The term Postmodernism is not merely awkward; it is conceptually troublesome. It relates itself too closely to Modernism, whereas, for instance, the term Victorianism does not relate itself either to Modernism or to Romanticism. More tellingly, it denotes temporal linearity and connotes belatedness, to which few postmodernists would admit. Finally, it perpetuates an idea of literary periodicity that postmodern thought iself seeks to overcome.

MAIEUTIC

Decidedly, Postmodernism is but a poor name for our desire, insufficient for the life we want to hold and bequeath. How, then, shall we call our time? The Age of Indeterminacy? The Age of Immanence? The Age of Indetermanence? Or, bluntly, the Atomic Age?

V. THE EVIDENCE OF OUR TIME

What evidence may we expect from our (postmodern) culture? Perhaps only evidence circumstantial: social bric-a-brac, intellectual *bricolage,* bright shards of a disestablished imagination, all jangling their peculiar themes and variations. I should like to hazard seven related themes, in advertence to that cultural jangle:

a. *Indeterminacy*. As in scientific so in cultural thought, indeterminacy fills the space between the will to unmaking (dispersal, deconstruction, discontinuity, etc.) and its opposite, the integrative will. Cultural indeterminacy, however, reveals itself with greater cunning and valency; choice, pluralism, fragmentation, contingency, imagination are only a few of its ambiguous aspects, as I shall presently have occasion to show.

b. *Process and Change.* In a technological world, all is flux; the time machine is the postindustrial machine itself, which accelerates both life and death. At its worst, process may transform the Logos into "instrumental reason"; we become "one-dimensional" (Herbert Marcuse). At its best, process permits change, surprise, innovation; it declares the openness of Being to Time (Martin Heidegger). Yet this metaphysical intuition rarely penetrates our polity. There, objects and even institutions become merely ephemeral; and in an "age of sensation" (Herbert Hendin), people seek satisfactions without commitment. Reification becomes suspect. Futurology on the rise (Herman Kahn & Co.) makes teleology obsolete. Thus process, more than any consensual goal or form of change, may come to be the sole source of value in history.

c. *The Diffractions of the Self.* From "loss of self" (Wylie Sypher), through the "Dionysian ego" (Norman O. Brown) and the "divided self" (R. D. Laing), to "protean man" (Robert Jay Lifton) and the "deconstructed self" (Leo Bersani), the identity of the individual is diffracted. Some practice the "mythotherapy" of changing masks (John Barth); a few emulate the old ways of the "new mutants" (Leslie Fieldler), surrendering themselves to orgiastic states of sex, psychedelics, and madness; many more cultivate the "new narcissism" (Peter Marin), vanishing quietly in their own silvered refractions. Such are the "games people play" (Eric Berne). Yet throughout contemporary arts, the ludic diffractions of the self generate brilliant new structures.

d. *The Displacements of Desire.* Desire has been liberated in all its violent and multifarious forms. Other ages may have been as explicit in their sensuality; none has so keenly understood the immanence of desire or so thoroughly made it into an object of reflection. Indeed, desire has become a kind of privileged theoretical discourse, an essential chatter of our culture. Neo- and post-Freudians, here as abroad, (Sandor Ferenczi, Wilhelm Reich, Melanie Klein, Jacques Lacan, Gilles Deleuze, Félix Guattari, Jean-François Lyotard, etc.) have helped to disseminate the languages of desire, perhaps even to encode them in the flesh. In America, such recent notions as "surplus repression" and "repressive desublimation" (Herbert Marcuse), "polymorphous perverse sexuality" (Norman O. Brown), "the erotics of texts" (Susan Sontag), and the "psychology of fragmentary and *dis*continuous desires" (Leo Bersani) may suggest the tropisms of love, its displacements in our personal and cultural lives.

e. *The Immanence of Media.* It may have begun with Gutenberg; it certainly will not end with McLuhan. The "work of art in an age of mechanical reproduction" (Walter Benjamin) and the "museum without walls" (André Malraux) presage larger tendencies in "mass culture" and "mid-cult" (Robert Warshaw, Dwight Macdonald), and point to "Voyager 1" (Carl Sagan), carrying the sounds of Bach, Beethoven, and Chuck Berry into the cosmic void. Closer at hand, media shape all our daily facts. These, in fact, dissolve into frames, events, "images" (Daniel Boorstin); or as in Watergate, they may vanish forever between public "mis-speakings" and private tapes. History itself is staged, more like a happening than a performance, before its own facts; the "politics of illusion" (Harold Rosenberg) prevail. From radio astronomy to the dispositions of our most secret heart, the immanence of media now effects the dispersal of the Logos.

f. *The Marriage of Earth and Sky.* Religion and science, myth and technology, intuition and reason, popular and high cultures, female and male archetypes (or stereotypes) begin to modify and inform one another; everywhere we may witness attempts to "cross the border, close the gap" (Leslie Fiedler). Beyond the "two cultures" (C. P. Snow, F. R. Leavis), beyond "mystics and mechanists" (William Irwin Thompson), beyond "arcadians and technophiles" (Ihab Hassan), lineaments of a new consciousness begin to emerge. Hence the un-"silent spring" of ecology (Rachel Carson), the "new alchemists" (John Todd and William McLarney), ideological or visionary "androgyny" (Carolyn Heilbrun, June Singer), the "Tao of physics" (Fritjof Capra), and perhaps even a "unitary sensibility" (Susan Sontag), calling for an epistemological shift in the order of our knowledge.

g. *The New Gnosticism, or the Dematerialization of Existence.* Here we encounter the most speculative stage in the dispersal of the Logos. Nature turns into "history" (Karl Marx), culture turns into "symbolic languages" (Lewis Mumford, Ernst Cassirer), and now languages begin to turn into "non-sensory communication" (José Delgado). This "gnostic tendency" (Ihab Hassan) assumes the increasing "etherealization " (Arnold Toynbee) or "ephemeralization" (Buckminster Fuller) or "conceptualization" (Ervin Laszlo) of existence. Mental constructs—Nietzsche would say "fictions"—become the primary resource of the earth; they are our knowledge. Mind insists on encompassing more mind in itself, on apprehending more and more of reality im-mediately. In this, the physicist (Gerald Feinberg), the mystic (Teilhard de Chardin), and the fabulator (Olaf Stapledon, Arthur Clarke, Alfred Bester, Theodore Sturgeon, Ursula LeGuin,

Samuel Delany, etc.) seem to be of one imagination compact. Yet we must ask: how problematic will this extension of consciousness prove, how demonic or simply illusory?

Throughout these seven themes, the play of indeterminacy and immanence may be constantly inferred, if not always heard or seen. But are these themes mere abstractions, figures in our own imaginary carpet? Not entirely so. I now return to the first of these themes, indeterminacy itself, to show how many versions of it our culture sustains in its optative, contingent, and manifold moods. Here are twelve versions of cultural indeterminacy, in the guise of a catalogue *déraisonné:*

Item: Society invites secession. Races, sexes, classes, languages, age groups make their claims and counter claims; values collide with values. Terrorism and totalitarianism, anarchy and bureaucracy, coexist. Between them, pluralism in America can still thrive. But Daniel Bell takes a gloomier view. Discord between the three realms of society—economy, polity, and culture—engender perilous contradictions. For Bell, "modernism is exhausted and the various kinds of post-modernism . . . are simply the decomposition of the self in an effort to erase individual ego." [*The Cultural Contradictions of Capitalism* (New York, 1976), p. 29.]

Item: In religion, both ecumenism and esotericism flourish. Zen Buddhism, Yoga, Tantrism, Hari-Krishna, Transcendental Meditation, the Arica and Naropa Institutes, Pythagoreanism, Sufism, Teilhardism, Kabalism, Hassidism, Gnosticism, Anthroposophy, Shamanism, Black and White Magic, Alchemy, Astrology, Spiritualism, Psychedelism, all besiege our shy souls. Churches admit women to the priesthood while Fundamentalists rage. Perhaps it is all summarized by David L. Miller, who quotes Nietzsche ("In polytheism man's free-thinking and many-sided thinking has a prototype set up: the power to create for himself new and individual eyes . . .") and who proclaims the joyous rebirth of many gods and goddesses. [*The New Polytheism* (New York, 1974), p. 1.]

Item: Gods and goddesses of the secular psyche are also reborn in their multitudes: Esalen, Gestalt Psychology, the Human Potential Movement, est. More significantly, Abraham Maslow probes the farther reaches of human nature; and James Hillman exposes the unitary myth of analysis, calling for a polytheistic psychology. Before them, we know, Norman O. Brown wrote poetically ("Everything is metaphor; there is only poetry") to free the body from the tyranny of genital organization, and to extol the openness of brokenness, though Brown also unfashionably assumed the oneness of all things: "To heal is to make whole." [*Love's Body* (New York, 1966), pp. 266, 80.]

Item: Man's rage for chaos, Morse Peckham speculates, may be a biological mechanism meant to counter the social need to impose order and closure. "To use an old expression," he says, "the drive to order is also a drive to get stuck in the mud." Art serves to resist this tendency, offering itself as a playful and disjunctive means of adaptation. "Art is the exposure to the tensions and problems of a false [imaginary] world so that man may endure exposing himself to the tensions and problems of the real world." [*Man's Rage for Chaos* (Philadelphia and New York, 1965), pp. xi, 314.]

Item: A philosopher of science, Paul Feyerabend, argues that "Science is an essentially anarchistic enterprise: theoretical anarchism is more humanitarian and more likely to encourage progress than its law-and-order alternatives." Learned, lucid, and antic, Feyerabend thinks of himself as a neo-Dadaist "prepared to initiate joyful experiments even in those domains where change and experimentation seem to be out of the question. . . ." [*Against Method* (London, 1975), pp. 17, 21.]

Item: Taking his cue from Leibniz, who believed that ours is only one among an infinitude of possible worlds, a mathematical prodigy of our times, Saul Kripke, has extended the boundaries of modal logic to distinguish between *kinds* of true statements in various "possible world semantics." Thus even the most formal modes of thought seem to entertain the optative mood; and mathematical logicians, like Kripke, challenge the orthodoxies of analytical philosophy. [Taylor Branch, "New Frontiers in American Philosophy, *New York Times Magazine,* August 14, 1966.]

Item: Originality in every field is now perceived as a tense tolerance of ambiguity, a tendency toward complexity and asymmetry. Frank Barron, who has devised many ingenious experiments for the study of creativity, notes: "Originality, then, flourishes where suspension [of disunity] is at a minimum and where some measure of disintegration is tolerable in the interests of a higher level of integration which may yet be reached." [*Creativity and Personal Freedom* (New York, 1968), p. 212.]

Item: In critical theory today, the central debate concerns the "limits of pluralism": the accent is on "the critic as innovator." [*Critical Inquiry,* 3, nos. 3 & 4 (Spring and Summer, 1977) and 4, no. 1 (Autumn, 1977); and the *Chicago Review,* 28, no. 3 (Winter, 1977).] Psychoanalytic critics also speak of a "third phase" of analysis, which risks intimacy and incompleteness in order to restore individual. As Norman N. Holland put it: "There can be as many readings as there are readers to write them. Can be and should be." ["Literary Interpretation and the Three Phases of Psychoanalysis," *Critical Inquiry,* 3, no. 2 (Winter, 1976), p. 233.] In general, antithetical critics, deconstructionists, critifictioneers, and paracritics (who shall all remain nameless) vie with one another in outrageousness while traditionalists glower and moderates wearily seek to reaffirm the "responsibilities" of criticism.

Item: In fact as in fiction, in society as in literature, fact and fiction jostle and blend; hence Capote's "non-fiction" novel, Styron's "meditation on history," Mailer's "history as biography," and the "new journalism" of Tom Wolfe, among countless others. This has led Mas'ud Zavarzadeh to theorize about a "fictual" genre which refuses "totalization," integration: "a zone of experience where the factual is not secure or unequivocal but seems preternaturally strange and eerie, and where the fictional seems not all that remote and alien, but bears uncanny resemblance to daily experiences." [*The Mythopoeic Reality* (Urbana, Ill., 1977), p. 56.]

Item: Nowadays, historians would rather serve Calliope than Clio. According to Hayden White, history is compounded of poetics and metaphysics: "the dominant tropological mode and its attendant linguistic protocol comprise the irreducibly 'metahistorical' basis of every historical work." [*Metahistory* (Baltimore, 1973), p. xi; see also Angus Fletcher, ed., *The Literature of Fact* (New York, 1976), and *New Literary History,* 8, no. 1 (Autumn, 1976).] So much for the new rhetoricians of time.

Item: The rhetoricians of space are architects, and they too speak of new "languages" far removed from the austere style, sharp, and pure, and linear, of high modernism. Charles Jencks says this of postmodern architecture: "The present situation tolerates opposite approaches. . . . If there is a single direction, I prefer the reader will discover that it is pluralistic: the idea that an architect must master several styles and codes of communication and vary these to suit the particular culture for which he is designing. I have called this 'adhocism' in the past, and I use the term 'radical eclecticism' here. . . ." [*The Language of Post-Modern Architecture* (New York and London, 1977), p. 7.] Indeed, as Jencks goes on to show, architecture has become witty edifices of various subcultures and "semiotic groups."

Item: Even semiotics, science of all signs, sign of our times, opens itself to the full ambiguities of social reality and recognizes the continual shifts of semantic fields within a culture. Such shifts, despite the regularity of linguistic codes, can become creative, altering the rules of the semiotic game. Indeed, Umberto Eco perceives the semiotic project itself under the aspect of a kind of indeterminacy. The project, he says, "will not be like exploring the sea, where a ship's wake disappears as soon as it has passed, but more exploring a forest where cart-trails or footprints do modify the explored landscape, so that the description the explorer gives of it must also take into account the ecological variations that he has produced." [Umberto Eco, *A Theory of Semiotics* (Bloomington, Ind., 1976), p. 29.]

No doubt, the variations of these cultural themes are countless, composed in our minds as the mind becomes part of what it comprehends. Some may seem vestiges of the Sixties, that prodigal decade now lost to us in its rhetoric and our own constraints. Yet in the end I believe indeterminacy to be neither a fashionable nor a factitious term but rather a decisive element in the new order of our knowledge. And on the other side of it lies immanence. This is vividly manifest in the arts.

MAIEUTIC

Is there not as much control, manipulation, torture, in our world as there is choice or indeterminacy in it? And this conjunction of indeterminacy and immanence, was it not in the mind of the great Romantics as well? There is a celebrated letter of 21 December 1817 in which a young poet reflects: "and at once it struck me what quality went to form a Man of Achievement, especially in Literature. . . . I mean Negative Capability, that is, when a man is capable of being in uncertainties, mysteries, doubts, without irritable reaching after fact and reason." What, then, has changed since Keats's time?

Perhaps our sense of immanence has become at once more semiotic and more technological; and our sense of indeterminacy, no longer the possession of a few, has become almost a decree of our cultural consciences. What else can such current titles as The Age of Discontinuity, The Age of Uncertainty, The Age of Anxiety, *or* The De-Definition of Art *mean? Why else should Charles Olson, in his fumid essay on* The Special View of History, *claim that Negative Capability is "crucial to post-Modern man"?*

The ambiguities of Empson, the paradoxes of Brooks, once described the style of a mannerist literature from a modernist perspective. Do indeterminacy and immanence now suggest our very concepts of self and world, language and reality, from another (postmodernist) vantage?

VI. IN THE ARTS

Virginia Woolf knew exactly when human character changed and modernism began: "In or about December, 1910." I confess to a vaguer sense of beginnings. When did the arts of indetermanence start? Whenever that (postmodernism) may have been, in the arts is now widely viewed and reviewed, not only in avant-garde magazines, but also in academic journals, both here and abroad.

Consider indeterminacy first: as in culture generally, indeterminacy in the arts has many guises. It may be called different things, from negative capability to parataxis. And it takes innumerable artistic forms: collages, montages, aleatory music, happenings, computer and topological art, earth art and body art, kinetic and process art, concept art, minimalism, concrete poetry,

For instance: *Trema*, 1 (1976); *Amerikastudien*, 22, no. 1 (1977); *Kritikon Litterarum*, 2 (1973) and 5 (1976), which include essay reviews by Manfred Pütz and Hartwig Isernhagen respectively.

"But today we do, indeed, find ourselves in a period in which the primary quality of the 'men of achievement'—of a Beckett, a Robbe-Grillet, a Grass, a Burroughs, a Godard—appears to be a Negative Capability, for they represent, generally, a firm disinclination to transfigure or to try to subdue or resolve what is recalcitrantly indeterminate and ambiguous in the human scene of our time. . . ." Nathan A. Scott, Jr., *Negative Capability* (New Haven, 1969), p. xiv. John Cage is also crucial here.

*

On black humor and the "metaphysics of

found objects and ready mades,
auto-destruc- tive sculpture,
absurdist, un- canny, and fantastic modes, partial, discontinuous, decrea- tive, ludic, or
self-relexive forms of every
kind, and many more. All these
"arts" tend, by diverse means,
to delay closures, frustrate expectations, promote abstractions, sustain a playful plurality of perspectives, and generally shift
the grounds of meaning on
their audi- ences.

multiplicity": "This new Pyrrhonism I have called . . . radical sophistication." Max Schulz, *Radical Sophistication* (Athens, Ohio, 1969), p. viii.

*

"antiformal imperatives of absurd time." William Spanos, *Existentialism 2,* p. 169.

*

"Chance as a supplement to necessity and necessity as the determinant of chance. Their interplay would be the game." Jacques Ehrmann, "Introduction: Games, Play, Literature," *Yale French Studies,* no. 41 (1968), p. 5.

*

On game theory and the systems approach to literature: "We call potential literature the research into forms, into new structures which can be utilized by writers as they wish." Raymond Queneau in *OULIPO* (Paris, 1973), p. 38.

*

"The change . . . is the sundering of art from artist—the complete and disciplined absence from the work of art *as we experience it* of any qualities or patterns which were intended by the artist. . . ." Louis Mink, "Art without Artists," in Ihab Hassan, ed., *Liberations* (Middletown, Conn., 1971), p. 80.

*

". . . modernism seems to stress the relationship between the creative sensibility and the work of art, between addresser and message, postmodernism that between message and addressee." Gerhard Hoffmann, Alfred Hornung, Rüdiger Kunow, " 'Modern,' 'Postmodern,' and 'Contemporary,' " *Amerikastudien,* 22, no. 1 (1977), p. 40.

*

"What the innovative artists and thinkers of this era have rebelled against is the very principle of a syntactically organized vision, the consciousness that requires

the organization of reality into relationships of subordination and domination. . . . Paratactical conventions try to resist any impulse to the hierarchical arrangement of images and perceptions and, as the roots of the word parataxis indicate, sanction their 'arrangement together, side by side'. . . ."
And again:
"The paratactical style is an intrinsically *communal* style, rather than a *societal* one; it is inherently democratic and egalitarian rather than aristocratic and elitist, and it is possible that the rebirth of parataxis in art and thought in this century does not represent the fall back into myth or the advent of a new totalitariansim so much as the demand for a change of consciousness that will finally make a unified humanity possible."
Hayden White, "The Culture of Criticism," in *Liberations,* ed. Hassan, pp. 67, 69.

Indeterminacy, then, has its own protocols and prepossessions in the arts. It favors paratactical styles; and, in the curious rhetoric of current French criticism, it tends to valorize metonymy over metaphor, syntagmatic over paradigmatic modes, play over presence, child over parents in a "displaced parental space."

The crucial statement here is: "For the displacement of origins, of parents, the reliance on play rather than a hierarchy of symbolic meaning, the joyous acceptance of absence rather than a morose and negative theology, language our only 'seigneur,' not even language as code but language as play, as joy—all these attitudes amount to a demystifying phrase: nothing more than human." Michel Benamou, "Displacements of Parental Space: American Poetry and French Symbolism," *Boundary 2,* 5, no. 2 (Winter, 1977), p. 483.

And for nearly everyone—which is always suspect—the crucial poetic unparents are: Stevens, Pound, Williams. Thus for Joseph Riddel, from Pater to Son is *Paterson,* or simply Language. *The Inverted Bell* (Baton Rouge, 1974), Ch. 1, esp. pp. 83 ff.

At the far limit of indeterminacy, however, the figurative state of silence—variously expounded by George Steiner, Susan Sontag, and me—reigns. Silence begins as "experiment" in literature, its urge to question and contest itself; and it moves through self-parody and self-subversion, radical irony, to the edges of speech. There, on the dark margins of consciousness, literature wants to consume or transcend itself wholly—in vain. And precisely there, on the margins of silence, the dream of immanence teases literature, teases all art, back into waking. As in *Finnegans Wake.*

"*Finnegans Wake* intentionally opens itself to the free play of language. . . . How will we read this curious(ity shop) of signs that is also a museyroom, a public house, a dreamspace? . . . And what is *it* that We and Thou had out? That meaning is dialogic? That first- and second-person, text and reader, dissolve—as Shem and Shaun into HCE, Issy in ALP, and ALP finally into HCE—into one intersubjectivity reading itself endlessly, or into one intertextuality expanding perpetually: into all-read-I? Charles Caramello, "Postface," in Michel Benamou and Charles Caramello, eds., *Performance in Postmodern Culture* (Madison, Wisc., 1977), p. 222.

Immanence is indeed implicit in the farthest reaches of dispersal, the dispersal of signs, the extension of consciousness. It has become, quite unmetaphysically, the quality of all expanding semiotic systems, including literature. Concerning the latter, Charles Altieri has argued persuasively that Coleridge and Wordsworth presage the symbolist and immanentist modes respectively; and it is immanence now that constitutes the ground of (postmodern) poetics.

"... postmodern poets have been seeking to uncover the ways man and nature are unified, so that value can be seen as the result of immanent processes in which man is as much object as he is agent of creativity."
And:
"While incarnation for the moderns exemplified the union of form and significant value on an otherwise empty and chaotic natural world, God for the contemporaries [postmodernists] manifests itself as energy, as the intense expression of immanent power."
Finally:
Distrusting symbolism and hence mediation—"postmodern poetics are radically Protestant"—"the postmoderns seek to have the universal concretized, to see the particular as numinous, not as representative." Charles Altieri, "From Symbolist Thought to Immanence: The Ground of Postmodern American Poetics," *Boundary 2,* 1, no. 3 (Spring, 1973), pp. 608, 610, 611.

Yet the point could be stated generally to include the other (postmodern) arts. In a society increasingly oriented toward systems rather than objects, art must often utilize transparent elements of these systems; it must shape, alter, or simply make visible the flow of communicable experience. Thus it becomes the negentropy of informational schemes rather than masterpieces crafted for the ages.

"In other words, if we extend the meaning of software to cover the entire art information processing cycle, then art books, catalogs, interviews, reviews, advertisements, sales, and contracts are all software extensions of art, and as such legitimately embody the work of art. The art object is, in effect, an information 'trigger.' " Jack Burnham, *Great Western Salt Works* (New York, 1974), p. 28.

The conception of art as an immanent system or field

betokens the crescive power of abstractions in every domain of culture, and once again recalls that overweening project: to generalize the condition of language and of art till the human environment itself becomes an immense signifier, till dumb matter begins to speak. Yet in many kinds of art—say the ecological art of Newton and Helen Harrison or the ritual art of Daryl Sapien and Michael Hinton—sensuous and even sensual actions become part of a sacramental, a vaguely pantheist and impersonal, vision. In still other cases, hermetic and systematic approaches to art prove uncannily congruent. Thus, for instance, the Hebrew letters of the *Sepher Yetzivah,* in Kabala, constitute in their staggering combinations all human sign systems as well as the laws of creation. Drawing on Kabalistic, gnostic, and alchemical lore, Burnham makes a startling case for analogies between esoteric wisdom and the works of Marcel Duchamp. Cryptic or furtive as some of these analogies seem, they hint at Duchamp's serene enigma: a unique admixture of indeterminacy and immanence, disjunctive wit and pervasive eroticism, held in the focus of an aesthetics of indifference."

Coincidentally, Susan Sontag emphasizes the gnostic and Kabalistic influences on Artaud. See her *Antonin Artaud: Selected Writings* (New York, 1976), pp. xlv-liii. Artaud and Duchamp, our precursors: two numinous artists, one cool, the other convulsive, masters of fragments, waiters upon the All.

"In essence, *The Large Glass* defines the means by which the powers of the Hebrew letters may be established whereas the Ready-mades use the powers of the letters in producing art yet to be made."
Also:
"Within the lore of cabalistic literature various permutations of the four elements represent *bound forms,* that is, they possess a mathematical and psychic cohesiveness that makes it impossible to separate or isolate the parts of language or artistic forms. . . . Duchamp deals with this. . . ."
And:
"So in the hermetic scheme followed by Duchamp, the notion of feeling the presence of God in an icon is vastly inferior to

sensing the presence of God in everything—just as witnessing the presence of God in perspective is a degraded form of iconization."

Finally:

"Hence by using the principles of classification devised by the Cabalists, we find the Bride divided into various 'living substances.'

FIRE:	Art involving complementarity
AIR:	Art using indeterminacy
WATER:	Art employing causality or implication
EARTH:	Art concerned with the principles of true physical and spiritual orientation."

Burnham, *Great Western Salt Works*, pp. 75, 79, 93, 115.

So much for Sel, author of may or may not the alchemical Salt rejoins Merphur—the volaprinciple and the principle—at the gynous wisdom. sentative of our champ, can the really be?

Marchand du *Salt Seller*, who have known of triangle, in which cury and Sultile, dispersing fixed, indrawing apex of andro-Yet how reprepoetics can Du-occult as system,

"Many postmodern fictions serve as 'esoteric writing' waiting to be deciphered, as if in terms of an initiatory rite: to read them, we must have mastered Seeing, which in turn enables us to transcribe our reading on to the world-text." Campbell Tatham, "Mythotherapy and Postmodern Fictions," in *Performance*, p. 153.

*

"Beyond its direct portrayal of the mind-in-creation, Kabbalah offers both a model for the processes of poetic influence, and maps for the problematic pathways of interpretation. More audaciously than any developments in recent French criticism, Kabbalah is a theory of *writing*, but this is a theory that denies the absolute distinction between writing and inspired speech, even as it denies human distinctions between presence and absence." Harold Bloom, *Kabbalah and Criticism* (New York, 1975), p. 52.

If nothing else, our movement engenders too many metaphors and systems, and these may help us to escape enslavement by the system of another. I confess to a richer sympathy for Kabala than Deconstruction, though none is compelled to choose one or the other. But the larger point here is this: whatever our philosophic persuasion may be, and whatever our attitude to Duchamp, we may still observe how the arts of indetermanence trace both center and circumference in our culture, how they continually play between self-reflexiveness and self-surrender.

Some names, alphabetically: A. R. Ammons, David Antin, John Ashberry, John Barth, Donald Barthelme, Christine Brooke-Rose, John Cage, Christo, Merce Cunningham, Jasper Johns, Allan Kaprow, Robert Morris, Alwin Nikolais, Nam June Paik, Thomas Pynchon, Robert Rauschenberg, Michael Snow, Robert Wilson, Andy Warhol, LaMonte Young, etc.

MAIEUTIC

Though the ironic geomancy of Duchamp cannot represent all our arts, let alone our culture in its various parts, his figure of the artist persists as a figura *in our midst. But now we may ask: is it not a mark of vexation or self-indulgence that we invoke science and the occult in such fits and starts?*

This is indeed the risk of indetermanence: it invites recuperation, cooptation by ideologies of every sort. At once underdefined and overextended, it may give to need or whimsy too great a scope. Yet need is also desire, a kind of hope. How shall we live with indetermanence, then, which is the epistemic equivalence of our violence, and still make of our disorders new knowledge?

VII. HUMAN AND INCONCLUSIVE

"Man is the measure of all things." "Many the wonders but nothing walks stranger than man." "What a piece of work is man."

The human measure has not changed much since Protagoras and Sophocles and Shakespeare—and yet it has altogether changed.

Consider the simple idea of measure: a meter. Sealed in its vacuum glass case, the platinum-iridium meter at Sèvres has served for more than a century as the standard of length. Now the standard is a spectrum wave length of light, the orange-red line of Krypton 86. Here is dematerialization of a kind. But we need to reckon further with Duchamp's "canned chance": three lengths of string, one meter each, allowed to fall freely from a meter's height on strips of dark blue canvas, to which they are carefully glued. Thus Duchamp provides us with three versions of an ideal length; or if you prefer, with a "work of art" entitled *3 Standard Stoppages*, courtesy of the Katherine S. Dreier Bequest. Perhaps everything I have tried to say about indetermanence lurks here, around these meters made of metal, gas, and curling string.

Let me now move to end. We may be living in liminal times, at the threshold of changes in the human measure more profound than we imagine; or we may be simply living through the ordinary nightmare of history from which there is no awakening.

Arthur C. Clarke: ". . . for the one fact about the future of which we can be certain is that it will be utterly fantastic." [*Profiles of the Future* (New York, 1972), p. xv.] Kenneth E. Boulding: "The twentieth century marks the middle period of a great transition in the state of the human race. It may properly be called the second great transition in the history of mankind." [*The Meaning of the Twentieth Century* (New York, 1965), p. 1.] *N.B.:* Clarke's and Boulding's works were first published in 1963 and 1964, respectively.

The openness of our time to time, its vulnerability to the future, has been noted by many authors, from futurologists like Alvin Toffler to poets like David Antin. Some, like Willis W. Harman of the Stanford Research Institute, go so far as to say: "As we grappled with the significance of contemporary revolutionary forces, we began to feel that the crucial gap is not between generations, nor between liberals and conservatives, but between those who anticipate a continuation of present trends and those who insist that a drastic change must occur." [*The Futurist*, XI, no. 1 (February, 1977), p. 8.]

Artists, though fewer in literature than in other arts, have also sensed this ending of a phase in Western history. This has led Leonard B. Meyer to say: "Man is no longer to be the measure of all things, the center of the universe. . . . for these radical empiricists, *the Renaissance is over. . . .* Whether the Renaissance is over for the rest of us—for our culture generally—only the future will tell. But whether it is over or not, the merit of considering the art and aesthetic of radical empiricism seriously is that it challenges us to discover and make explicit the grounds for belief and values which we unconsciously take for granted." [*Music, the Arts, and Ideas* (Chicago, 1967), pp. 83 ff.] Meyer first published this essay in 1963; he saw then the indeterminacy, not the immanence.

But there is no doubt that rancorous afflictions are visited upon humanists across the nation, around the world. Whence these miseries? Others more informed than I on the sociology or economics of the Humanities may know the facts. I had it in mind only to note a certain cultural ethos, a certain epistemological shift, which I thought pertinent to the anxious order of our knowledge. I mean the order of indetermanence, a term finally no less uncouth than postmodernism itself, which I hoped to displace by a more precise token of our historical energies.

The cardinal question of course remains: how in practice to found a human or posthuman vision—call it inconclusively human—or an anxious order of knowledge? Predictably, I have no answer, though I have some urgent hunches and guesses. We may begin by acknowledging the realities of change if only to challenge them, remembering always that true challenges require self-exposure. We may also insist on a larger scope for our moral and intellectual ambitions. Humanists once prided themselves on taking the entire human universe, with all its wonder, cruelty, and crankiness, as province to their imagination. How many still do or can?

Walter Kaufmann: "In their serious work, scholastics prefer to address only those who agree with them on essentials. As a result we are losing a whole dimension of discourse." And: "Those who really wish to work on the frontiers of knowledge must cross the frontiers of their departments." [*The Future of the Humanities* (New York, 1977), pp. 42, 43.]

Arthur Schopenhauer was more scornful: "He who holds a professorship may be said to receive his food in the stall; and this is the best way with ruminent animals"; then goes on to say: "It is precisely minds of the first order that will never be specialists. For their very nature is to make the whole of existence their problem. . . ." [*The Art of Literature* (Ann Arbor, Mich., 1960), pp. 40, 42.]

Concomitantly, we may restore our sense of an audience, of a human *other* to which we address our speech, if only to transgress against expectations, if only to cry, "No, do not understand me too easily." This is to say that humanists may honor the responsive intelligence, and honor true style against jargon and babbling sophistication. At the same time, we may remain mindful, without brutalizing our own minds, of the imperatives of action in our lives, of the conflicting demands, say, of justice and freedom. What silent ideologies constitute the culture of indetermanence, and to what praxis or commitment are we then drawn? Finally, we may learn to dream.

What does it mean for humanists to dream? Perhaps it means to confess human desire and so transmute it into life's still uncreated forms. Grandiose dream! More modestly, it may mean to acknowledge imagination, the power of sympathy, acknowledge our own hope and gall. Yeats, we recall, rebuked the scholars: "Bald heads forgetful of their sins." But humanists are scholars and more than scholars: they know what turbulence it takes to make the spirit whole. Though knowledge is rightfully their primary call, humanists on a transhumanized earth may, like artists, mediate between culture and desire, history and hope. And who is there to say that in some penultimate scheme, the human urge to Know—so profound, mysterious, and possibly mad—may not be a version of what Gnostics long ago called Love?

From
THE SERBELLONI JOURNAL
I

Is it not for us to confess that in our civilized attitude towards death we are once again living psychologically beyond our means, and must reform and give truth its due?

Sigmund Freud

The Serbelloni Journal

In March and April of 1978, my wife and I spent six weeks at the Rockefeller Foundation's Bellagio Conference and Study Center, or the Villa Serbelloni, as it is still known in Italy.

Bellagio is a small town on Lake Como, rising on a promontory that separates two branches of the lake; the Villa itself covers some fifty acres at the very "point that divides the winds," which blow from hulking Alps in the north. The region has lain athwart the path of conquerors, drawn plunderers and tourists for centuries. Its beauty survives them.

As Resident Scholars at the Serbelloni, we were offered an apartment, the resources of a reference library to which previous scholars had added their own works over the years, and the tact and time to complete a project. The scholars, from various fields, from countries the world over, assembled in the *salone* after dinner to converse.

My project was the present work. But as in the year I had spent at the Camargo Foundation, I kept a journal, noting ideas and events that seemed to impinge, however abstractly, on that work. The journal was briefer as the time of our residence was shorter; the journeys away from Bellagio more hurried and rare. I had the sense, that spring, of my time somehow outrunning nature, and of the civility of the Serbelloni as but a whisper of permanence. Change, in science or art or politics, and once again in the intimations of mortality, loomed large in the interior landscape. So did that transformer of Change itself: human gnosis.

The portal of the Villa Serbelloni carries the insignia of Torre e Tasso. *The morning mail—erratic, a Tristero conspiracy in reverse—brings an invitation to the Yale International Conference on Gnosticism. The program includes:*

"Gnosis and Alchemy"
"Gnosis and Psychology"
"Seminar on Sethian Gnosticism"
"Seminar on Valentinian Gnosticism"
Etc.

Not exactly my kind of gnosis. Still, "I wish it were here"—who would renounce Bellagio for New Haven in March?—rather than "wish I were there." For we still believe: "you cannot be in two places at once." Really?

True, the Italian mail nowadays overcomes the space/time continuum haphazardly. But what if the Conference on Gnosticism were carried on Telstar? The old Gnosticism (religious) becoming the "content" of the new (technological)? Yet Telstar is only the Book projected; and the prime projector is not a Medium but Imagination. An example:

> It has been my aim to set down just enough to awaken that faculty of imagination, without which our travels, like all the rest of life, are dull and uninteresting; while, with it for companion, the past is reanimated, the dead leave their graves to play their parts over again, the great silences grow eloquent, the waste places of the world become astir once more with all the passions of human life.
> (T. W. M. Lund, *Como and the Italian Lake Land,* 1887.)

Beyond space, beyond time, beyond the grave. Could Gnosticism, Sethian, Valentinian, or Phibionite, offer more?

■

The Villa Serbelloni: itself an exemplum of the noetic tendency. From granite to thought, from fortress to study center, its history the very mystery of History.

A lichened castello *still commands the promontory. Settlements go back to Celtic and Roman times: Pliny the Younger builds his famous villa near Como. Later the Longobards: red-bearded warriors hew rude ramparts large as their wanderlust. Then Christian princes: in the eleventh century, someone raises a church tower, more tower than church, on the south side of the present Villa—the tower now houses our marbled bathroom. The next four centuries: Como and Milano, Guelphs and Ghibellines, Viscontis and German mercenaries, wreak havoc on one another and on the Bellagio fortress hill. Till the Sforzas, well-named, wrest the Duchy of Milano, the whole northern region.*

1489: the Bellagio Castle passes to Marchesino Stanga, Treasurer of Duke Ludovico Sforza. Stanga erects a "kingly palace," receives Empress Maria Bianca, receives later the Emperor himself. "As usual, Maximillian disappointed his splendor-loving subjects by appearing in a gray hunting costume, like 'the pettiest German baron' and accompanied by an entourage of only 200 persons." Brief respite.

Siege and rapine follow: the French come, then the Spaniards, the "wicked and unbridled Cavargnoni" (local pirates) burn and loot throughout. Stones fall and rise again with new mortar, mixed with blood. Violence with repetition and difference—as in language.

The sixteenth century: Count Francesco Sfondrati of Milano acquires the fief. After his wife's death, he becomes a cardinal, "trusted diplomat for Charles V and Pope Paul III." He builds, landscapes, plants orange, lemon, and laurel trees, olive groves and vineyards. His grandson, Duke Ercole Sfondrati, proves munificent: "he put a supply of grain on a flat rock standing above the level of the lake, to which people could row for supplies. The result was that not a single case of the plague occurred in Bellagio, although Milano lost three-fourths of her population."

1788: the last Sfondrati bequeathes his estate to Alessandro Serbelloni, scion of another great Milanese family. Further construction, embellishment: roads, tunnels, grottoes, the Polenta Pavilion "where the noon meal of the traditional corn mush was ladled out to the impoverished workmen." Stendhal and the Princess Metternich visit the place before the last Serbelloni sells it, end of the nineteenth century. The Villa Serbelloni (not to be confused with the current Grand Hotel Villa Serbelloni on the lake below) becomes a luxurious hotel. History hurtles. . . .

1930: the Principessa della Torre e Tasso (née Ella Walker, daughter of Hiram Walker, the whiskey king) buys the entire estate; it becomes her summer residence.

1959: the Principessa bestows the Villa Serbelloni on the Rockefeller Foundation, which makes it an "international study and conference center."

"1978": Sally and I are "here," writing, reading.

From battlements to books?

Nothing linear. Already, in the Middle Ages monks learned and taught by tallow candles; and towers stood over the cliffs of Como, exchanging tidings from afar. (Those grim, grey stones were somehow made to speak.) And all that pillage, rapine? Was it a kind of deep barter, perhaps some wild equivalent of our "seminars," for which we still obscurely yearn? History did slouch toward the crossroads of violence to be born. But it also allowed Pliny the Younger another kind of moment:

> Why not . . . hand over to others the cares of daily life and in this lofty, undisturbed retreat devote yourself to intellectual pursuits?

This has become the Villa's motto, its charge.

(All quotations from "The Point that Divides the Wind: A Brief History of the Villa Serbelloni," by Betsy Olson, based on the research of John Marshall. Private pamphlet.)

■

Every morning, I slouch from our tapestried bedroom, along the lemon-bright corridor, to my small dark study at the other end of the Villa. I sit at my desk to "finish a book." Retrograde task!

When the book is finished, the last page seldom knows the first—the manuscript is typed and retyped—it goes out to the publisher—interminable wait—galleys, then page proofs, arrive—the book finally "appears"—its author has died.

"Death of the author?" It is sufficient to think of print as process. It may take three years to write a book; it may take as long to publish it. We are still very far from technological gnosticism, im-mediate mind. But Germans and Japanese manage far better than we do.

The book as delay: the author as impersonator of his dead self. Still, the book lives on in print. The author has exchanged "real time," his mortality, for another kind of time, his "immortality."

I sharpen my pencil and think of Yeats. His "masterful images" may have grown in "pure mind"; but they began in the "foul rag-and-bone shop of the heart." What, I wonder, do scholars of the Serbelloni—myself included—dispense in that shop?

■

Our bedroom window faces south. Breakfast comes on a neatly piled tray: coffee or tea, butter, honey and marmalade, rolls, fruit, cheese. Sally sits facing the Lecco arm of the lake, I the Como arm. The morning ferry at the dock below begins to churn, tugging on its hawser. An aliscafi *streaks by, leaving a vanishing trace, white spume on blue water. In the distance, the Monti Tremezzo and—farther, higher still—Monte San Primo show a jagged line of snow on their peaks. The terraced gardens of the Serbelloni are beginning to break into pale green. Sally suddenly asks: "Why are we really here?"*

Later in my study, overlooking a grottoed and darkly wooded part of the estate, I ponder her question, which I translate: "What is nature to idea, what this scene of loveliness to the sullen mind?"

Freud somewhere remarks: "In the last resort, what has left its mark on the development of organisms must be the history of the earth we live in and its relation to the sun." And this from Eliot:

> The dance along the artery
> The circulation of the lymph
> Are figured in the drift of stars
> Ascend to summer in the tree

Blood and sun, lymph and tree. Is it wholly accidental that this Villa, place of introspection, should be situated so brilliantly in nature? What ancient intuition, what imperative of evolution, is here recognized, institutionalized, by the Rockefeller Foundation?

Perhaps Mind must still return to Nature in order to think what it thinks out of Nature. Perhaps the Laws of Nature yield themselves best to Mind in certain circles of Nature's grace.

(Filippo Meda on the Villa in Ercole Sfondrati's time: "I called on the Duke . . . and felt that I was enjoying the delights of the Terrestrial Paradise.")

Or perhaps Mind is most in harmony with itself where mind-perceived harmonies of Nature abound. The premise of creativity in this place, in any case, disdains the Faustian study, the poet's garret, the monkish cell.

Except that my study is dark, and our bedroom window narrow.

■

All is dapple, shadow, shimmer today. Clouds scud over the lake and mountain scapes: wind-driven, changing shapes. Sometimes the sun breaks away, thickening the brown-green shade at this hill's base, yellowing that far hill's slope. The peaks are in the light, but the eye always returns to apricot villages and silver groves below. What pulls our sight down? Gravity of spirit, as Faust knew in his old age?

> Hinaufgeschaut!—Der Berge Gipfelriesen
> verkünden schon die feierlichste Stunde;
> sie dürfen früh des ewigen Lichts geniessen,
> das später sich zu uns hernieder wendet.
> . . .
> Nun aber bricht aus jenen ewigen Gründen

ein Flammenübermass, wir stehn betroffen:
. . .
so dass wir wieder nach der Erde Blicken,
zu bergen uns in jugendlichstem Schleier.

Faust feels the gravity of light.

(Was the Original Act one of Gravity rather than Light, the binding act, Love preceding Lucidity to make the universe in its variousness whole?)

Yet light and gravity, as Einstein has taught, are not strangers to one another: the first bends in the heavy presence of the other, as sky curves to meet earth at the horizon. Still, it was photism, not Gaia's invisible weight, that inspired Gnostic cults. Such cults return in a new light. The Britannica *(Fifth Edition) says: "In modern times there have been self-consciously Gnostic groups, especially in Europe; the basic source of their ideas seem to lie not in early Gnosticism but in a kind of Faustian Romanticism."*

We have come some way since Goethe's "More light!" Our photism derives more from electric technologies and scientific theories than from myths and mystical cults. Once the Indo-Germanic races, according to Ernst Cassirer, worshipped "light as an undifferentiated, total experience," preceding even the sense of "individual heavenly bodies, which figure only as its media, its particular manifestations." Now we are told, by Jacques Merleau-Ponty and Bruno Morando, that when matter and antimatter collide, "two photons [are] emitted in two opposite directions, each of which has an energy of $h\nu = mc^2$*." And serious physicists like J. D. Bernal can speculate that consciousness itself may "vanish in a humanity that has become completely etherialized . . . ultimately perhaps resolving itself entirely into light." More soberly perhaps and nearer at hand:*

> All the greatest exponents of civilization, from Dante to Goethe, have been obsessed by light. But in the seventeenth century, light passed through a crucial stage. The invention of the lens was giving it a new range and power. . . . [And so on to Galileo, van Leeuwenhoek, Huygens, Spinoza, Descartes, and Newton.] Vermeer used the utmost ingenuity to make us feel the movement of light. . . . [This, together with the Dutch painter's delight in material objects] often achieves what I can only call a spiritualization of matter.
> (Kenneth Clark, *Civilization.*)

> I sense light as the given of all presences, and material as spent light. . . . I believe that consciousness is in all life.
> (Louis Kahn, "Architecture: Silence and Light," in *The Future of Art.*)

> [With Teilhard, Pauwels and Bergier, and Lévi-Strauss in mind] . . . their "worlds of image" are somehow similar: in all three instances we are confronted with a kind of mythology of matter, whether of an imaginative, exuberant type . . . or a structuralist, algebraic type. . . .
> (Mircea Eliade, *Occultism, Witchcraft, and Cultural Fashions.*)

These "new mythologies of matter" imply photism and hylozoism as well—as in Findhorn and Lindisfarne? But though they may valorize solar seed, the spermatic word, they tend more toward a General Field theory, uniting the various forces of the cosmos, than to the strange, erotic practices of Tantric religion or Gnostic Phibionites.

("I will not be ashamed to say those things which they are not ashamed to do, in order that I may cause horror in those who hear about their shameful practices," Epiphanius says of the latter.)

All these have the same theoretical speed: electricity, magnetism, telephone, television, laser, radar, radio telescope, electronic microscope, computer—and Eliot's "light upon the figured leaf."

Still, perhaps we should sometimes cry: "Less light!" and so discern more scrupulously the lineaments of this earth and our own mortality.

■

We dine at the Villa by candlelight and crystal chandeliers. Bright talk, discreet tinkle of silver. Succulent North Italian cuisine with fit wines, including Serbelloni's own. Always, just attention to the senses; in work as in leisure, an answerable regimen. The influence of Betsy and Bill Olson, of course, more hosts than directors of the Bellagio Center. But the influence of whom or what else?

In great houses, Yeats thought, beauty is bred of custom and ceremony. Something of these pervades the Serbelloni, mixed with American practicality. Foundations, after all, possess neither the murderous munificence of princes (Borgias, Medicis, Sforzas) nor the spiritual tautness of monasteries (Iona, Cluny, Assisi). Prodigal sometimes, they remain always pragmatic. Yet something here maintains a climate of intellectual civility, not quite snobbish, not entirely casual.

Still, where scholars of wit congregate, malice can not lag too far behind. The scholars come and go, whispering at Bellagio of The Magic Mountain *and* Last Year at Marienbad. *(I introduced the "Serbelloni Villans"—so they are locally called—to the "Marienbad game" of Nim.) We think of epithets for this patrician place, so different from our homemade world: Arcadia, Utopia, Plutopia, Gastrotopia, Logotopia—in fact, every* topos *but*

Pornotopia. We discuss colleagues, newly arrived, recently departed. We sparkle, or think we sparkle, seldom violating Good Taste.

Gossip as a kind of mythomania; malice as a form of play. Play of conservative minds?

(My colleagues here do seem "established," even the young philosopher who sits in a study next to mine, writing urgently of a new conservatism for our time.)

Gossip and malice: anti-Promethean, both predicated, as is conservatism, on the sense of limit, of limitation—finally, one's own. Yet culture itself is never simply conservative: the violence of creation and decreation in it exceeds nature's, "red in tooth and claw."

I have called myself "amateur of change." Yet I will not play a postmodern Jacobin. Radicals, quite like their reactionary counterparts, lack the courage of Oedipus; ignoring their desire, these narrow Prometheans deny complicity in their fate. Perhaps politics can now preserve its authenticity only in its contradictions and our own.

(For myself, I favor radical change and suspect rational utopian schemes; distrusting power, I suspect it all the more in "Power to the People"; neither anarchist nor mystic, I admire both, as well as visionary conquerors; more protestant than catholic in taste, perhaps even a touch antinomian, I have no disapprobation for "great houses," Penhurst, Coole Park, or the Serbelloni.)

Needed: a redefinition of political terms (radical/reactionary, liberal/conservative, leftist/rightist), even a nomenclature of change. Needed more: a new conception of change.

Perhaps all change is finally *"change for change's sake." In nature as in culture, in the cosmos, change is a function of death, agent of becoming, ultimate avant-gardist. To know for whose or what's sake change finally works were to know the sense of the universe.* Finally. *Meantime, we need to discover a human order adequate to the "history of the earth," and to all that nature has striven to create out of nature: mind.*

■

To Milano for Easter weekend. Despite the Brigate Rosse, the wobbling lira, the parliamentary crisis, the "trains ran perfectly on time," the taxis were cleaner than in America. The city, on holiday, has begun to lose its wealthy inhabitants to hideouts in Piedmont, Lombardy, Aosta. La Scala is on strike, The Via Monte Napoleone, its shops like luxurious tombs, has begun to thin. We walk the streets, vaguely oppressed. "It's the city," Sally blurts. "History as failure."

Milano: city of power, often brutal. Like Attila, who sacked it in 452; like its wolfish Longobardian kings; like Barbarossa who razed it in revenge on the Guelphs; like the cruel Viscontis, so shadowy, or the Sforzas with jowly and sated faces; like the still menacing Castello Sforzesco, crushing the city's skyline. Yet Ludovico ("Il Moro") brought Leonardo and Bramante here and boasted Pope Alexander was his chaplain, the Emperor Maximillian his general, the Signoria of Venice his chamberlains, and Charles VIII of France his courier.

Another Milano, almost spiritual: founded by superstitious Celts; Constantine proclaiming Christianity in the Edict of Milano in 331; Ambrose of the honeyed tongue, scourge of Arians, adopted patron saint of the city; Botticelli's Madonna and Child at the Poldi-Pezzoli, delicate in her radiance and subtle, without prettiness; the horizontal Christ of Mantegna, at the Brera, enormous head, pallid body, leading the startled eye to some infinity behind the canvas; and Michelangelo's last, unfinished work, the Pieta Rondanini, sheltered in an alcove of ashstone at the Sforzesco, bent with a sadness heavier than all gravity, compassion in every curve, every line returning to the earth more love than earth ever gave to man.

Milano now: a confrontation best seen at dusk in the Piazza del Duomo. On one side: the white marble cathedral, encrusted grime still being scraped from the apse, a vast dowager, lacy with gables, pinnacles, lancettes, pedestals and statues, majestic if a little squat; on the other side, a neon jungle or forest of signs, CINZANO, FIAT, OLIVETTI, gaudy prayers of another kind; and between them, the piazza space, grey, swooping clouds of pigeons, frisbee clowns, ragazzi *howling melodiously as high-heeled girls click by.*

And at the edge of all this, the outer edge, Sally reminds me, lies Antonioni's wasteland: colossal cisterns, chimney stacks, truck lots, concrete warehouses, factories of corrugated steel, all in a red haze (Gary, Detroit, Hackensack). At the center, wealth, invisible fireball; desolation and fallout in expanding circles all around.

The evening papers reported nothing new about Aldo Moro.

■

I think with anger of my favorite heteroclite, Giordano Bruno, who said: "The actual and the possible are not different in eternity."

And in the present? What saves the actual, actualizes the possible, and guards us against eternity?

■

Easter has passed, spring continues.

Spring, they say in Bellagio, "is a little late this year." In Milwaukee, it has not even begun. But they celebrate the Resurrection, here as there, on the same day. Why is Christ more punctual than Ceres or Prosperpine?

Spring is here now, the improbable transformation. Soft, new tints against the old sepia and brown of tree trunks; out of the warming earth, bud, sprite, and bloom. On the Serbelloni terraced grounds you may see: flowering quince, almond, plum, peach, chestnut, cherry, and apple trees; magnolia, myrtle, mimosa, dogwood, syringa, clematis, camelia, oleander, laburnum, wisteria, azalea, and rhododendrons; beds of tulip, pansy, iris, daffodil, saxifrage, narcissus, orchid, primrose, and violet, cut in formal shapes; and in the dank underbrush, the anemone hepatica, blue in the shade. The cypresses, here and there, frame the landscape of spring; rising straight, they curl at the top in memories of wind and ice.

I breathe this Italian spring, and think back of a wintry day in Connecticut: deep snow, the woods stark, grey and white birches peeling against a ragged sky, the streams almost frozen, trickling blue-black beneath the ice. Dead of winter, they say, and I had come to visit a woman dying.

I brought a dozen perfect yellow roses from the airport. She protested the gift, pleased, while she put them in an earthen pot she had turned. She wanted to burden no one; her self-pity, if any survived her convent childhood, remained invisible; over the years, her solitude became essential. We played a record I had also brought, sonatas for violin and clavier, in the glassed-in parlor. The winter sun filtered through the birches. I kept thinking: "Mozart and terminal cancer in one room." She bragged shyly about her "other" healthy organs. When she looked at the late light on the snowdrift outside, she said: "It's beautiful." I wondered: "What world she sees there with those slate-green eyes?" Before I left, she gave me a sliced apple to "freshen my mouth."

■

"Death is love itself; in death absolute love is being revealed. It is the identity of the Divine and the human. . . ," Hegel wrote. Liebestod? *Or simply philosophy deflecting grief?*

We come to our awareness of death late: the child of four, the paleolithic adult, Ernest Becker (now dead) claimed, lack it strangely. Still more strange: by death possessed, we scarcely comprehend it. A biological barrier or mental wall stands between mind and its own future. Yet this opacity of foresight may be the most Promethean of all our gifts, the motive of all our metamorphoses.

Spring is change, verdant; death duskier, deeper in transformation.

Death in-forms our theories,
shapes our stories.
It

is our radical
transaction with the universe—or perhaps simply a threshold, an openness.
The crack in our being
that makes Being complete?
This "little bit of nature," this "thinking reed": desire, adventure, grief.

■

4

THE GNOSIS OF SCIENCE:
A Paratactical Pastiche

GNOSIS. *pl.* (rare) gnoses [Gr. investigation, knowledge (in Christian writers *esp.* a higher knowledge of spiritual things). . . .]

GNOSTIC. *adj.* and *sub.*
A. *adj.*
1.a. Relating to knowledge; cognitive; intellectual.
b. *non-use.* Believing in reality of transcendental knowledge; opposed to *agnostic.*
c. Possessing esoteric spiritual knowledge.
d. In humorous or slang use: clever, knowing.
2. Pertaining to the Gnostics; having an occult or mystic character.

Oxford English Dictionary

The Nobel laureate George Wald tells a breathtaking story. Someone asked: "Why is the solar system 4.5 billion years old?" Someone answered: "Because it took us that long to know it." To which Wald adds: "If we have come to the point of giving that answer, how much longer have we got to go?" Enormous query. Here are all the elements of our gnosis: science, imagination, the cosmos itself, rendered by mind (conscious, unconscious) under the aspect of time.

Does change imply one or more beginning(s)? Though Derrida may deny Origin, current cosmologies find origins inevitable. The Steady State Theory of the universe—continuous "creation" of matter, continuous expansion, no end or beginning—now seems to many scientists untenable. Instead: the Big Bang Theory, all matter in the universe packed into an unimaginable mass, at unspeakable temperatures, exploding at a certain "moment," say twenty billion years ago, expanding into infinite "space." (There doesn't seem to be enough mass in the cosmos, some scientists argue, to reverse the expansion into contraction, and so justify a Pulsing Theory of the universe.)

The universe seems to have had "a beginning."

It is still bathed in the faint radiation of its "beginning," radiation discovered in 1965 by Arno Penzias and Robert Wilson of the Bell Telephone Laboratories.

It is "expanding." Hubble's Law of 1929: the farther (from us) a galaxy, the faster it moves. The law conforms to Einstein's earlier Theory of Relativity. More than that, it confirms a single yet changing cosmos.

We do not at this time know why or whence or whither. Here is Robert Jastrow, Director of NASA's Goddard Institute for Space Studies:

> Theologians are generally delighted with the proof that the universe had a beginning, but astronomers are curiously upset. Their reactions provide an interesting demonstration of the response of the scientific mind—supposedly a very objective mind—when evidence uncovered by science itself leads to a conflict with the articles of faith in our profession. . . . As usual when faced with trauma, the mind reacts by ignoring the implications—in science this is known as "refusing to speculate"—or trivializing the origin of the world by calling it the big bang, as if the universe were a firecracker. ("Have Astronomers Found God?" *New York Times Magazine*, June 25, 1978.)

The universe defies all our trivializations. Yet miraculously it defies neither mind nor its speculations. The gnosis of science is here to stay—and change.

* * *

Like the imagination, science is a powerful agent of change. Knowledge may be power and it may be virtue; but it is also self-conscious process, awareness in mutability.

The noetic process is certainly older than Plato's Academy. It coincides with language, that Promethean gift or impatience which sparked socialized human consciousness. This same process, stone-slow at first, has become vertiginous in our epoch. Knowledge has grown into an "industry" so vast and problematic, Kenneth Boulding argues, as to project the human race into a new phase of its planetary history; and as the first great transition was from precivilized to civilized societies, so is the second—we are now in its throes—toward "postcivilization":

> The key to the evolutionary process, whether in biology or in society, lies in a set of related phenomena associated with teaching, learning, and printing. This indeed is the secret of life. The gene operates as a three-dimensional printer, for it has the ability to produce exact copies of itself in the material world. Printing is a process by which order can be copied and spread. When a teacher teaches a class, furthermore, the students know more at the end of the hour and the teacher knows no less. Indeed, by a process which is even more mysterious, the teacher knows more too. The impact of man in the evolutionary process arises because of the capacity of his images—that is, the knowledge present in his mind—to grow by a kind of internal breeder reaction: the imagination. It is this which has given the human nervous system such a fantastic social-evolutionary potential, a potential of which we have probably used up 1 percent in the brief history of the human race.
> (*The Meaning of the Twentieth Century.*)

Writing confidently in 1964, Boulding may have underrated the growing afflictions of "information."

A XEROX ADVERTISEMENT

There is an energy crisis and a food crisis and any number of other crises, all caused by vanishing resources.

But there is one that involves not a shortage, but an excess. A crisis where the resource isn't dwindling, but growing almost uncontrollably.

That resource is information.

. . .

You see, Xerox doesn't just copy information anymore. We help you manage it.

(*Time.*)

Still, Boulding's insight into imagination—the interactive power of images and concepts—remains crucial to human gnosis.

* * *

"We help you manage it."

Science, science extended by its sundry technologies, is under grave suspicion. The suspicion, aggravated by "the greening of America," is nothing recent. Already in 1960, Gerald Holton, picking up C. P. Snow's theme of "the two cultures," 1959, deplored "the cultural psychosis engendered by the separation of science," and called for its "reciprocal contact with the concerns of most men." Science has much "advanced" since then, advancing at the same time its alienation. We fear the archetypal Mad Scientist, from Victor Frankenstein to Dr. Strangelove; we mistrust the archetypal Sorcerer's Apprentice, the technocrat run amuck, who ravages our environment. "Ah," Hermann Hesse exclaimed, "in fifty years the earth will be a graveyard of machines, and the soul of the spaceman will simply be the cabin of his own rocket." The hyperbole avows our presentiment that science, even in its most benign technological reaches, must radically alter the human measure, that measure so curiously constant, despite all history, from neolithic times to our own.

Nor are the strictures against science simply intuitive; they are theoretical as well. Here, as in so much concerning the critique of modernism, Nietzsche claims priority. For him, the nineteenth century witnessed the victory of the scientific *method* over knowledge; the positivist stance took for fact what was already interpretation. Logic itself, which grew from "the herd instinct in the background," became a mode less of agreement than dominion. The conceptual ban it imposed on contradictions, Nietzsche notes in *The Will to Power,* proceeded "from the belief that we are *able* to form concepts, that the concept not designates the essence of a thing but *comprehends* it—in fact, logic (like geometry and arithmetic) applies only to fictitious entities that we have created." Thus science appears as a "seduction by 'number and logic,' " "seduction by 'laws,' " into a "sovereign ignorance." Science is fiction, Nietzsche says—we shall return to this—and science, indeed all knowledge, is both power and desire: "a species grasps a certain amount of reality in order to become a master of it, in order to press it into service."

In this insight, Marx and Nietzsche for a moment meet. All science, all technologies even more, presuppose ideologies, human interests; this is a primary assertion of Socialism, from Karl Marx to Jürgen Habermas.

Not all who so argue are Marxists. In his *Adventures of Ideas,* for instance, Whitehead remarks: "In considering the history of ideas, I maintain that the notion of 'mere-knowledge' is a high abstraction which we should dismiss from our minds. Knowledge is always accompanied with accessories of emotion and purpose." Similarly, Michael Polanyi argues, in *Personal Knowledge,* that a "heuristic function" is central to the achievement of science; in this "function" or "passion," the mainspring of scientific originality, "cognitive content is supplemented by a conative component." Nonetheless, the Marxist critique of the politics of knowledge remains the most thorough; and it has begun to influence scientists themselves. Thus Robert M. Young, Director of the Wellcome Unit for the History of the Biomedical Sciences at Cambridge University, concludes: "Science therefore becomes the ideology of power, a totalized world view which produces a fatalism on the one hand, and amenability to technological manipulation on the other." Yet with few exceptions, such as Alvin W. Gouldner's *The Dialectic of Ideology and Technology,* the empirical tradition of American sociology continues to ignore the politics of technotopia.

Anxious to refute Nietzsche's skeptical reduction of knowledge—a reduction based on a mistaken identification of science with positivism—Habermas counters:

> The connection of knowledge and interest, conceived naturalistically [which Nietzsche did], may dispel objectivist illusion in every form, but only to re-justify it subjectivistically.

Instead, Habermas wishes to reaffirm the possibilities of both knowledge and interest:

> Because science must secure the objectivity of its statements against the pressure and seduction of particular interests, it deludes itself about the fundamental interests to which it owes not only its impetus but the *conditions of possible objectivity* themselves. . . . If knowledge could outwit its innate human interest, it would be by comprehending that the mediation of subject and object that philosophical consciousness attributes exclusively to *its own* synthesis is produced originally by interests. The mind can become aware of this natural basis reflexively. Nevertheless, its power extends into the very logic of inquiry.
> (*Knowledge and Human Interest.*)

Science, in this view, is not simply fiction; but neither is it free from interest, nor does it constitute the only form of cognition. The issue here is scientific abstraction, objectivity; or as Habermas would say, the issue is "the connection of *theoria* and *kosmos,* of *mimesis* and *bios theoretikos* that was assumed from Plato through Husserl."

As we have seen and shall see again, science is increasingly conscious of *kosmos.* This is not to say that science now escapes the charge of abstraction; or that it renounces entirely the dream of objectivity. The charge of abstraction, leveled by Goethe and

Nietzsche, and later (equivocally) by Freud, is made again by Norman O. Brown. Repression begets civilization, civilization begets abstraction, abstraction begets death—that is the relentless logic of Brown's early book:

> The basic mechanism for producing this desexualization of life, this holding of life at a distance, is, as we have seen, negation; sublimation is life entering consciousness on condition that it is denied. The negative moment in sublimation is plain in the inseparable connection between symbolism (in language, science, religion, and art) and abstraction. Abstraction, as Whitehead has taught us, is a denial of the living organ of experience, the living body as a whole. . . . *(Life Against Death.)*

For Brown, the utopian task is to construct a "Dionysian ego," and thus to dissolve the distinctions on which all abstract systems rest. Yet abstractions in modern art or science, as Werner Heisenberg knows, may themselves be part of a larger project to reveal the invisible fabric of the one and the many, of the universe in its multitude.

As for the dream of objectivity, it finds articulation in a man who seems the very antithesis of Brown: the Nobel laureate and austere biologist Jacques Monod. Candidly, Monod admits the threat of science:

> The fear is the fear of sacrilege: of outrage to values. A wholly justified fear. It is perfectly true that science outrages values. Not directly, since science is not judge of them and must ignore them; but it subverts every one of the mythical or philosophical ontogenies upon which the animist tradition, from the Australian aborigines to the dialectical materialists, has made all ethics rest: values, duties, rights, prohibitions. (*Chance and Necessity.*)

Different as Brown and Monod seem, both assent to a central thesis: that science, which depends upon abstraction (Brown) and the postulate of objectivity (Monod), nihilates history. Their conclusions, thereafter, vary. For Brown, the human race must rise through metaphor from history to mystery; his metaphor is the resurrection of the body. For Monod, our race must wither into the truth of objectivity and so affirm the basic tenet of a new ethical system, the stringent ethic of knowledge.

Metaphor or Objectivity. How final is this dualism? How intrinsic to culture or consciousness?

* * *

The imagination, we have seen and shall see again, is key to science. Why, then this persistent wrangle between the descendants of the Two Cultures? Or between Art and Technology, Fiction and Fact, Heart and Head, Past and Future, Faith and Reason, Earth and Sky, etc.? Do such schisms somehow assuage the crisis of identity that some disciplines evince?

The human animal is an odd, or rather, even, creature. Two handed, two eyed, bifurcated, double brained, and sometimes Janus faced, it insists on a dichotomous, if not schizoid, destiny. And so dualisms and diremptions of every kind rule our lives, especially in the West. Created in languages, these contraries thrive on the babel of tongues.

Self and Other: psychoanalysts, dealers in dreams, and immunologists, caretakers of cells, recognize the distinction as cause for wars both large and small. Thus we make our enemies, better to know ourselves.

But there may be a greater enemy within (not Original Sin): a "paranoid streak" occasioned by the coexistence of old (reptilian, limbic) and new (cortex) brains in the human animal, strangers each to each. (See Paul D. Maclean, of the National Institute of Mental Health, in Arthur Koestler and J. R. Smythies, eds., Beyond Reductionism.*)*

Yet dualisms are also dynamic, dialectical; they aspire to overcome themselves. The result, if not unity, is a continuous search for wholes. Thus new conjunctions match the disjunctions of the age, and convergences rush there where divergences strain. This is manifest in such diverse regions of culture as contemporary art, technology, science, religion, and philosophy.

Two examples may suffice.

* * *

A region of conjunction: art and technology.

We have come to take modern and postmodern art for granted, and so sometimes forget how much of it is complicit in both science and technology. Yet the history of the avant-gardes in our century is a history of technological symbiosis, of tools becoming statements, concepts becoming styles, processes becoming environments. The artist-engineer, of whom Leonardo was paragon, is reborn in many and curious guises under the sign of the lathe, the dynamo, the computer. Even so sober, so skeptical, a critic as Edmund Wilson is led to wonder in his conclusion to *Axel's Castle,* written nearly half a century ago:

> And who can say that, as science and art look more and more deeply into experience and achieve a wider and wider range, . . . they may not arrive at a way of thinking, a technique of dealing with our perceptions, which will make art and science one?

Consider for a moment the artistic movements of the twentieth century:

Cubism
Futurism
Suprematism
Constructivism
Dadaism
Merzism
De Stijl
The Bauhaus—

or independent masters such as Duchamp or Calder. To varying degrees, all *assumed* technology, took it for artistic meaning *and* method. Light, motion, sound, mass, time, space, new technics and new materials, all were explored.

And later, during and after the Second World War when the center of artistic gravity moved to New York, and after Abstract Expressionism had run its course:

—John Cage, Milton Babbitt, David Tudor, etc.
—Barnett Newman, Robert Rauschenberg, Jasper Johns, Andy Warhol, Frank Stella, etc.
—David Smith, Robert Morris, Tony Smith, etc.
—Merce Cunningham, Alwin Nikolais, etc.
—Allan Kaprow, etc.

and again:

—Nam June Paik, Billy Klüver, Gyorgy Kepes, Christo, James Seawright, Bruce Nauman, Lejaren Hiller, Alan Sonfist, John Whitney, Charles Scuri, etc.
—PULSA, USCO, EAT, ANONIMA, etc.

Though Wilson was seldom prophetic, in this he was proleptic: a new scale, a new kind, of association between art and industry, art and media, art and concept—be it system or game theory, Kabalism or linguistics—seems to have taken place. The point is well made by Gyorgy Kepes:

> Technology today does not simply imply a physical imple-

ment, a "machine," mechanical or electronic, but a systematic, disciplined, collaborative approach to a chosen object. There is a new technology that Daniel Bell has called "intellectual technology," this is what artists must accept and understand. The medium, in this case, is not in itself the message; it becomes a message when it is in vital dialogue with our most authentic contemporary needs.
(In Douglas Davis, *Art and the Future.*)

The "intellectual technology" to which both Kepes and Bell refer is simply current knowledge—a reminder of Boulding—knowledge constituted by science as by imagination, extended by technology as by art. Yet even Kepes could not have foreseen the most recent contributions of technology to art. These include computer-controlled synthesizers that can imitate the sounds of an entire "symphony," video "paintings" and holographic "sculpture," laser "scenic designs" for theater and dance, and assorted wonders that lead Alexis Greene to predict in the *New York Times* (February 26, 1978): "The future museum-goer may be able to 'walk' through computer simulations of ancient Rome or 19th century London, much the way airplane pilots in training 'fly' into simulated airports."

It would be intriguing to explore parallel tendencies in the verbal arts, from Concrete Poetry and OULIPO (*Ouvroir de Littérature Potentielle*), through the experiments with "the book" of Max Bense, Helmut Heissenbüttel, Michel Butor, Philippe Sollers, Maurice Roche, Christine Brooke-Rose, Raymond Federman, Harry Mathews, Walter Abish, Eugene Wildman, Italo Calvino, among others, to that magnum opus of science and imagination, technology and myth, gone paranoiac: *Gravity's Rainbow.* Intriguing and perhaps too digressive.

In his essay, "The Electronic Novel," Strother B. Purdy focuses on the image of the electric grid that appears in certain novels, from J. M. G. Le Clézio's *La Guerre* to Pynchon's *Gravity's Rainbow.* The grid implies immanence as well as the void, the totality of human thought and the abyss. In the "electro-mysticism" of Pynchon's Kurt Mondaugen, for instance, the appropriate prayer is: "In the name of the cathode, the anode, and the holy grid"; and the ultimate quest is for a *vide:* "the pure, the informationless state of signal zero." "With Le Clézio," Purdy writes, "the stress is also on the near infinity of surrounding objects and message sources, with a greater emphasis on the resultant dissolution of individual identity. . . ."

Thus in art as in other human endeavors, the effect of technology is dispersal of language, an extended circuitry of awareness, a problematic immanence of mind. Such immanence may evoke thoughts of God and the Devil, Negentropy and Entropy, Being and Nothingness.

* * *

A second region of conjunctions: religion and science.

To the chagrin of purists in various disciplines, such conjunctions have become a cultural fad—a "fad," perhaps, more significant than purists allow. Thus in an issue of the *Saturday Review* (December 10, 1977), subtitled "God and Science: New Allies in the Search for Values," the historian Martin Marty writes:

> Strangest of all, in place of the ancient set piece war between belief and unbelief, we are now seeing internecine warfare *between* old school religionists and a newer breed of theologians cautiously open to scientific advances, and *between* hard core, slide rule scientists and their colleagues who are open to the new findings about mind and consciousness.

While these "internecine wars" rage, the subject has lent itself to scientific experiment, epistemological speculation, and spiritual quest—as well as hocus, knavery, and legerdemain. Witness the popular works of Arthur Koestler, most notably *The Roots of Coincidence,* or the testaments of William Irwin Thompson, written with greater panache.

The author of several books in the last decade, Thompson engages (somewhat glibly, often with acumen) issues of cultural and intellectual convergence. In an earlier work, *At the Edge of History,* he ruminated on the confluence of "mechanists" and "mystics," the culture of M. I. T. and that of Esalen meeting in a new "Pythagorean science." In a later work, *Passages about Earth,* Thompson addressed himself to the same topics with inspirational zeal. Dropping out of the university and circling the globe in his search of wise heads—including Paolo Soleri, Ivan Illich, Gopi Krishna, Carl Friedrich von Weiszächer, Doris Lessing, David Spangler—he ends by founding his own Lindisfarne Association in an attempt to wed the freemasonry of science with the ancient spirit of Iona and Lindisfarne. But Thompson's interest in Tantric Yoga and Celtic Christianity concern us here less than his angled perception of a new kind of science, which he calls Pythagorean, rather than Archimedean, knowledge.

As if he were illustrating Thompson's thesis, Lawrence LeShan juxtaposes two statements, one from the *Pali Canon,* a document of mystic Buddhism, the other from J. Robert Oppenheimer's *Science and Common Understanding:*

> Vaccha asked the Buddha:
> "Do you hold that the soul of the saint exists after death?"
> "I do not hold that the soul of the saint exists after death."
> "Do you hold that the soul of the saint does not exist after death?"
> "I do not hold that the soul of the saint does not exist after death."
> "Where is the saint reborn?"
> "To say he is reborn would not fit the case."
> "Then he is not reborn."
> "To say he is not reborn would not fit the case."

■

> "If we ask, for instance, whether the position of the electron remains the same, we must say 'no'; if we ask whether the electron's position changes with time, we must say 'no'; if we ask whether the electron is at rest, we must say 'no'; if we ask whether it is in motion, we must say 'no.' "
> (*The Medium, the Mystic, and the Physicist.*)

But what can juxtapositions really prove? The marriage of Earth and Sky? A mutation in archetypes? Some sudden shift in epistemic categories? Hardly. Still we may suspect that pop religion, pseudo science, and cultural fashion do project images of desire, figments of the real, perhaps even histories of the future. Here, at any rate, is a cento on this spiritual theme:

—Albert Einstein, quoted in Philipp Frank's *Einstein,* admits: "The most beautiful emotion is the mystical. It is the sower of all true art and science. He to whom this emotion is a stranger, who can no longer wonder and stand rapt in awe, is as good as dead."
—Fred Hoyle, in *The New Face of Science,* asks why scientists do what they do: "The real motive of course is a religious one. Finding out about the world is essentially a religious concept."
—Werner Heisenberg, in *Physics and Philosophy,* hazards: "The Pythagorean school was an offshoot of Orphism, which goes back to the worship of Dionysus. Here has been established the connection between religion and mathematics which ever since has exerted the strongest influence on human thought."
—Erwin Schrödinger, in *My View of the World,* asserts: " 'There is but *one* monad.' Then what does the whole of monadology turn into?—the philosophy of the Vedanta (or perhaps the more recent but certainly independent one of Parmenides). Briefly stated, it is the view that all of us living beings belong together. . . ."

—Raymond Ruyer, in *La Gnose de Princeton,* discusses a movement variously inspired by Samuel Butler, Alfred North Whitehead, Arthur Eddington, James Jeans, E. A. Milne, Carl Friedrich von Weizsäcker, and Fred Hoyle, which now embraces scientists, mathematicians, doctors, and clergymen, all concerned with a cosmological vision, rigorously scientific as it is, playfully metaphoric, a panpsychic vision that proclaims: "It thinks in the universe!"
—Fritjof Capra, in *The Tao of Physics,* offers innumerable correspondences between quantum physics and Eastern mysticism, and quotes Niels Bohr: "For a parallel to the lesson of atomic theory . . . [we must turn] to those kinds of epistemological problems with which already thinkers like the Buddha and Lao Tzu have been confronted. . . ." This is also the theme of Denis Postle's *The Fabric of the Universe.*
—Norbert Wiener, in *God & Golem, Inc.,* presents "valid analogies between certain religious statements and the phenomena studied by cybernetics," especially the phenomenon of "creative activity, from God to the machine." See also Gersholm Scholem, "The Golem of Prague and the Golem of Rehovoth," *Commentary* (January, 1966).
—Ludwig von Bertalanffy, in *Robots, Men and Minds,* writes: "The scientist can say . . . that *Homo sapiens* is the highest product of terrestrial evolution. The mystic says essentially the same thing when claiming evolution to be God becoming aware of Himself. . . . Teilhard de Chardin has only given it a modern and not necessarily the best expression."
—Pierre Teilhard de Chardin, in *The Phenomenon of Man,* remarks: "Like the meridians as they approach the poles, science, philosophy and religion are bound to converge as they draw nearer the whole."
—Wolfgang Pauli and C. G. Jung, in *Naturerklärung und Psyche,* collaborate to explore the influence of archetypes on scientific concepts, including "synchronicity," "acausality," and the "space-time continuum." Pauli, like Weizsäcker, also speculates on the "complementarity" of Asiatic religions and quantum physics.
—William Irwin Thompson, in *Evil and World Order,* argues: "To see technology in proper scale, we need cosmic consciousness, and that consciousness comes more often from meditation than from reading Marx or Freud."
—Margaret Mead, in *Twentieth Century Faith,* says: "Exploration of the forms that man's imagination takes—even in the simplest primitive societies . . . suggests that there may be a biological basis in man, and in man alone, for the . . . sense of wonder or the cosmological sense."
—Harvey Cox, in "The Virgin and the Dynamo Revisited," suggests that technology provides images which replace traditional symbols of authority and that the "divine substance" may begin to "flow away" from human to technological repesentations.
—*Time* magazine speaks casually of the "greening of the astronomers"; and physicists, like Murray Gell-Mann, draw whimsically on *Alice in Wonderland, Finnegans Wake,* and the *Eightfold Path of Buddha* to describe the most elusive particles of matter.

—The physicist David Bohm (University of London) and the neurologist Karl Pribram (Stanford University), in *Brain Mind Bulletin*, July 4, 1977, theorize: "Our brains mathematically construct 'concrete' reality by interpreting frequencies from another dimension, a realm of meaningful, patterned primary reality that transcends time and space. The brain is a hologram, interpreting a holographic universe."
—The New Alchemists, John Todd and William McLarney, like their ancient predecessors, hope to deal with nature reverently, even mysteriously. In other words: the resexualization and resacralization of both nature and technology. Not only a Tao but also an Eros of science: the hieratic impulse in ecology.
—Science fiction writers—the names are legion but they surely include Olaf Stapledon, Stanislaw Lem, Arthur Clarke, Alfred Bester, Theodore Sturgeon, Ursula LeGuin, Samuel Delany, Philip Dick, Roger Zelazny—project worlds in which science and vision conspire to realize all the potentialities of (human) Being.
—Current studies address spiritual and "paranormal" phenomena of every kind: acupuncture, biofeedback, psi, psychedelics, yoga, meditation, mysticism (Buddhist, Neo-Platonist, Christian, Kabalistic, Hassidic, Sufi), shamanism, anthroposophy, astrology, magic, etc.

* * *

No doubt, Western culture may appear to us, in this Spenglerian moment, a vast Sargasso Sea, with all manner of things—sinister, ridiculous, and sublime—floating in it. But the moment may not be one of decadence; it may rather prove one of painful planetization, during which various attitudes are possible. Some, like members of the Zetetic Society—perhaps more dogmatic than truly skeptical—fear a reversion to fascism or superstition. Others, like Mircea Eliade, see in occultism, witchcraft, and cultural fashion a fundamental drive: "to go beyond one's parents' and grandparents' world of meaning . . . [in the hope of] discovering a new and creative mode of existence in the world." Still others, like Boulding, believe that in a technological age "the foreshadowing of things to come" is revealed "in the experience of the mystics and the groupings of man in religion." Finally, there are those, like Thompson, who would enlarge their cognitive perspectives of culture, who are "willing to take in science, politics, and art, *and* science fiction, the occult, pornography."

Admittedly, there are as many perils as possibilities in such curious conjunctions. What ethical, psychological, or political demands will they suddenly make? When epistemologies shift and distinctions blur, when facts and fictions begin to merge, when reality becomes derealized, dematerialized, there is a chance that baleful exigencies will replace habitual codes and constraints. Such exigencies not only raise the familiar specter of totalitarian rule; they further remind us that all change—most particularly that change empowered by new sciences, new technologies—is cause for *mortal* anxiety.

Change may threaten us with death; it offers us rebirth as well. And on closer look, some "new conjunctions" turn out to be very old indeed, as Marjorie Nicholson shows in *Science and Imagination*. Still, the trend that began with Copernicus, Tycho Brähe, Kepler, Galileo, Bacon, Huygens, Descartes, Leibniz, and Newton has now accelerated prodigally in our century. In so doing, it has burst the paradigms of nineteenth century mechanistic, materialistic, deterministic science; or to put the matter more cautiously, in the words of Max Planck, the law of causality is now considered neither false nor true but rather a "heuristic principle," intended to help scientists "achieve fertile results." Of this we can be certain: the cosmology of Newton and Laplace differs strikingly from the one Einstein has bequeathed. Furthermore, new theories of evolution challenge hallowed assumptions about Darwinian natural selection. Finally, the fields of cybernetics, on the one hand, and of brain research, on the other, raise cardinal questions about the nature of human intelligence, about the reflexive enigma of consciousness itself. Are we struggling through an epistemic shift, traversing an interparadigmatic age? Or is it all some cultural delusion of the times? Or perhaps simply an ancient metaphysical yearning?

No answer should easily satisfy the skeptical mind; and none can alleviate the revulsion of the positivist temper for the questions themselves. Yet there is a need for intellectual adventure in every civilization, as Whitehead knew, though adventure may risk the uncertainties of metaphysics; still, he thought, "metaphysical understanding guides imagination and justifies purpose."

Again, the imagination is key! But it is an imagination working through both the experiments and models of science to give us a phantasmic vision of reality: hadrons and tachyons, quarks and quasars, neutrinos and neutron stars. It is an imagination that transgresses boundaries, affirms the sovereignty of thought. Yet it is neither "mystical" nor "idealistic" in the traditional acceptance of these words. For sacred and profane, idealistic and materialistic, are no longer perceived as adequate to a full description of reality. The eminent biologist, J. B. S. Haldane, astutely observes: "Materialism . . . includes many forms far more subtle than the crude materialism of fifty years ago, and if you are willing to concede enough unexpected properties to so-called dead matter it becomes distinctly idealistic."

Uncannily, the radical epistemology of Nietzsche—deicide and surely no mystic—anticipates this emergent perspective:

> At last, the "thing-in-itself" also disappears, because this is fundamentally the conception of a "subject-in-itself." But we have grasped that the subject is a fiction. The antithesis "thing-in-itself" and "appearance" is untenable; with that, however, the concept "appearance" also disappears.

And in 1888 (!) most amazingly this:

> Physicists believe in a "true world" in their own fashion; a firm systemization of atoms in necessary motion, the same for all beings. . . . But they are in error. The atom they posit is inferred according to the logic of the perspectivism of consciousness—and is therefore itself a subjective fiction. This world picture that they sketch differs in no essential way from the subjective world picture; it is only construed with more extended senses, but with *our* senses nonetheless—
> (*The Will to Power.*)

What is this emergent perspective? Toward what paradigm does the imagination now strain? Tropical, systemic, and epistemological concerns all seem complicit in the new gnosis of science, as traditional boundaries begin to dissolve—even the distinction between presence and absence, existence and nothingness, is now challenged in quantum physics—and consciousness appears boundless, if not already immanent in the universe. The evidence comes from physics, biology, cybernetics, no less than cosmology.

* * *

On the physical universe.

Only four decades ago, the much quoted statements of Arthur Eddington and James Jeans—on the universe being "mind stuff," on its seeming "more like a great thought than like a great machine"—provoked something of a scandal. Yet since Einstein's simple equation, $E = mc^2$, set the sky of Hiroshima on fire, every schoolchild now knows that matter and energy are convertible into one another. This ghostly reciprocity has further moved into the heart of quantum physics. The new view of matter, Erwin Schrödinger says, recalls some aspect of Berkleian philosophy:

> The casting aside of all models and the wholesale employment of mathematics . . . comes very close to the Berkleian standpoint and, in the theory of wave mechanics, reduces the last building stones of the universe to something like a spiritual throb that comes as near as possible to our concept of pure thought.
> (*Science Theory and Man.*)

Heisenberg concurs; for him, modern physics "takes a definite stand against the materialism of Democritus and for Plato and the Pythagoreans." This dematerialization of the atom into mathematical forms also alters our idea of "objective" measurement; for the measuring device intrudes upon what it seeks to measure, and the intrusion becomes critical as the measurement attempts to become more precise. But what, precisely, is being measured? Probabilities, "tendencies to exist." When Heisenberg explores the vanishing interstices of the atom, he seems to hear the one and the many dissolve into the sheer music of number. Thus he muses:

> Perhaps there was no such thing as an indivisible particle. Perhaps matter could be divided further, until finally it was no longer a real division of a particle but a change of energy into matter, and the parts were no longer smaller than the whole from which they had been separated. But what was there in the beginning? A physical law, mathematics, symmetry? In the beginning was symmetry! This sounded like Plato's *Timaeus*. . . .
> (*Physics and Beyond.*)

Perhaps this is what Henry Adams called "physics stark mad in metaphysics"; perhaps it is no more than an acknowledgment, in Geoffrey Chew's words, that in contemporary science "the existence of consciousness, along with all other aspects of nature, is necessary for self-consistency of the whole." Of this we can be more certain: the middle distance, the sensible world in which we live and die, is but a fragment of a universe flung out to the farthest galaxies, withdrawn into its smallest particles. The categories of perception which guide us through that earthly distance may be the result of long biological adaptation to our environment; but now the brain has evolved far enough to perceive realities beyond our common senses. Non-iconic, often non-verbal, immaterial, the scientific vision of the cosmos now proceeds by metaphors and models, effective fictions of concord with nature, to which nature herself responds with varying degrees of kindness. Thus, for instance, a theoretical physicist, Paul Dirac, may calculate the "existence" of a particle, a positron, say, or metropole, years before its "capture." Thus, too, the mathematician Adrian Dobbs can postulate psitrons, which move in a second time dimension and possess an imaginary mass ($\sqrt{-1}$), and so may travel faster than light without violating the Theory of Relativity. Such particles would seem to suggest, Dobbs says, an actual state or entity "surrounded in imaginary time with an array of objective probabilities, which are not necessarily actualised, but nonetheless influence the actual course of events." As for quasars, they may be "white holes," *Time* magazine reports, "portals through space and time linking our universe and a mirror image universe composed of anti-matter." We seem to inhabit a virtual universe, of black and white holes in space, yet one not a whit less "real" for that. Potentialities and possibilities become realities in the very act of perception if the perceived data can be referring to a coherent model of our making.

No doubt, all thought is a kind of fiction making, though some fictions prove more useful and pleasing than others. In acknowledging this, the new epistemologies acknowledge a fundamental aspect of metaphor in art as in science. Metaphors do not only create and recreate human reality; they also delimit zones of thought and solve problems even as they generate new ones. Indeed, from the chemist Kekulé van Stradonitz, discover of the benzine ring, through Poincaré, Einstein, Planck, Bohr, Schrödinger, Heisenberg, Dirac, and even Monod, among countless others, scientists have testified to the power of dream, imagination, and artful elegance in their discoveries; and some, like Bohr, attributed their scientific persuasiveness to the "intensity" or "force of . . . [their] own imagination." Mysteriously, the useful and pleasing, the true and the beautiful, prove correlative in a certain intellectual light. And the correspondence between consciousness and cosmos—the "simplicity of natural laws has an objective character," Heisenberg believed—continues to provide the faith on which science, on which all gnosis, ultimately rests.

* * *

On biological evolution.

Einstein wondered about the reciprocity of mind and nature, the comprehensibility of the universe. Yet that reciprocity, we have noted, is itself part of the evolution of life on earth. Thus natural selection may help explain the resonance between the brain and the physical reality which includes it. Having eliminated all serious competitors except himself,

—an amendment to the Endangered Species Act now enables human beings, for the first time ever, to decree the end of a given species, thus confirming J. D. Bernal who noted, back in 1929, the tendency of nature to "pick some particularly happy development and allow it to expand in the place of and even at the expense of her earlier efforts"—

man is left to reproduce, and compete with, himself. And to extend his consciousness. Without assuming teleology, Sagan arrives at this Teilhardian conclusion:

> The entire evolutionary record on our planet, particularly the record contained in fossil endocasts, illustrates a progressive tendency toward intelligence. There is nothing mysterious about this: smart organisms by and large survive better and leave more offspring than stupid ones.
> (*The Dragons of Eden.*)

More than that, the increase in intelligence has become a qualitative factor: physiological activities of the brain now manifest themselves in psychological and spiritual phenomena, and are so perceived directly by consciousness. Yet as Sagan also warns, the human race, having created the technology of self-extermination, now puts its intelligent destiny in doubt. Thus an interstellar message may serve to reassure us that a wise society could still prosper even with a technology more advanced than our own.

If consciousness was once a product of biological evolution, has it now established itself as a heterocosm, ruled by laws of its own? Nearly two centuries ago, Goethe understood that theorizing was inherent in all human experience, and that the highest achievement was to "comprehend that everything factual is already theory." Rapturously, he wrote to Herder:

> I must also tell you confidentially that I am very close to the secret of the reproduction and organization of plants, and that it is the simplest thing imaginable. This climate offers the best possible conditions for making observations. To the main question—where the germ is hidden—I am quite certain I have found the answer; to the others I already see a general solution, and only a few points have still to be formulated more precisely. The Primal Plant is going to be the strangest creature in the world, which Nature herself shall envy me. With this model and the key to it, it will be possible to go on forever inventing plants and know that their existence is logical; that is to say, if they do not

actually exist, they could, for they are not the shadowy phantoms of a vain imagination, but possess an inner necessity and truth. The same law will be applicable to all other living organisms.
(*Italian Journey*.)

Heisenberg transposes the idea into modern science:

I am reminded of Goethe's attempt to derive the whole of botany from a single, primordial plant. . . . Following Goethe, we could call nucleic acid a primordial living being, for it, too, is an object and at the same time represents a biological blueprint. If we talk like that, we are, of course, right back with Plato's philosophy. Our elementary particles . . . are the original models, the ideas of matter.
(*Physics and Beyond*.)

And the biophysicist, Lecomte du Noüy generalizes the idea still further:

Man is capable of *creating* an unreal world by drawing the elements from within himself and no longer from his surroundings or from his experience. It is not a question of utilitarian adaptation, but of an absolutely new intellectual construction in which material reality is only a pretext. Behind the facts perceptible to his senses, behind his discernible universe, man invents another conceptual universe which becomes indispensable to enable him to think, to interpret experience, and eventually *to dominate the first*.
(*Human Destiny*.)

The gravest questions, however, concern not the evolution of consciousness but the direction that consciousness may give to evolution. Here Darwinians and Lamarckians, Mechanists and Vitalists, Reductionists and Holists, continue a debate that seems more acrimonious the more philosophical it becomes. The challenge, if not to the theory of evolution itself, is to the Darwinian doctrine of natural selection. Once again, Nietzsche uncannily prefigured the challenge: arguing against Darwin, he discounted the influence of "external circumstances," insisting on the "tremendous shaping, form-creating force working from within" organisms that, nonetheless, found a limit to their evolution. Many species have indeed evolved into high complexity only to recede and vanish from the earth. Will Nietzsche also prove prophetic about the human race—"man as a species is not progressing"—or will consciousness guide it to a rare destiny?

George Bernard Shaw, himself an unabashed Lamarckian, envisioned an apotheosis of mind. At the end of an unconscionably long play in search of immortality, *Back to Methuselah,* the She-Ancient presages: "The day will come when there will be no people, only thought." But as Haldane remarks, Shaw's biology remains unconvincing: his characters reach maturity in four years and live to be a thousand whereas increasing "neoteny" and "caenogenesis," or "foetalization," would require a prolonged childhood:

> If human evolution continued in the same direction as in the immediate past, the superman of the future would develop more slowly than we, and be teachable for longer. He would retain in maturity some characteristics which most of us lose in childhood. Certain shades of the prison house would never close about him. He would probably be more intelligent than we, but distinctly less staid and solemn.
> (*The Causes of Evolution.*)

Otherwise put: "Except ye . . . become as little children, ye shall not enter into the kingdom of heaven." Shrewdly, Haldane finds the race of Olaf Stapledon's *Last and First Men* more scientifically persuasive. Though the Last Men live to be a quarter of a million years, their "childhood" and "adolescence" span millenia and their "adulthood," extending into aeons, extends also into both time and space by the most complex forms of telepathy.

Yet science fiction now seems no more preternatural than science. What precisely impels and constrains the evolution of life? How is the role of consciousness in biology defined? Two current ideas come to mind: internal selection and teleology or, more cautiously, teleonomy. Internal selection is believed to act more decisively in evolution than Darwin supposed:

> Thus we define *"internal selection" as the restriction in the directions of evolutionary change by internal organizational factors, i.e., selective processes acting directly on the early consequences of the genotype which insures that . . .* [certain mutations] *survive up to the point at which Darwinian external selection enters.*
> (Lancelot Law Whyte, *Internal Factors of Evolution.*)

> We could ask whether the aim to be reached, the possibility to be realized, may not influence the course of events. . . . In other words, the kind of accident which plays so important a role in Darwinian theory may be something very much subtler than we think, and this is precisely because it agrees with the laws of quantum mechanics.
> (Werner Heisenberg, *Physics and Beyond.*)

Thus life imposes restrictions on a level prior to adaptation and external chance. But chance itself may be too crude a concept, inviting refinement, admitting purpose. Odious as this last possibility is to most biologists, it haunts the edge of their consciousness. Even Monod is compelled to introduce the concept of "teleonomy"—the structural tendency of organisms to "act projectively—realize and pursue purpose"—in his "objective" frame. Purpose, project, program: concepts that, without ruling variability, resist the rule of randomness. Thus François Jacob, in *La Logique du vivant,* also argues that what evolves is neither matter nor energy but forms, organizations, "unities of emergence," integrating themselves into the larger pattern of things. Integrating themselves according to what principle or plan? Here we may allow various savants to risk their own speculations:

> Everywhere but in man, consciousness has had to come to a stand; in man alone it has kept on its way. Man, then, continues the vital movement indefinitely, although he does not draw along with him all that life carries in itself. . . . *It is as if a vague and formless being, whom we may call, as we will* man *or* superman, *had sought to realize himself, and has succeeded only by abandoning part of himself on the way.* (Henri Bergson, *Creative Evolution.*)

> I prefer to speak of the "history of nature." In this I remain close to the concept of evolution for which . . . Gopi Krishna as well as Aurobindo and Teilhard de Chardin are indebted to the evolutionism of the nineteenth century. The spiritualizing of this concept . . . seems to me inescapable if man is included in evolution. . . . (Carl Friedrich von Weizsäcker in Gopi Krishna, *The Biological Basis of Religion and Genius.*)

> If we are bold enough to extrapolate at long range . . . we might say that, in the prudent words of Sir Isaac Newton, everything takes place as if the descent of the material universe toward an inert chaos and toward annihilation were compensated by the simultaneous ascent of an imponderable universe, that of the spirit. . . .
> (Lecomte de Noüy, *Human Destiny.*)

> In open systems, we have not only *entropy production* owing to irreversible processes taking place in the system; we also have entropy transport, by way of introduction of material which may carry high free energy or "negative entropy." Hence the entropy balance in an open system may well be negative. . . . This is what actually applies in living organisms.
> (Ludwig von Bertalanffy, *Robots, Men and Minds.*)

> Though intelligence can arise only from life, it may then discard it. Perhaps at a later stage, as the mystics have suggested, it may also discard matter; but this leads us into realms of speculations which an unimaginative person like myself would prefer to avoid.
> (Arthur C. Clarke, *Profiles of the Future.*)

The opinion, therefore, which seems to me to be most justifiable is that life in all its forms is the phenomenal disturbance created in the world of matter and energy when mind comes into it. Living matter is the outward and visible sign of the presence of mind, the splash made by the entry of mental existences into the sea of inert matter.
(Joseph Needham, ed., *Science, Religion & Reality.*)

Jorge Borges, in his recent bestiary of mythical creatures, notes that the idea of round beasts was imagined by many speculative minds, and Johannes Kepler once argued that the earth itself is such a being. In this immense organism, chemical signals might serve the function of global hormones, keeping balance and symmetry in the operation of various interrelated working parts, informing tissues in the vegetation of the Alps about the state of eels in the Sargasso Sea, by long, interminable relays of interconnected messages between all other kinds of other creatures.
(Lewis Thomas, *The Lives of a Cell.*)

We have already seen reasons to doubt whether mind has played any important part in guiding evolution, nor should I expect it to appear in the absence of brain. My suspicion of some unknown type of being associated with evolution is my tribute to its beauty, and to that inexhaustible queerness which is the main characteristic of the universe that has impressed itself on my mind during twenty-five years of scientific work.
(J. B. S. Haldane, *The Causes of Evolution.*)

Obviously, no precise consensus emerges from the authors of this collage; and all would wish to qualify their statements by such nuances as contexts must provide. Still, their paramount concern is the evolutionary destiny of mind, which has begun to act on the genetic system directly. Once a product of cosmic change, mind now finds itself prime agent of change in the cosmos. Or say: the new matrix, womb of creation, abiogenesis.

In mid-sixteenth century, in *De generationibus rerum naturalium,* Theophrastus Paracelsus wrote directions for abiogenesis; and as myth blended into alchemy, so did the latter become literature first and fact after.

1832

Wagner: The glass vibrates with sweet and powerful tone;
It darkens, clears: it *must* arrive at being.
. . .
Homunculus: How goes it Daddy? It was then no jest.
Come, press me tenderly upon thy breast.
(Goethe, *Faust II.*)

1932

Tall and rather thin but upright, the Director advanced into the room. . . . "These," he waved his hand, "are the incubators." And

opening an insulated door he showed them racks upon racks of numbered test-tubes. . . . Still leaning against the incubators he gave them . . . a brief description of the modern fertilizing process . . . where the Alphas and Betas remained until definitely bottled; while the Gammas, Deltas, and Epsilons were brought out again . . . to undergo Bokanovsky's Process.
(Aldous Huxley, *Brave New World.*)

1969

The hopes and hazards we anticipate in BSP [biosocioprolepsis] are all based on the fact that man, who has already learned to remake his physical environment, will now acquire—or have thrust upon him—the capacity to remake himself. The dust of the earth, having become conscious of the dust of the earth, will be able to recreate itself without benefit of the original creative breath. . . .
(Albert Rosenfield, *The Second Genesis.)*

1978

Oldham, England, Wednesday, July 26 (AP)—Doctors at Oldham General Hospital last night delivered a baby girl believed to be the world's first child conceived outside the womb, the hospital announced. . . .

"Her condition at birth was normal," the hospital said in a statement issued after midnight.

The parents are John Brown, a 38-year-old truck driver, and his wife, Lesley, 32, of Bristol, England.

Mrs. Brown became pregnant through fertilization of an egg with her husband's sperm in a glass dish.
(*New York Times,* July 26, 1978.)

* * *

From the first paranoiac paramecium to superconscious being is a journey immense. But Blake believed: "Everything which exists today was imagined long ago"; and also: "What is now proved was once only imagined." Will the gnosis of science reveal that time is a noetic fiction, an illusion that constitutes consciousness (Kant) but also separates it from Being (the mystic tradition)?

*Past, Present, Future: divisions of the mind that subatomic particles now habitually cross (Dobbs) and cosmic messages regularly defy (Hoyle). Even the "singularity," which is the birth of the universe, is conceived as a moment in which "*everything *is reversed," expansion and contraction, past and future, as "images are reversed in a mirror" (Jacques Merleau-Ponty). Yet men still conduct their psychomachia of "priority" and "belatedness." Is this a particular failing of humanists (scientists, a Watson or Crick, say, may* *claim priority though rarely will admit belatedness)—humanists schooled in a complex bias of retrospection? Or is this disposition rather due to the Western sense of death?*

Heidegger thought that "authentic history" finds its weight neither in the "past" nor in the "today" but in the Geschehen *or process of Existence, originating in the "future," the "Being-toward-death." Is such "authentic history" metaphysically cybernetic? Is Being itself?*

* * *

On cybernetics.

Evolution, as geneticists conceive it, is an immense cybernetic process rather than a machine, a process now abetted by human languages, and so made infinitely more complex. In that process, as Erich Jantsch and C. H. Waddington agree, embryonic forms evolve into "self-transcendent systems" that possess qualities akin to natural languages:

Erich Jantsch:
. . . the human world, analogous to physical and biological evolution, incorporates a basic principle of *self-transcendence*, of venturing out by changing its own physical, social, and cultural structures—above all, by changing its own consciousness.
(*Evolution and Consciousness.*)

C. H. Waddington:
Biological systems, in their genetic and evolutionary processes, transcend themselves in a way comparable to that in which a natural language can discuss its own structures (and becomes in doing so a metalanguage), a possibility which is not open to a completely formal language.
(*Evolution and Consciousness.*)

The far prospect of evolution may be dematerialization, images "masterful" and "complete" that must grow in "pure mind" (Yeats). But the far prospect is far indeed; the nearer prospect is a problematic diffusion of language, a mottled immanence of mind, a painful transhumanization of the earth, which Foucault allows himself only to intimate. Thus symbolism, the central force in anthropogenesis, finally leads to the "dispersal of man" in innumerable shapes. Such dispersals have already engendered a new semiotic or systemic awareness, a new ecology of signs.

There is an epistemology of modernism that questions the object as it questions the word, thereby questioning the sign. Art, in questioning mimesis, redefines and loosens its relation to the signified, aspiring, however, as if by compensation, to the most radical and most enveloping signification of all, to that of an absolute presence.
(Annette Michelson, in *On the Future of Art: Sponsored by the Solomon R. Guggenheim Museum.*)

Physical reality seems to recede in proportion as man's symbolic activity advances. Instead of dealing with the things themselves, man is in a sense constantly conversing with himself. He has so enveloped himself in linguistic forms. . . .
(Ernst Cassirer, *An Essay on Man.*)

I have stated these things not because I want to write a science fiction concerning itself with the possibility of telegraphing a man, but because it may help us understand that the fundamental idea of communication is that of the transmission of messages. . . .
(Norbert Wiener, *The Human Use of Human Beings.*)

As already mentioned, it makes more sense to say that insofar as men are controlled, it is by the totality of signs in their culture and not by their economic relations alone. Thus the theory of signs, semiology, takes on a fundamental importance. . . .
(Charles Jencks, *Architecture 2000.*)

Today, should you want the information in a man's head you will find it cheaper and more convenient to transport the man rather than to transmit the information. In the future the reverse will very likely be the case. . . . Transmit the information electronically. . . . Actual physical travel could very well become confined to vacationing and to other personal issues.
(Fred Hoyle, *The New Face of Science.*)

The new ecology of signs is inescapably cybernetic. The dispersal of languages, in science and art, now provokes us to ask: what is intelligence? Such provocations may at times conceal a certain bionic impatience: the "human measure" is deemed obsolete. This impatience, present even in so sensitive a futurist as J. D. Bernal or Arthur Clarke, reminds us that a Promethean *hybris* animates profound change.

Still, this fact remains: systems theory, including cybernetics, has now altered the categories of knowledge as praxis. The trend is toward holism, and from direct action toward indirect control. Algorithmic orders, subject to recursive and computational rules, increasingly assume the management of reality—and of the future. As Ludwig von Bertalanffy says:

> Suitable data being fed in, the machine runs according to preestablished rules, and eventually a result drops out which was unforeseeable to the individual mind with its limited capacities. This is the essence of mathematical reasoning, prediction in science and control of nature in technology.
>
> . . . there are, however, gloomy aspects of symbolic universes. The conceptual anticipation of the future which allows for true purposiveness at the same time creates anxiety, fear of future and death, unknown to animals.
>
> Owing to their immanent dynamics or laws, symbolic

> systems may become more potent than man, their creator.
> (*Robots, Men and Minds.*)

This is not the place to join the issue of human against artificial intelligence; nor is it the time to vex once more the old Cartesian conundrum of the *res cogitans* and *res extensa.* We know that the nervous system appears to be using a system of notation radically different from that of the computer (John von Neumann); the brain can employ both natural and mathematical languages, both logical and arithmetic orders. We know, further, that the brain contains a staggering number of "bits," and that a single human chromosome comprises the "information" of a library of four thousand volumes, each containing five hundred pages. We have recently come to know something about the right and left brains, the location of memory, sensations, motor impulses, the functioning of dreams. But we know, above all, that our knowledge of the brain is still paltry; and that more paltry still is our understanding of that energy we call mind, which is "different from that of neuronal potentials that travel the axone pathways" (Wilder Penfield). Indeed, as some logicians would argue, no mind can finally comprehend itself, just as no logical system can provide an integral description of its own structure. How, then, may we expect to compare man and machine? Donald G. Fink gives this modest analogical answer:

> Just as we can visualize the concept of infinity . . . so can we visualize a machine and program whose hierarchy of abstractions contains one echelon above the highest echelon of natural thought. Further, we may conceive that this extra echelon need not be "thought out" by man. . . . It *might* be produced by extrapolation from previous designs. In this sense, intelligent machines may forge into the unknown.
> (*Computers and the Human Mind.*)

The answer depends finally on our definition of intelligence and of human nature itself, both of which may be now subject to redefinition. The physicist David Bohm articulates an extreme view when he claims that all our models of human nature have a "limiting and distorting influence"; such "models will drop away, and there will be no specifiable limit to human nature." Yet the view emerging from cybernetics is no less Protean: human beings are organizations of messages, possessing the ability not only to perpetuate themselves but also to alter the very conditions of their perpetuity. According to Warren McCulloch—physician, neurologist, psychologist, logician, poet, and original cybernetician—machines can do the same:

> Turing showed that a computing machine having a finite number of parts and states can compute any computable number. Pitts and McCulloch (1943) proved the theoretical equivalence of all Turing machines, whether they be made of neurons or any other hardware. From this it follows, as von Neumann said, that we can build a machine that will do with information anything that brains do with information—solve problems, suffer emotions, hallucinate on sensory deprivation, what you will—provided we can state what we think it does in a finite and unambiguous manner.
> (*Embodiments of Mind.*)

Can we really state it so? The proviso is crucial; for in it all the tentativeness that McCulloch banished returns.

But the issue before us is not the parity of biological and electronic intelligences; it is rather cognitive change. What we call change is but the self-creation of knowledge; what we call future is but the virtual action of information upon itself; and language emerges as the feedback loop between cultural and biological evolution, accelerating, disrupting, both. Thus humanity achieves its (brief? sinister? sublime?) negentropic moment on this particular mote of the universe.

* * *

The moment is one of transhumanization; the clues are everywhere. Norbert Wiener, for instance, conceives human beings as gnostic and self-creating "communicative organisms," seeking continually a "new equilibrium with the universe and its future contingencies." From this cybernetic conception the transhumanization of the earth proceeds. To "speak," in the widest sense of articulation, may sometimes be to speak trivially or even to lie. Yet to speak seems ineluctably to create the conditions of further speech, further interplay, further cognition or recognition—and even wider love. This is not to deny the power of "silence," "noise," or "misunderstanding," tributes all to the perversity of consciousness in search of its own farthest limits. Still, however perverse human consciousness may seem (therein lies its freedom), the transhumanization of the earth moves apace. Behind that movement looms a planetary vision, shared anxiously by artists and scientists, doctors and engineers, mystics and businessmen, shared even by some rare politicians. And despite all the acute lacks and current exigencies of the earth, the vision refuses old temptations of domination and power. At once archaic and electronic, mythic and cybernetic, religious and scientific, a new epistemological factor is implicit in it. This factor, emerging from the biological and cultural evolution of consciousness, now asserts itself in an idea of mind as part of a larger "mind," organism as part of a vaster "organism." The idea is current in the works of such technological visionaries as Buckminster Fuller, Paolo Soleri, Marshall McLuhan, and Arthur C. Clarke. It is also encountered in the works of various scientists, speaking in a philosophic mood: J. D. Bernal, Gerald Feinberg, Lewis Thomas, José Delgado, Erwin Schrödinger, Ludwig von Bertalanffy, Gregory Bateson, Lancelot Law Whyte, and of course—perhaps more mystic than scientist—Teilhard de Chardin.

Connections between two or more minds would tend to become a more and more permanent condition until they functioned as dual or multiple organisms. The minds would always preserve a certain individuality, the network of cells inside a single brain being more dense than that existing between brains. . . . The complex minds could, with their lease of life, extend their perceptions and understanding and their actions far beyond those of the individual. . . . The interior of the earth and the stars, the inmost cells of living things themselves, would be open to consciousness through these angels, and through these angels also the motions of stars and living things could be directed. (J. D. Bernal, *The World, the Flesh, and the Devil.*)

On the millenial nature of the goal of extending consciousness. . . . The goal I propose is essentially to transcend what we are now, in the respect most important to us.
(Gerald Feinberg, *The Prometheus Project.*)

The human brain is the most public organ on the face of the earth, open to everything, sending out messages to everything. . . . We pass thoughts around, from mind to mind, so compulsively and with such speed that the brains of mankind often appear, functionally, to be undergoing fusion. . . . The whole dear notion of one's own Self . . . is a myth.
(Lewis Thomas, *The Lives of a Cell.*)

Human relations are not going to be governed by electrodes, but they could be better understood if we considered not only environmental factors but also the intracerebral mechanisms responsible for their reception and elaboration.
(José Delgado, *Physical Control of the Brain.*)

No Self stands alone. Behind it stretches an immense chain of physical and . . . mental events . . . by so much that a thousand words would not exhaust it, by all that, I say, the Self is not so much linked with what happened to its ancestors, it is not so much the product . . . but rather, in the strictest sense of the word, the SAME THING as all that. . . .
(Erwin Schrödinger, *My View of the World.*)

As matter dematerialized, so mind was dementalized. In a process quite similar to that of physics, reality was extended beyond the limits of direct experience. Consciousness, Descartes's *res cogitans,* is but a small sector of psychic events; unconscious happenings emerge with quite fluid boundaries, into experienced consciousness.
(Ludwid von Bertalanffy, *Robots, Men and Minds.*)

The cybernetic epistemology which I have offered you would suggest a new approach. The individual mind is immanent but not only in the body. It is immanent also in pathways and messages outside the body; and there is a larger Mind of which the individual mind is only a subsystem. The larger mind is comparable to God and is perhaps what some people mean by "God," but it is still immanent in the total interconnected social system and planetary ecology.
(Gregory Bateson, *Steps toward an Ecology of Mind.*)

The twentieth century will be seen to display a convergence towards a new universal attitude towards man and his problems, culminating in, and supported by, a scientific synthesis of unprecedented scope transcending the separation of subject and object. I foresee a new logic of process coherent with nature and history, which will put spirit into method. Since life imitates art, why should not history respond to this conjecture?
(Lancelot Law Whyte, *Focus and Diversions.*)

Is it not conceivable
that Mankind, at the end
of its . . . folding-in upon itself, may reach a critical level of maturity where, leaving
Earth and stars to lapse slowly
back into the dwindling mass of
primordial energy, it will detach itself
from this planet and join the one, true, ir-
reversible essence of things, the Omega
point?
(Teilhard de Chardin, *The Future of Man.*)

In fairness to these writers, we may note that their view is integrative rather than totalitarian; it accepts the idiomorphic, the optative, the phenotypical, the concrete. Even in Teilhard's radiant vision of "Noögenesis," the "supreme synthesis" allows individuation, permits the most complex liberty. Yet his vision and theirs may offend gloomy humanists by a certain presumption of cosmic optimism. Transhumanization in a time of torture and terrorism, of poverty, pollution, and exponential population, may seem criminally utopian; and the extension of consciousness may prove less a divine than a demonic boon. It was, after all, a Madman who proclaimed the "death of God" in Nietzsche's *The Gay Science,* and asked: "Shall we not ourselves have to become gods merely to be worthy of it?"

Are our leaders or politicians any more sane? Scientists often wonder, and like Bronowski they may cry: "Our conduct as states clings to a code of self-interest which science, like humanity, has long left behind"; or like Hoyle: "There is an alliance between the social organizations and the primitive parts of our brains against the higher parts of our brains."

How, then, may change recover from itself continuous value? How can vision create value before it is valued? Perhaps only if Process prove a trope of Being, the Future a figure of Desire, and Language itself the form our Immanence takes. This is certain: without a tomorrow, we die today, yet today is all we are vouchsafed.

* * *

The gnosis of science is a gnosis of change. C. P. Snow thought scientists had the future in their bones; their paradigms must alter or break. Not that scientists accede to change in their beliefs without malice or passion; examples of their ferocity in this respect abound. Consider (Arthur) Clarke's Law: "When a distinguished but elderly scientist states that something is possible, he is almost certainly right. When he states that something is impossible, he is very probably wrong." Still, the most innovative scientists possess a euchronic sense; their openness to Time, Ernst Bloch would say, invokes the principle of Hope; and like all true artists they know that creation, future-slanted, is prophecy self-surprised. Thus we may doubt that the human race already has exhausted its "primitive wishes" in earlier inventions, as Dennis Gabor claims. Though immanent in the present, the future is and must remain to us virtual, fictive. There can be no final preparation for the Unknown. Or as Lewis Thomas put it: "The future is too interesting and dangerous to be entrusted to any predictable, reliable agency." Or reliable agony, we may add.

Once, H. G. Wells attempted heroically to preview the shape of things to come. In his late and crotchety book, *Mind at the End of Its Tether,* he put forth his "stupendous propositon" nakedly: "The end of everything we call life is close at hand and cannot be saved." Yet the book was republished, under the same cover, with Wells's *The Happy Turning,* which ends: "There shines a world 'beyond good and evil,' and there, in a universe completely conscious of itself, Being achieves its end." Complementarity, it seems, applies to prophecy as well(s). For time may be that fictive dimension of consciousness wherein science and imagination, complementary now as magic and art were once long ago, reveal their teleological unity of action, which we call change.

Change? "For self-transcendent systems, Being falls together with Becoming," Erich Jantsch says. And the search for the One and the Many, which mind began even before the Pythagoreans, then comes to an end? There may be intelligences in the universe that will resolve such questions into more intelligent questions.

("Viewed in terms of the cosmic game, it is of no significance at all whether it takes one year, or a thousand years, to establish interplanetary communication," Fred Hoyle says.)

But for us, we can only hope that the earth will transmute itself, as Rilke sang, and "arise in us invisibly." Perhaps this has already taken place. Lofted into outer space, how many of us have seen those mysteriously colored pictures of our planet, taken with special infrared and ultraviolet cameras, revealing strange configurations? Now the earth seems a beating heart, now a floating brain, now a kidney, or perhaps a new secret organ of which we are still unaware. An organ, or perhaps fruit, of the serene "Eros of the universe," as Whitehead might say?

Some Say Big Bang was Really "Serene"

Mountain View, Calif.—UPI—NASA scientists say the big bang explosion that some believe marked the start of the universe was orderly and smooth, not violent and chaotic. . . .

"Our measurements give a picture of an extremely smooth process. The big bang, the most cataclysmic event we can imagine, on closer inspection appears finely orchestrated," the scientists said. "Either conditions before the beginning were very regular, or processes we don't yet know about worked to make the universe extremely uniform."
(*Milwaukee Journal*, July 26, 1978.)

From
THE SERBELLONI JOURNAL
II

One after another his victorious thought comes up with and reduces all things, until the world becomes at last only a realized will,—the double of the man.

Ralph Waldo Emerson

Today's adventure is yesterday's: I sit in my dark Serbelloni study sharpening No. 2 pencils to start my day. Some pencils are coated white, some red or green, but these merry colors (Italy's flag) drop into the wastepaper basket, lying there in monochrome whorls of wood.

A parable of one's writing? From chromatic possibilities of the unsaid to the fated hue of everything we say or do? This may be the sour, the "merely personal," view. Whitehead thought that the "process of creation is the form of unity of the Universe," and conceived "the Divine Eros as the active entertainment of all ideals."

Can this mean that though character is fate and fate character, there is still in language—as in the universe language posits to itself—a sense of wholeness and diversity that every creative act only palely reflects?

I hold a pencil shaving to the light: a small rainbow transpires through the roseate wood.

■

Emerson says: "And as the eye is the best composer, so light is the first of painters. There is no object so foul that intense light will not make it beautiful." What of objects in the mind, where light never penetrates, mind being light's other self? Or is mind light's corruption, at best its sophistication? This may be too pure and Gnostic a view, which Eric Voeglin calls a spiritual disease, metastasis, *in contrast with spiritual conversion,* metanoia.

But what is the deadlier disease: lying against time, purity, or lying for time, politics? We need not choose.

■

Four weeks have passed at the Serbelloni. Have we become inured to its sophistications?

Tonight, the dinner conversation touches gingerly on Nixon. A European scholar—suave, pin-striped, silver-haired—speaks ironically of our former President's detractors; another, with a glint in his eye, concurs. Sally and I exchange looks over the candles. She amuses herself by asking: "In what circle would Dante have placed Nixon?" The conversation politely veers.

Later, I recall the statement of an English friend: "You've got to realize Europeans are delighted whenever anything goes wrong in America. They're grateful to Nixon. Besides, it's an opportunity for them to show off their moral and political sophistication."

The paradoxes run deep. Culturally more innovative, America also seems more politically immature than Europe—at the same time that it is becoming "the Hapsburg Empire of the postmodern world" (Sally). But what does "politically immature" mean? Illusion and obsessiveness: illusion in the private sphere (sex, love, money, success, etc.), obsessiveness in the public realm (law, morality, religion, ideology, etc.). Illusions and obsessiveness (Rousseau and Calvin): they make for that massive (Nixonian) hypocrisy so characteristic of our nation.

Do they also make for our violence (in war, crime, sport, divorce)?

■

The Lepontine Alps, for a change, bar the cold rain-clouds from the north: a bright day. We join an outing to the Isola Comacina: launch, lunch, ramble through ruins and brambles, photographs. The island, no more than two kilometers in circumference, is uninhabited now. Yet it once served as a funnel through which three millenia of history passed, leaving behind in lacustrine mud a deposit of legend and bones and stones—as well as Kodak wrappers, Coke bottles, German sandals, beached by the annual tide of tourists. "Kilroy was here!"

So were many others: Greeks, Celts, Romans, Byzantines who fortified the island against the "barbarians" till the Longobards, under King Authari, captured it in 585, thus ending the last vestige of Imperial Rome in northern Italy. How is history made? T. W. M. Lund renders this quaint account:

> We find ourselves midway in the sixth century. The Emperor Justin reigns at Constantinople. His court is honeycombed by intrigue. Narses, a eunuch, has reconquered Italy for the Empire. A general of consummate skill and bravery, he has done what his predecessor Belisarius was recalled for not doing. He has entirely crushed the Goths. Totila is slain. His successor, Teja, is defeated. Their power lies in ruins, but the avarice of Narses has raised up enemies for him. Threats of revolt lead to his recall. The Empress Sophia adds insult to injury: "Arms for men, " is her sneering sarcasm; "for women and eunuchs the distaff and spindle. Narses will find them ready for him upon his return."
>
> There is sting in the taunt which enters deeply into his soul. Wounded to the quick, he swears that he will spin a thread which all her skill will not avail to unravel. He plans a sweet and ample revenge. Retiring to Naples, he makes overtures to the Lombards, a powerful German nation, to invade and occupy Italy, describing the country in glowing terms likely to excite the cupidity of those Northern warriors.

> They came, those men of enormous stature, long-bearded and loosely clad, with blue eyes looking out from under a yellow shock of hair, fierce, brave, passionate, licentious, striking hard and gripping fast; they came, and the wrongs of Narses were expiated by the loss of Italy to the Empire. The Italians yielded almost without resistance, partly from the panic inspired by the warlike fame of the invaders, partly from the feeling that no change of masters could be for the worse. (*Como and the Italian Lake Land.*)

The view is of a romantic nineteenth-century English clergyman. Yet however history may make or remake itself (epic, tragedy, romance), it reaches us sometimes as farce (Marx). Our guidebook, The Villa Serbelloni: Tours in and around Bellagio, *concludes the story that Lund's* Como and the Italian Lake Land *could not complete:*

> After the first World War, the owner of the Isola left it in his will to Albert I, King of the Belgians, who gave it to the Italian government, which in turn rented it to the Accademia di Belle Arte of Milan. A few houses have been built inconspicuously among the trees near the outer shore as retreats for art students.
>
> The restaurant until recently connected with the ancient Convent of Saints Faustino and Giovita now has an imposing new building at the southwestern extremity of the island. There the concessionaire, the famous Signor Nessi, after regaling you with fine food and wine, will tell you the history of the Isola Comacina while he mixes the delectable witches' brew with which he daily exorcises the evil spirits of the past.

So much for the Isola, once known as Crisopoli for its fabulous plunder; respected for its spiritual authority (six churches, including a nameless biapsidal chapel that may have held the remains of Agrippino, Bishop of Como, in 616); and renowned for its Maestri Comacini [*from* Comacinus *(Como), or* cum-macina *(with machine), or* co-macini *(associate masons)*] *who spread through Europe during the Dark Ages, building their cupolaed churches, subtle harmonies of circle and square, with enduring art.*

Now Signor Nessi, wearing a funny red-striped, festive cap, asks Sally to step up and help ladle flaming brandy into the caffè diavolo, *"delectable witches' brew." Is she the witch, then, or Clio? Perhaps the question is not altogether trivial so long as we lack a convincing hermeneutics of history.*

■

Scientists now believe that Nature is patient of interpretations in terms of those laws which happen to interest us. Imagination, intuition, dream, elegance, beauty, interest: these, rather than the word "truth," occur most often in the discourse of workers at the edge of knowledge. Emerson, too, more than a century ago—the tradition reverts to Pythagoras and Plato—saw that all Nature is metaphor, which it is the function of Culture to (re)cognize, and saw Science as the intellectual burden of that recognition. Nature, he believed, was gradually coming into Mind, leaving "matter like an outcaste corpse."

("Idealism" is now as obsolete as "Materialism." We know as little about the Oversoul as about the Thing in Itself; we know only that perceptual and cognitive relation we call consciousness, bright interplay between unknowns. Yet in certain intellectual circles, "materialist" still implies approbation—it's "hard"—and "idealist" contumely—it's "soft." Hard and soft have their uses. Even Princeton's Saul Kripke, among philosophers perhaps our premier logician, now concludes: "Materialism, I think, must hold that a physical description of the world is a complete description of it. . . . No identity theorist [materialist] seems to me to have made a convincing argument against the intuitive view that this is not the case.")

Emerson also saw History under the aspect of Mind:

> The instinct of the mind, the purpose of nature, betrays itself in the use we make of the signal narrations of history. Time dissipates to shining ether the solid angularity of facts. . . . Who cares what the fact was, when we have made a constellation of it to hang in heaven an immortal sign?

True, History, which begins as the biography of historians, may dissolve finally into legend. But a large part of it remains obdurate, resistant to Mind. (Offal, rubbish, grafitti in the Comacina ruins.) History: a tale told by all, signifying everything? Perhaps we can not finally interpret History precisely because we are the makers of it. And we die.

Perhaps all of our gnosis comes to this: the mind is (insufficient to?) itself.

■

A true heretic is "out of his mind," wants *to go out of it. This is less madness than vision. Giordano Bruno rudely wrote:*

> Only a complete fool can believe that in infinite space, in the innumerable worlds, most of which surely enjoy a better

fortune than ours, there is nothing but the light we perceive. It is simply silly to assume there are no living creatures, no other minds and no other senses than those known to us. (*L'Infinito Universo e Mondi.*)

This "assumption" is as close to the Imagination as it is to Heresy. No wonder the good Prior of the Carmelite Convent in Frankfurt, where Bruno took refuge in 1590, thought that this "universal man did not possess a trace of religion," and "was chiefly occupied in writing and in the vain and chimerical imagining of novelties." Bruno burned, in 1600, in the Campo di Fiori in Rome, saying to his judges at the Inquisition: "Perhaps your fear in passing judgment on me is greater than mine in receiving it."

Decidedly, this brother of fire was a hothead, and not altogether respectable. Yet he understood, in his charred flesh, that Change is fearsome, heretical, imaginary, and profoundly teleological. The last, one believes only when (at least slightly) "out of one's mind."

■

Bad days: winter has returned, my pencil drags, halts on the page. We decide on an overnight trip. Friends urge us to visit Padua, see the frescoes of Giotto at the Capella degli Scrovegni and the great wooden horse, imputed to Donatello, in the Palazzo della Ragione. We might as well push on to Venice. The road to Como snakes narrowly between mountain and lake, every curve a symphony of horns and brakes. Beyond, the autostrada *stretches easily to Milano, Verona, Padua, Venice.*

Venice proves a mistake. A frigid wind lashes the lagoons; the green, watery veins of "La Serenissima" swell balefully; the Piazza di San Marco floods, exciting only Sally. There are no tourists yet; the calles *are shadowier than ever. (But at Antico Martini, the next table has four boisterous German businessmen feasting call girls and their pimp, a vulpine face like Mosca's.) The Scuola di San Rocco is capriciously closed; I can barely re-imagine its swirling Tintorettos. Somehow this time—we have loved Venice—the cold and mold repel me. I ask Sally: does anything remain unfelt or unsaid about this (ef)fluent city?*

Padua the next day. Though the sky is still bleary, the sullen mood has begun to lift. This, for us, is a new city. We know no one here; parks, buildings, streets, and faces are all strange. Marco Polo could not have felt more the tingle of otherness, access of freedom. Travel: brief moment of self-forgetfulness, self-remaking. Only brief: the analogical mind soon takes over, the self slips back in its case. These are our machines for living.

But there is also the anagogical mind—here in the Scrovegni—which no machine can contain. Giotto's subject is the Christian epic, from the

Expulsion of Joachim to the Last Judgment. Row upon row on both walls of the nave, under a blue star-spangled vaulting, each scene stands in its childlike frame. Yet with the first step into this place we move into boundless space. Let art historians speak of Giotto's "realism," his "strong line," his "simplicity"—

like Dante, his contemporary, Giotto possessed heroic grace, true affluence of being:

Come fontana piena
che spande tutta quanta
cosı lo mio cor canta

—those angels with almond eyes, and those saints with long gazes, will not return till humankind meets something in intergalactic spaces. Is this the moment humanity now faces?

We walk out of the chapel silent, happy, breathing freely. Though Venice ruled here, and all the way to Bergamo, its golden wiles and styles left no enduring mark on Padua. We find the Palazzo della Ragione, a robust Renaissance structure standing squarely between the Piazza della Frutta and the Piazza delle Erbe. It is market day, and the arcades of the Palazzo burst with fruits, vegetables, cereals, sweets, cheese, poultry, fish, and hung meat, including shanks of cavallo. *The entire area teems with people (where do the poor hide?) come to barter their needs with shout and shove.*

A stately stone stairway on the flank of the Palazzo leads us straight up to the main portal. We enter a timbered hall as large as a hangar—the entire second floor of the building—yet somehow lived, warm odor of oak, echo of public passions. There stands Donatello's (?) enormous horse, haunches rippling with an energy no wood can hold, great eyes staring down from a height Hercules could not half reach, neck, richly maned, curved as if to raise the high-beamed roof still higher. The whole figure could belong to a constellation of stars. And yet something appears almost too noble, too willed, in this stallion's stance, something less elemental than psychological, as if the creature could mount a human nightmare in the night and engender a grostesque form.

Donatello after Giotto: only a century later, and already tainted by modern consciousness? And in Venice later still: Titian and Tintoretto. Is all Europe then in decay after Dante and Giotto? (Hamlet and Lear were never so gay as the archaic figure of Apollo.) I resist the conclusion of decadence, knowing that history, like any writer, has its bad writing days.

Perhaps all cycles are but partial perceptions of something that, though it may change, neither grows nor decays.

■

Discreet bustle in the corridors, muted excitement. Carabinieri *seal off the Villa's entrance; serge-suited men, brandishing antennas, deploy themselves over the grounds. Cars, launches, helicopters. The scholars assemble in the* salone *to receive the news: the King and Queen of the Belgians will visit the Bellagio International Conference and Study Center for two days. They will be accompanied by Herman Liebaers, Grand Maréchal of the Court, formerly Director of the Royal Library in Brussels. The President of the Rockefeller Foundation, Dr. John Knowles, and his wife will fly in from New York to welcome them.*

The royal visit is no holiday: a center of advanced studies is contemplated in Belgium. Other such centers are under study; researchers have come to research the researchers. Thus power works in paradigms as knowledge does. And knowledge, since shamans, priests, and bards, continues to serve power ambivalently. But this King and Queen prove too gracious for carping minds. Courtly and curious, they speak fluently half a dozen languages and listen in them better than they speak. They put everyone at ease—in the proudest republican still lurks a fairy tale of childhood, with wondrous kings and queens.

Their Majesties send word: they would be most grateful if the resident scholars, each, would grant them an hour the next morning. I spend my hour with Queen Fabiola. We meet punctually at ten in the salonetta. *Where would I like to sit? This chair or that? Perhaps with my back toward the light? (How fine to* offer *all the advantages. Would Dr. Knowles have done the same? Or has he read Michael Korda's* Power, *on the popular art of intimidation?) And what would I really like to talk about?*

The hour passes; we speak of "my project" and sundry things. Clear-eyed and subtle, Queen Fabiola moves gracefully in words. (Santayana: "Eloquence is a republican art, as conversation is an artistocratic one.") Yet she favors the spiritual over the spirituel, *feels beyond abstractions pity and pain. She says things like this: "Power is example, perhaps the most personal, the most consecrated, a king and queen can set. My husband and I try to express it in our love." And this: "The final aim of power may be humility"; and after a moment: "And isn't humility knowledge that everything is in relation to all else?"*

Later, in my study, I think back on that hour, order and concern, immeasurable misery out of sight. I think of Belgium, its old colonies in the Congo ("The horror. The horror."), and of its quotidian dis-ease (Flemish and Walloon) carried from one generation to another—

once as a boy, on the beach at Ostende, I was accosted terrifyingly by a band of bigger boys demanding in Flemish to know which language I spoke, and escaped only by muttering in English—

and of the world's torn body, which no spiritual

salve seems to heal. I think of Fabiola, childless, the Spanish woman now Queen; and of another, Theodolinda, who Christianized her first husband, King Authari—widowed, she remarried King Agilulf, friend of Pope Gregory the Great—and whose square Lombard tower still stands across the lake in Varenna, with clear sightlines to Bellagio as well as to far points north and south and west, signaling into the night.

From pain is spirit born, which spirit must then deny; from an old stone tower, light chatters of the human hour. To the cry of pain or cry of power, History gives no reply.

Unless the words of the Chorus Mysticus, addressed to the Mater Gloriosa, may apply:

das Unbeschreibliche
hier is es getan;
das Ewig-Weibliche
zieht uns hinan.
(*Faust II.*)

■

We are leaving the Serbelloni the next morning: I stop at the second floor Regency parlor to take my leave of Ella Walker. Her full portrait, in the fresh bloom of youth, hangs over the marble mantlepiece, looking mistily across the room to her mother's portrait: two oval faces, straight-lipped, their moral features limned in a thousand pages of Henry James, identical except for time and the falcon look in the older woman's eye.

(The Gothaisches Genealogisches Taschenbuch: *Hellena Holbrook Walker, born in Detroit, 17 August 1875; married first to Manfred, Count of Matuschka, Toppolczan, and Spaetgen, in 1897; marriage annulled by the church in 1925; married again, in 1932, to Alexander Karl Egon Theobald Lamoral Johann Baptiste Maria, of the cadet line of Thurm and Taxis, who died in 1937; buried with him at the ancestral castle, Duino, in 1959.)*

Titles, words to slow death by, turning time into place. Eponyms. A Bellagio street commemorates the Principessa—old villagers still recall her sweetly—and turquoise tiles over the Serbelloni welcome all in her name. We go through the ages living in each other's houses, leaving only such traces as language, gnostic babble, vouchsafes.

■

We are packing. Sally asks: "How is your Prometheus?" *I look up, quote Emerson whom I have been rereading: " 'The Prometheus Vinctus is the romance of skepticism.' So much for the gods—and our writing."*

I snap a suitcase shut, ready to travel, remembering that my mother, for six months before her death, always kept a fully packed suitcase in her bedroom.

5

PROMETHEUS AS PERFORMER: TOWARD A POSTHUMANIST CULTURE?

A University Masque in Five Scenes

—for Anima

He goes from death to death, who sees the many here.

The Vedanta

*

Beauty is the translucence, through the material phenomenon, of the eternal splendor of the "one."

Plotinus

*

To the eyes of a man of imagination, Nature is imagination itself.

William Blake

*

The mystery of the world is its comprehensibility.

Albert Einstein

*

Our mission, unfinished, may take a thousand years.

Mao

*

This demiurgic enthusiasm springs from the obscure presentiment that the great secret lay in discovering how to "perform" faster than Nature. . . . Fire turned out to be the means by which man could "execute" faster, but it could also do something other than what already existed in Nature.

Mircea Eliade

*

The presupposition of the Promethean myth is the transcendent value which a naïve humanity attaches to *fire* as the true palladium of every rising culture. That man, however, should not receive this fire only as a gift from heaven, in the form of the igniting lightning or the warming sunshine, but should, on the contrary, be able to control it at will—this appeared to the reflective primitive man as sacrilege, as robbery of the divine nature. . . . The best and highest that men can acquire they must obtain by a crime, and then they must in turn endure its consequences. . . .

Friedrich Nietzsche

*

God help thee old man [Ahab, "true child of fire"], thy thoughts have created a creature in thee; a vulture feeds upon that heart for ever; that vulture the very creature he creates.

Herman Melville

*

From women's eyes this doctrine I derive:
They sparkle still the right Promethean fire. . . .

William Shakespeare

* * *

THE CHARACTERS IN ORDER OF APPEARANCE

PRETEXT: who opens and presumably explains the nonaction.
MYTHOTEXT: *who is obsessed with the story of Prometheus.*
TEXT: who carries the burden of the intellectual narrative.
HETEROTEXT: **who speaks only to quote from various authorities.**
CONTEXT: who pretends to be a historian.
METATEXT: WHO ENJOYS COMMENTING ON TEXT AND CRITICIZING COLLEAGUES.
POSTEXT: who vainly attempts to conclude the nonaction.
PARATEXT: (inaudible in print): who breaks the frame now and then with his comments, and who has already appeared as a version of the speaker.

PRETEXT

[appearing from nowhere, speaking rather superciliously]

Good ladies and gentle men:

This masque reflects upon the lineaments of an emergent culture. Call it posthumanist culture—or call it nothing at all. It remains the matrix of our lives, and of our evolving destiny. There is a matrix larger still: the universe itself, everything that was, is, and will become. What a performance! Yet who can account for it? No one—not even a Titan—not even Prometheus.

Still, this masque endeavors to unmask Prometheus, maker (arsonist) of our history. He served, after all, to link Divine Space and Human Time, Sky and Earth, the One and the Many. He prefigured the fate of our own flawed and fateful consciousness.

One word more. The form of this entertainment can deceive no one. To name it "a university masque" is merely to grant its Author the benefit of his equivocations (multivocations). Great Tom Eliot defined in a few notes a whole humanist culture. This Author prefers to play voice against voice and text against text, hoping thus to perform the indefinitions of a posthumanist moment. Still, the Author remains One and his Audience Many—that, too, is in the nature of performance.

But no more pretexts; the masque follows in five stark scenes.

SCENE THE FIRST

FROM MYTH TO POLITICS: THE QUESTION OF THE ONE AND THE MANY

MYTHOTEXT

[in a voice resonant with the archetypes]

Prometheus, son of Iapetus, Titan turncoat and trickster. There are many versions of his story, but the main outlines are familiar. He sided with the new Olympian gods (Zeus & Co.) against his own chthonic kind. Yet Prometheus, that forethinker, could never leave well enough alone.

Some say he created men out of clay and mortar, Prometheus plasticator; *some say he only gave them fire. The fire was stolen from the smith-god Hephaestus—or was it taken from Apollo's sun? It was stolen, in any event, and hidden in a (phallic) fennel stalk. But this fire was no simple element: it was knowledge and imagination, the alphabet, medicine, and all the arts. Stolen fire, red forbidden fruit. We owe everything to a crime. "Prometheus's double nature is always acknowledged; as by Coleridge who said that he was the Redeemer and the Devil jumbled into one" (Denis Donoghue,* Thieves of Fire*). Byron's Manfred also makes the proud point:*

> *. . . Slaves, scoff not at my will!*
> *The mind, the spirit, the Promethean spark,*
> *The lightning of my being, is as bright,*
> *Pervading, and far darting as your own. . . .*

Ah, but the doubleness of this Luciferian trickster is not merely theological; it is political and epistemological as well. And it is doubleness that wants to become one again. Socrates here is our authority: "There is a gift of the gods . . . which they let fall from their abode, and it was through Prometheus, or one like him, that it reached mankind [*no emphasis on theft here*]*, together with a fire exceeding bright." This gift, Socrates goes on to say in the "Philebus," is a perception that "all things . . . consist of a one and a many, and have in their nature a conjunction of limit and unlimitedness."*

Thus the One and the Many formally enter Western thought, though the question may have haunted earlier philosophers since Thales of Milesia.

TEXT

[forcefully]

Thank you, Mythotext, you have led us from myth to politics through philosophy. Your image of Prometheus mirrors our own present, in which the one and the many, the ecumenical will of humankind and its will to secession, hold their bloody play under the twin aspects of totalitarianism (torture) and anarchy (terrorism). Convergences and divergences, conjunctions and disjunctions, centers and margins, are visible everywhere; on the one hand various myths of totality, on the other, diverse ideologies of fracture. Thus, the more Marshall McLuhan proclaims "the global village," or Buckminster Fuller "spaceship earth," or Norman O. Brown "the mystic body of mankind," the more Jacques Derrida and his *confrères* insist upon *différance* and the metaphysics of fragments.

The news, alas, seems to favor Derrida. *E pluribus unum?* Our planet continually splinters, breaks according to ideology, religion, class, race, language, sex, and age. The earth splits into blocks, blocks into nations, nations into provinces, provinces into tribes, tribes into families, families into feuding individuals—and individuals, soon enough, alas, into random atoms. Can it be fortuitous that atoms themselves have been split into the tiniest, the shiest particles, particles that seem a mathematical whisper, a mere breath? Whose breath? The breath of the universe?

No doubt, convergence and divergence are but two aspects of the same reality, the same process. Totalitarianism and anarchy, torture and terror, summon each other. And the more communication threatens to become global, the more individuals, insisting on their quiddity, will discover the deep and obscure need for misunderstanding. But is this all we can expect from our earth and sky, our brief moment of sodality?

There are poets and philosophers, scientists and mystics, who lead us to expect more. They believe in some richer relation between the one and the many, the universal and the concrete. Like Blake, in his prophecy called "America," they envision a movement "beyond struggling afflictions," toward "another portion of the infinite." Like Whitman, they sing of an "orbic vision," in which the inner divisions of consciousness and the external divisions of humankind are healed and made whole—made whole but *not* homogeneous, healed but *not* rendered uniform:

> "Have you thought there could be but a single supreme?
> There can be any number of supremes . . .
> All is eligible to all."

Is this the project of the Promethean consciousness? To perceive the parity, nay the identity, of parts and wholes?

HETEROTEXT

[chiming in]

Text and Mythotext, listen to some other voices of the "orbic vision," speaking variously of the concrete and the universal:

G. W. F. Hegel in *The Phenomenology of Mind:*

This simple force [concrete spirit in government] allows, indeed, the community to unfold and expand into its component members, and to give each part subsistence and self-existence of its own. Spirit finds in this way its realization or its objective existence. . . . But spirit is at the same time the force of the whole, combining these parts again within the unity which negates them . . . and keeping them aware that their life only lies in the whole.

*

Karl Marx in *The Economic and Philosophic Manuscripts of 1844:*

Man, much as he may therefore be a *particular* individual . . . is just as much the *totality*—the ideal totality—the subjective existence of thought and experienced society present for itself. . . .

*

Henri Bergson in *Creative Evolution:*

On the other hand, this rising wave is consciousness, and, like all consciousness, it includes potentialities without number which interpenetrate and to which consequently neither the category of unity nor that of multiplicity is appropriate, made as they both are for inert matter.

*

Teilhard de Chardin in *The Future of Man:*

If there is any characteristic clearly observable in the progress of nature towards higher consciousness, it is that this is achieved by increasing differentiation, which in itself causes ever stronger individualities to emerge. . . . In other words, in a converging Universe, each element achieves completeness, not directly in a separate consummation but by incorporation in a higher pole of consciousness in which alone it can enter into contact with all the others.

*

Werner Heisenberg in *Across the Frontiers:*

. . . we seem to inhabit a world of dynamic process and structure. Therefore, we need a calculus of potentiality rather than one of probability, a dialectic of polarity, one in which unity and diversity are redefined as simultaneous and necessary poles of the same essence.

*

Jacques Monod in *Chance and Necessity:*

The weight of an allosteric enzyme molecule capable of the same performances is of the order of a 10^{-17} of a gram. Which is a million billion times less than an electronic relay. That astronomical figure affords some idea of the "cybernetic" (*i.e.,* teleonomic) power at the disposal of a cell equipped with hundreds or thousands of these microscopic entities, all far more clever than the Maxwell-Szilard-Brillouin demon.

Hegel and Marx and Bergson, Teilhard and Heisenberg and Monod, a motley crew. But do they not all sing, each in his key, the same song of singleness in variousness?

TEXT

[severely]

Heterotext, do be sensible. Your voices are a little too obscure and worse: mystical. There is nothing supernatural in the process leading us to a posthumanist culture. That process depends mainly on the growing intrusion of the human mind into nature and history, on the dematerialization of life and the conceptualization of existence. In that sense, we need not wait for the end of History, as Hegel thought, to witness the synthesis of the Concrete and the Universal, Slave and Master, Individual and State. Each of us, by virtue of Desire, Imagination, and Language, provides some awkward version of the Concrete Universal. For what is the human animal, as Monod himself says, but the most distinctive organism on earth, and at the same time the most self-transcendent—I mean the most capable of abstracting itself through language and rising equivocally through layers of consciousness?

As for you, Mythotext, I must tell you this: Prometheus may be a vague metaphor of a mind struggling with the One and the Many, yet I prefer to view his struggle in narrower perspective. His mind is where Imagination and Science, Myth and Technology, Language and Number sometimes meet. Or to put it both prophetically and archetypically: Prometheus presages the marriage of Earth and Sky. Only then, perhaps, will posthumanism see the dubious light of a new day.

[no one answers Text; the scene closes]

SCENE THE SECOND

From Lascaux to Henry Adams: A Historical Collage

CONTEXT

[entering ponderously, gravid with history]

Allow me to have my turn, young texts; this matter you so ardently discuss requires a less hurried perspective. Posthumanism seems to you a sudden mutation of the times; in fact, the conjunctions of imagination and science, myth and technology, earth and sky, have begun by firelight in the caves of Altamira and Lascaux. Aeschylus, we know, wrote in *The Daughters of Danae:* "The pure sky [Ouranos] desires to penetrate the earth, and the earth is filled with love so that she longs for blissful union with the sky." But before Aeschylus, during those awesome invasions of ice from the north, did not some prehistoric Prometheus sharpen his foresight so that the race may survive the dread of famine and cold? And before that even, did the foresight of Prometheus transform the lives of our human ancestors from dreaming to waking? Yet unlike Mythotext here, I am less concerned with myth and archaic time than with history. From the Pythagoreans, through medieval alchemists, to the European Renaissance, a rich hermetic tradition has opened itself to both science and mystery.

MYTHOTEXT

[interrupting]

So much hermetic knowledge throughout history—and so little wisdom! Why then did the Promethean fire fail humankind? Is it merely because it was stolen, a power unearned, exceeding the reach of human piety? Thus Shaftesbury, in The Moralists, *speaks of Prometheus: "who with stol'n Celestial Fire, mix'd with vile Clay, dids't mock Heaven's Countenance. . . ." Or is it rather because the "gift" itself lacked an essential element: civic wisdom? In Plato's dialogue, Protagoras tells how Epimetheus, having squandered all the divine gifts on animals, found nothing more to give humankind. While Epimetheus sat puzzling about this, "Prometheus came to inspect the work, and found the other animals well off for everything, but man naked, unshod, unbedded, and unarmed. . . . Prometheus, therefore, being at a loss to provide any means of salvation for man, stole from Hephaestus and Athene the gift of skill in the arts together with fire. . . . In this way, man acquired sufficient resources to keep himself alive, but had no political wisdom. This was in the keeping of Zeus, and Prometheus no longer had the right of entry to the citadel where Zeus dwelt. . . ."*

CONTEXT

[ponders the interruption, then decides to ignore it]

The European hermetic tradition included Albertus Magnus, Paracelsus, Giordano Bruno—authors whom that "New Prometheus," Dr. Victor Frankenstein, studied profoundly before turning to shallower things. Surprisingly, this same hermetic tradition affected some eminent scientists, not in fiction but in history. Kepler, we know, wrote the horoscope of Wallenstein in 1609. Even the great Newton spent much of his earlier life in alchemical and Faust-like pursuits. "His deepest instincts," wrote Lord Keynes, "were occult, esoteric, semantic." But the outstanding example of the conjunction between science and imagination, technology and art, remains Leonardo da Vinci, who has haunted so many minds since the Renaissance. Both Freud and Valéry saw in Leonardo more than a total and meditative curiosity; they also saw in him something approaching a unified consciousness, perhaps even the radical process of consciousness itself, made incarnate. This has led Roger Shattuck to say in "The Tortoise and the Hare":

> At the very moment when . . . Western consciousness was hardening into a division between reason and feeling, two of the greatest contemporary minds were saying precisely the opposite in terms that recapitulate the history of modern European thought. They assert, in effect, that the experience of four hundred years tells us urgently and insistently not to divide up the mind.

HETEROTEXT

[also interrupting]

You quote nearly as much as I do. Quote then Erich Neumann in *Art and the Creative Unconscious* on Leonardo:

> Unknown to himself, his whole life was directed by the tendency toward integration of his personality, which experienced itself in the likeness of a godhead encompassing in itself the higher and the lower, heaven and earth.

Here is your sky and . . .

CONTEXT

[interrupting the interrupter]

At that same turning point of the twentieth century, Henry Adams, who thought that energy is the effort of every multiplicity to regain its unity, recorded his own intuition of the undivided mind. Dating his words exactly in the year 1900, Adams wrote in a famous passage of his *Education:*

> Copernicus and Galileo had broken many professional necks about 1600; Columbus had stood the world on its head toward 1500; but the nearest approach to the revolution of 1900 was that of 310, when Constantine set up the Cross. The rays that Langley disowned, as well as those he fathered, were occult, super-sensual, irrational; they were a revelation of a mysterious energy like that of the Cross. . . .

METATEXT

[clipped, logical, almost prissy]

MYTH, PHILOSOPHY, AND HISTORY ARE ALL VERY NICE. BUT THIS COLLAGE—SHALL WE GENEROUSLY SAY OF SIGNIFICANT MOMENTS?—MUST LEAVE THE AUDIENCE NONPLUSSED. PERMIT ME, THEREFORE, TO SUMMARIZE THE INACTIONS OF THIS MASQUE. INSOFAR AS I CAN UNDERSTAND MY LEARNED AND LOQUACIOUS COLLEAGUES, THEY WISH TO MAINTAIN THAT:

1. THE COSMOS IS PERFORMANCE, POSTHUMANIST CULTURE IS A PERFORMANCE IN PROGRESS, AND THEIR SYMBOLIC NEXUS IS PROMETHEUS;

2. PROMETHEUS IS HIMSELF THE FIGURE OF A FLAWED CONSCIOUSNESS STRUGGLING TO TRANSCEND SUCH DIVISIONS AS THE ONE AND THE MANY, COSMOS AND CULTURE, THE UNIVERSAL AND THE CONCRETE;

3. WITH REGARD TO POSTHUMANISM ITSELF, THE MOST RELEVANT ASPECT OF THE PROMETHEAN DIALECTIC CONCERNS IMAGINATION AND SCIENCE, MYTH AND TECHNOLOGY, EARTH AND SKY, TWO REALMS TENDING TO ONE;

4. THIS DIALECTIC, HOWEVER, HAS A HOARY HISTORY; THE LANGUAGES OF IMAGINATION AND THE LANGUAGES OF SCIENCE HAVE OFTEN MINGLED AND CROSSED IN CERTAIN EPOCHS AND IN CERTAIN GREAT MINDS OF THE PAST;

5. BECAUSE BOTH IMAGINATION AND SCIENCE ARE AGENTS OF CHANGE, CRUCIBLES OF VALUES, MODES NOT ONLY OF REPRESENTATION BUT ALSO OF TRANSFORMATION, THEIR INTERPLAY MAY NOW BE THE VITAL PERFORMING PRINCIPLE IN CULTURE AND CONSCIOUSNESS—A KEY TO POSTHUMANISM.

[Text, Mythotext, Context coldly nod their approval; the scene ends]

SCENE THE THIRD

CONTEMPORARY CULTURE

TEXT

[delighted to hold forth again]

Humanists are a little Epimethean, I fear; the astonishing convergences of imagination and science, myth and technology in contemporary culture have tended to elude them. Nor have the great modern minds which currently command the greatest authority—I mean Marx and Freud, Sartre and Lévi-Strauss, Heidegger and Husserl—particularly illuminated this question. (William James may prove a curious exception.) Yet, more and more, the evidence suggests that the "two cultures" of C. P. Snow and F. R. Leavis, of abstract, sky-haunted technophiles dominated by the male principle, and moist, earth-bound arcadians ruled by the female principle, are slowly becoming obsolete as consciousness evolves, through many setbacks and contradictions, to include them both.

HETEROTEXT

[stammering a little with excitement]

Excuse me, one may be permitted to speak more amusingly of this matter. William Irwin Thompson remarks in *Evil and World Order:*

In these declining years of the Magnus Annus the most interesting minds seem to have moved long ago; now only the "intellectuals" are left wrapped in their greatcoats of Europe and dreaming of leftist politics or the "new creations" of the avant-garde; but these are the warm dreams that come charitably to all those who are about to freeze to death.

Surely that is your point!

TEXT

[insufferably patronizing]

Yes, Heterotext, it is vaguely to the point. But it remains for us to chart the movement of "the most interesting minds," map out the areas of their problematic convergence. I would suggest four regions in contemporary culture:

a. the creative process
b. the symbiosis of art, science, and technology
c. the twilight zones in science
d. the search for a unified sensibility.

Perhaps you can recite for us, Heterotext, the current bibliography on these topics.

HETEROTEXT

[with alacrity, without the stammer]

I will do more: I will quote, then query, then cite a few bibliographic references.

A. On the Creative Process:
§ Quotations:
—Max Planck: "The pioneer scientist must have a vivid intuitive imagination for new ideas, ideas not generated by deduction, but by artistically creative imagination."
—Erwin Schrödinger: "I need not speak here of the quality of the pleasures derived from pure knowledge; those who have experienced it will know that it contains a strong esthetic element and is closely related to that derived from the contemplation of a work of art."
—Carl Sagan: "There is another aspect of science, one that is infrequently described except among the practitioners themselves: science as a supreme art form. The creative endeavor in science carries the same emotional exhilaration as the painting of a great work of art or the writing of an epic poem."
—Jacques Monod: "I am sure every scientist must have noticed how his mental reflection, at the deeper level, is not verbal: to be absorbed in thought is to be embarked upon an *imagined experience. . . .*"

§ Queries:

What, then, are the roles of dream, play, imagination, and aesthetic sensibility in scientific, mathematical, artistic creation? Which traits do creative personalities share, regardless of their fields? What indeed do we mean by creativity? Can neurological research on the one hand and psychological theory on the other move toward a unified concept of brain and mind?

§ References:

Frank Barron, *Creativity and Personal Freedom*
Sigmund Freud, *The Interpretation of Dreams*
Brewster Ghiselin, ed., *The Creative Process*
Arthur Koestler, *The Act of Creation*
Wilder Penfield, *The Mystery of the Mind*
Jean Piaget, *Biology and Knowledge*
Steven Rose, *The Conscious Brain*
Hans Seyle, *From Dream to Discovery*
Paul Valéry, *The Art of Poetry*

B. On the Symbiosis of Art, Science and Technology:

§ Quotations:

—Marcel Duchamp to Stieglitz: "You know exactly how I feel about photography. I would like to see it make people despise painting until something else will make photography unbearable."

—Werner Heisenberg: "In this respect they [scientific idealizations] may be compared to the different styles of art, say of architecture or music. A style of art can also be defined by a set of formal rules which are applied to the material of this special art."

—Jacob Bronowski: "Art and science are both uniquely human actions. . . . they derive from the same human faculty: the ability to visualize the future, to foresee what may happen . . . and to represent it to ourselves in images. . . ."

—Douglas Davis: "Art and technology are two parts of the triad that makes one structure, and science is the third."

§ Queries:

To what extent are various technologies integrating themselves into our art forms? Has technology begun to affect not only particular genres—cybernetic or op art, electronic music, video, contemporary dance—but also the very definition of art? Indeed, is it possible that science and technology may be transforming human consciousness itself, so as to make art, as we have known it, gradually obsolete? In short, where will Marinetti's Futurism finally lead?

§ References:

Jonathan Benthall, *Science and Technology in Art Today*
Jack Burnham, *Beyond Modern Sculpture*
John Cage, *Silence* and *A Year from Monday*
Douglas Davis, *Art and the Future*
Marcel Duchamp, *Complete Works*

Gyorgy Kepes, ed., *Structure in Art and Science*
Marshall McLuhan, *Understanding Media*
Thomas Pynchon, *Gravity's Rainbow*
Jasia Reichardt, *The Computer in Art*
Wylie Sypher, *Technology and Literature*
Robert Wilson, *Einstein on the Beach*

C. On the Twilight Zones in Science:

§ Quotations:

—Carl Friedrich von Weizsäcker: "the [yoga] concept of *Prana* is not necessarily incompatible with our physics. *Prana* is spatially extended and vitalizing. Hence above all it is moving potency. The quantum theory designates something not entirely remote from this by the term 'probability amplitude.' "

—Gunther Stent: "Since John Cage had pointed out to me the analogy between the genetic code and the *I-Ching,* I have looked into this matter a little more. To my amazement I found that the 'natural order' of the *I-Ching* hexagrams generates a table of nucleotide triplet codons which shows the same intercodon generic relations as Crick's table!"

—Arthur Koestler: "The rapprochement between the conceptual world of parapsychology and that of modern physics is an important step toward the demolition of the greatest superstition of our age—the materialistic clockwork universe of early-nineteenth-century physics."

—Lyall Watson: "All the best science has soft edges, limits that are still obscure and extend without interruption into areas that are wholly inexplicable."

§ Queries:

What changes in the logos (rationality) of the sciences may be expected as their frontiers expand? What are the epistemological as well as social implications of current experiments with transcendental meditation, biofeedback, parapsychology, artificial intelligences, and cosmic consciousness?

§ References:

Ludwig von Bertalanffy, *Robots, Men and Minds*
Fritjof Capra, *The Tao of Physics*
C. G. Jung & Wolfgang Pauli, *Naturerklärung und Psyche*
Arthur Koestler, *The Roots of Concidence*
Gopi Krishna, *The Biological Basis of Religion and Genius*
Lawrence LeShan, *The Medium, the Mystic, and the Physicist*
Raymond Ruyer, *La Gnose de Princeton*
C. H. Waddington, ed., *Biology and the History of the Future*
Lyall Watson, *Supernature*

D. On the Search for a Unified Sensibility

§ Quotations:

—Charles Lindbergh: "Decades spent in contact with science and its vehicles have directed by mind and senses to areas beyond their reach. I now see scientific accomplishment as a path, not an end; a path leading to and disappearing in mystery."

—Robert Pirsig: "The Buddha, the Godhead, resides quite as comfortably in the circuits of a digital computer or the gears of a cycle transmission as he does at the top of a mountain or in the petals of a flower."

—Aldous Huxley: "Man cannot live by contemplative receptivity and artistic creation alone. As well as every word proceeding from the mouth of God, he needs science and technology."

—Margaret Mead: "We need a religious system with science at its very core, in which the traditional opposition between science and religion, reflected in grisly truth by our technologically desecrated countryside, can again be resolved, but in terms of the future instead of the past."

§ Queries:

To what extent do the diverse careers of an astronaut like Michael Collins, a writer like Thomas Pynchon or Norman Mailer, a musician like John Cage or Jimi Hendrix, a historian like William Irwin Thompson, an anthropologist like Margaret Mead, and a Zen cyclist like Robert Pirsig reflect an authentic quest in our post-industrial society for an infinitely optative yet unified sensibility? And again, what are the personal, political, and philosophical implications of such a quest?

§ References:

Michael Collins, *Carrying the Fire*
Aldous Huxley, *Literature and Science*
Norman Mailer, *Of a Fire on the Moon*
Margaret Mead, *Twentieth Century Faith*
Joseph Chilton Pearce, *The Crack in the Cosmic Egg*
Robert M. Pirsig, *Zen and the Art of Motorcycle Maintenance*
William Irwin Thompson, *Passages about Earth*

[having overextended its mind with queries, Heterotext suddenly stops; Mythotext grasps the opportunity]

MYTHOTEXT

[scornfully]

Cultural chatter! Quote as they may, neither Text nor Heterotext have hit the mark. There is another "region of convergence," old as consciousness, new as the latest bauble of science or gewgaw of technology. I mean language itself, though some call it the Word, consummate technic of mind, eternal myth of awareness. Technic and myth join in an image of fire, tongues *of fire. Yet these tongues are not only Pentecostal; they flutter as well in every Promethean breath. That sacred alphabet Prometheus gave to men may have been the least dubious of his gifts.*

Speak of convergence, speak of language.

[the scene ends]

SCENE THE FOURTH
The Future of Vitruvian Man

TEXT

[now determined to assert himself and quote as much as Heterotext]

At present, posthumanism may appear variously as a dubious neologism, the latest slogan, or simply another image of man's recurrent self-hate. Yet posthumanism may also hint at a potential in our culture, hint at a tendency struggling to become more than a trend. The Promethean myth, after all, contains an enigmatic prophecy. How, then, shall we understand posthumanism?

We need first to understand that the human form—including human desire and all its external representations—may be changing radically, and thus must be re-visioned. We need to understand that five hundred years of humanism may be coming to an end, as humanism transforms itself into something that we must helplessly call posthumanism. The figure of Vitruvian Man, arms and legs defining the measure of things, so marvelously drawn by Leonardo, has broken through its enclosing circle and square, and spread across the cosmos. "Stands he not thereby in the center of Immensities, in the conflux of Eternities?" Carlyle ominously asked. Less than a century after, Pioneer 10 carries the human form and the human sign beyond the solar system into the intergalactic spaces; and Carl Sagan wryly speculates, in *The Cosmic Connection,* about the future of human intelligence, babbling its childhood to the universe.

This expansion of human consciousness into the cosmos, this implication of mind into farthest matter, becomes awesome when astrophysicists reflect upon the "origin" of the universe. As Sir Bernard Lovell, Professor of Radio Astronomy at the University of Manchester, put it:

> The transference from the infinities of density and size at time zero [when the universe began] to the finite quantities encompassed by the laws of the physical world may lie beyond scientific comprehension. Does man face this difficulty because he has externalized the object of his investigation? Is there reality in these externalized procedures? What is man's connection with the universe of atoms, stars, and galaxies? . . . Indeed, I am inclined to accept contemporary scientific evidence as indicative of a far

> greater degree of man's total involvement with the universe. . . . A remarkable and intimate relationship between man, the fundamental constants of nature, and the initial moments of space and time seems to be an inescapable condition of existence.
> (*New York Times Magazine,* November 16, 1975.)

This cosmological view, I think, requires from us a genuine alteration in our modes of feeling and thought and performance, an alteration that must go beyond, say, Albert Schweitzer's "reverence before life," and beyond the *participation mystique* attributed to primitive man.

But this cosmological extension of human consciousness (which both Teilhard de Chardin and J. D. Bernal long, if differently, perceived) is not the only force tending toward posthumanism. Indeed, the re-vision of man is currently promoted by certain prescient humanists as well as by most scientists. Thus, for instance, Claude Lévi-Strauss, both humanist and scientist, finds it necessary to remind us that the "world began without the human race and . . . will end without it." Michel Foucault taunts us that "man is an invention of recent date. And one perhaps nearing its end." And Jacques Derrida previews an emergent human structure, no longer turned toward the origin, "which affirms play and attempts to move beyond man and beyond humanism."

Yet, Derrida, Foucault, and Lévi-Strauss, I am convinced, mean not the literal end of man but the end of a particular image of us, shaped as much by Descartes, say, as by Thomas More or Erasmus or Montaigne. That is why contemporary thought emphasizes so much the dissolution of the "subject," the annihilation of that hard Cartesian ego or consciousness which distinguished itself from the world by turning the world into an object. The Self, structuralists and poststructualists insist, following the intuition of Nietzsche, is really an empty "place" where many selves come to mingle and depart.

A similar perception, deriving from biology more than psychology or philosophy, persuades Elisabeth Mann Borgese that human nature is still evolving:

> One might even say that whether postmodern man is still *Homo sapiens* remains to be seen. A species that can fly is different from one that cannot. A species that can transport itself out of earth's biosphere to other planets is different from an earthbound species. A species that can transplant vital organs from one member to another, blurring the boundaries between this individual and that individual and

> between life and death, is different from a species whose members cannot do this.
> (*Center Magazine,* March/April 1973.)

Projected out of this world and into the universe, the physical and mental possibilities of evolution become even more staggering. "Only a minute fraction, an inconceivably small fraction of all possible forms of life have existed on earth," writes James F. Danielli, Director of the Center for Theoretical Biology at SUNY-Buffalo. "It is inconceivable that the terrestrial organisms we now have are representative samples of the organisms which can exist" (*Center Magazine,* October 1972). Concretely, this means that the re-vision of human destiny must ultimately consider that destiny in a vast evolutionary scheme.

More soberly, more immediately perhaps, a posthuman philosophy must address the complex issue of artificial intelligence, which some of us know only by the familiar name of HAL (the supercomputer in Kubrick's *2001,* so strangely human, that is, at once so sinister and pathetic in every circuit and bit). But artificial intelligence is not merely a figment of science fiction; it almost lives in our midst. There is an anecdote about Alan Turing, the young mathematical genius who died in 1954 and whose work provided John von Neumann with the basis of modern computer theory—a somber anecdote that we do well to ponder. It is told by the wife of one of Turing's closest colleagues:

> I remember sitting in our garden at Bowdon about 1949 while Alan and my husband discussed the machine and its future activities. I couldn't take part in the discussion . . . but suddenly my ear picked up a remark which sent a shiver down my back. Alan said reflectively, "I suppose, when it gets to that stage, we shan't know how it does it."
> (*New York Times Magazine,* February 15, 1976.)

Yet the human brain itself does not really know whether it will become obsolete—or simply need to revise its self-conception. The argument explored by Arthur Koestler, in *The Ghost in the Machine,* that the human brain may be radically flawed—may be, that is, an organ inadequate to its task, a "mistake" among countless other "mistakes" of evolution—remains a hypothesis, perhaps itself more mistaken than the brain which conceived it. Will artificial intelligences supersede the human brain, rectify it, or simply extend its powers? We do not know. But this we do know: artificial intelligences, from the humblest calculator to the most transcendent computer, help to transform the image of man, the concept of the human. They are agents of a new posthumanism, even if they do no more than the IBM 360-196 that can perform in a few hours all the arithmetic estimated ever to have been done by hand by all mankind. Inevitably, such posthumanism implies the dispersal of the classic human image. The individuality of the body, according to Norbert Wiener, is that of a flame rather than of a stone. In *The Human Use of Human Beings,* Wiener goes farther:

> We have already suggested . . . that the distinction between material transportation and message transportation is not in any theoretical sense permanent and unbridgeable.
>
> This takes us very deeply into the question of human individuality.

All these visions finally boggle the minds of poor humanists like ourselves. Yet they are not the visions of science fictionists and future shockers, intended to amuse and terrify us—even as they make the best-seller lists. These visions are immediate and concrete. Technology and the pharmaceutical industry have already altered most performances in the Olympic Games; and those Bionic Women from the German Democratic Republic may point to a future more golden than all their medals. And when the figure of Leonardo's Vitruvian Man appears on the cover of our *TV Guide* nowadays, under it runs the caption: "Compared with the real bionic people we expect in the not-too-distant future . . . The Six Million Dollar Man is Just a Tin Lizzie" (28 August 1976).

What then will the future, in its middle distances, bring to us?

[long pause as Text tries to penetrate Time; the scene slowly fades and ends]

SCENE THE FIFTH

The Warnings of the Earth

MYTHOTEXT

[enters in outrage]

*This optimism is more kitsch than vision, and it makes for a revolting in*humanism*. Here is an editorial from an engineering magazine (the IEEE's* Spectrum*):*

> *As a subsystem, man leaves much to be desired. What other system has no significant prospect of miniaturization or ruggedization, can work at full capacity only one quarter of the time, must be treated as non-expendable, requires a critical psychological and physical environment, cannot be decontaminated, and is so unpredictable?*

You easily forget: Prometheus was a trickster and thief. In the end, Text here seems to side more with Goethe, Percy Bysshe Shelley, and Gide, in their romantic interpretation of the myth, than with wise Aeschylus, Mary Shelley, or Kafka. But to open oneself with hope to the Promethean endeavor is also to recognize its error and terror, its madness within.

Consider for a moment. We know that Iapetus was father to Prometheus. But, pray, who was his mother? Was it Asia, or Themis, or perhaps Clymene, "shapely daughter of Ocean"? Accounts differ. Yet their differences do not obscure a certain point: the shameless misogyny of the myth. Epimetheus, we know, takes Pandora to wife. Fashioned exquisitely by Hephaestus, she is sent as the cunning revenge of Zeus. Hesiod put it brutally: "Gods and men were speechless when they saw how deadly and how irresistible was the trick with which Zeus was going to catch mankind. This was the origin of the damnable race of women. . . . They have no place where the curse of poverty is; they belong with luxury" (Theogony)*. But the curse is not simply economic; Epimetheus, against the advice of his brother, opens Pandora's box, and all the ills of mankind ensue.*

From the start, great writers have sensed that Prometheus must do more than overthrow the patriarchic Zeus; he must also recover the female principle within his own consciousness. Thus Aeschylus included in his work both Themis and the watery nymph Io; Nietzsche perceived in the "Titanic impulse" some covert affinity between the Promethean and the Dionysian; and Percy Bysshe Shelley gave Asia a creative role, placing love at the very heart of his work.

The Earth must be heard. Yes, Earth must be heard, else Consciousness will turn the Sky into fire.

TEXT

[placatingly]

Calm yourself, Mythotext, I concur, I freely concede the point. I, too, know the Jungian text:

> Consciousness thus is torn from its roots and no longer able to appeal to the authority of the archetypal images; it has Promethean freedom, it is true, but also a godless *hybris*. It does indeed soar above the earth, even above mankind, but the danger of an upset is there, not for every individual, to be sure, but collectively for the weak members of such a society, who then, again like Prometheus, are chained to the Caucasus by the unconscious.
> (*The Secret of the Golden Flower*.)

Obviously, the marriage of Earth and Sky may never find a happy consummation. It may also beget monsters and mutants. We know all too well the litany of our failures: pollution, population, power that serves only to suppress—in short, man's deadly exploitation of nature and himself. Some, for instance, say that the technological capacities bungled in Watergate would make the "Miracle, Mystery, and Authority" of the Grand Inquisitor seem like childish play. Others caution of present and "future shock"; of cloning, parthenogenesis, transplants, prosthesis; of the alteration of memory, intelligence, and behavior; of the creation of chimeras, androids, and cyborgs. Others, still, simply prophesy of famine and global war. From D. H. Lawrence and Friedrich Junger to Lewis Mumford, Rachel Carson, Jacques Ellul, and the Club of Rome, men and women of vision have warned against dehumanization and have challenged rampant technology—Marx having preceded them with his famous doctrine of alienation. I know all this.

Yet even Jung's devoted disciple, Erich Neumann, says:

> Our conception of man is beginning to change. Up to now we saw him chiefly in a historical or horizontal perspective, embedded in his group, his time, and his cultural canon . . . but today we are beginning to see man in a new perspective—vertically—in his relation to the absolute. (*Art and the Creative Unconscious.*)

Yet even Heidegger was equivocal on technological being. He sternly warned that technology was no longer empowered by human reality—*"Die Technik in ihrem Wesen ist etwas, was der Mensch von sich aus nich bewältig"*—warned that it no longer corresponded to the human measure—*"wir haben noch keinen Weg, der dem Wesen der Technik entspricht"* (*Der Spiegel,* 31 May 1976). How, then, could the human race "spare the earth, receive the sky, expect the gods, and have a capacity for death," Heidegger wondered? Still, beyond those necessary warnings, he sensed the transformative capacity of the human, and paraphrased Rilke: "Not only is man by nature more daring than plant and beast. Man is at times more daring even 'than Life itself is.' " Will this daring lead us to "where all ground breaks off—into the abyss"? Or will the transhumanization of the human mean our "childhood's end" (Arthur Clarke)?

HETEROTEXT

[quietly]

I wish to quote from Arthur Clarke's *Profiles of the Future.* Speaking of the future races, Clarke says:

> They will have time enough, in those endless aeons, to attempt all things, and to gather all knowledge. They will not be like gods, because no gods imagined by our minds have

ever possessed the powers they will command. But for all that, they may envy us, basking in the bright after-glow of Creation; for we knew the universe when it was young.

MYTHOTEXT

[still gloomy]

Text mentions the capacity for death; Heterotext speaks of the future. Prometheus is connected with both. In the "Gorgias," Socrates claims that Prometheus had also given men exact foreknowledge of their death. But Hades, god of the underworld, complained to Zeus, and the gift was revoked. Could it be that for once Zeus acted with tact? Robbed of human mortality, how can Earth give continual birth? Without death, how can there be surprise or generation?

Yet the motives of Zeus were seldom pure. We know that after aeons of pain, Heracles delivered Prometheus from his bondage on Tartarus; for Prometheus knew a secret vital to the rule of Zeus. Some say Zeus was finally toppled, others maintain a reconciliation ensued, and a few still whisper that the sick centaur, Chiron, offered to resign his gift of immortality and take the place of Prometheus under the vulture. Perhaps Kafka, after all, puts it best:

> *Everyone grew weary of the meaningless affair. The gods grew weary, the eagles grew weary, the wound closed wearily.*
>
> *There remained the inexplicable mass of rock. —The legend tried to explain the inexplicable. As it came out of a substratum of truth it had in turn to end in the inexplicable.*

[hush; last scene ends]

POSTEXT

I come at the end, though there are no ends; I come only after. And what I must say has already been said, and will be said many times thereafter.

Is it not finally plain? Prometheus, gnostic, dreamer, prophet, Titan transgressor and trickster, giver of fire, maker of culture—Prometheus is our performer. He performs Space and Time; he performs Desire. He suffers.

We are ourselves that performance; we perform and are performed every moment. We are the pain or play of the Human, which will not remain human. We are both Earth and Sky, Water and Fire. We are the phoenix form of Desire. Everything changes, and nothing, not even Death, can tire.

[Here ends the Masque.]

Index